Macromedia® Flash™ MX ActionScript™ For Dummies®

Cheat Sheet

Actions Keyboard Shortcuts*

Note: Actions panel must be open before shortcut is executed.

Action	Windows	Macintosh	Action	Windows	Macintosh
Break	Esc+br	Esc+br	loadVariables	Esc+lv	Esc+lv
Call	Esc+ca	Esc+ca	on	Esc+on	Esc+on
Comment	Esc+//	Esc+//	onClipEvent	Esc+oc	Esc+oc
Continue	Esc+co	Esc+co	play	Esc+pl	Esc+pl
Delete	Esc+da	Esc+da	print	Esc+pr	Esc+pr
Do While	Esc+do	Esc+do	removeMovieClip	Esc+rm	Esc+rm
Duplicate Movie Clip	Esc+dm	Esc+dm	return	Esc+rt	Esc+rt
Else	Esc+el	Esc+el	setProperty	Esc+sp	Esc+sp
Else If	Esc+ei	Esc+ei	setvariable	Esc+sv	Esc+sv
Evaluate	Esc+ev	Esc+ev	startDrag	Esc+dr	Esc+dr
For	Esc+fr	Esc+fr	stop	Esc+st	Esc+st
for..in	Esc+fi	Esc+fi	stopAllSounds	Esc+ss	Esc+ss
FSCommand	Esc+fs	Esc+fs	stopDrag	Esc+sd	Esc+sd
Function	Esc+fn	Esc+fn	trace	Esc+tr	Esc+tr
getURL	Esc+gu	Esc+gu	unloadMovie	Esc+um	Esc+um
goto	Esc+go	Esc+go	var	Esc+vr	Esc+vr
if	Esc+if	Esc+if	while	Esc+wh	Esc+wh
loadMovie	Esc+lm	Esc+lm	with	Esc+wt	Esc+wt

D0752040

For Dummies: Bestselling Book Series for Beginners

Macromedia® Flash™ MX ActionScript™ For Dummies®

Cheat Sheet

Panel Keyboard Shortcuts

Panel	Windows	Macintosh
Actions panel	F9	F9
Align panel	Ctrl+K	Cmd+K
Color Mixer	Shift+F9	Shift+F9
Color Swatches	Ctrl+F9	Cmd+F9
Info panel	Ctrl+I	Cmd+I
Library	F11 or Ctrl+L	F11 or Cmd+L
Movie Explorer	Alt+F3	Option+F3
Property Inspector	Ctrl+F3	Cmd+F3

Other Useful Flash Keyboard Shortcuts

Command	Windows	Macintosh
Convert to Symbol	F8	F8
New Symbol	Ctrl+F8	Cmd+F8
Frame	F5	F5
Remove Frames	Shift+F5	Shift+F5
Keyframe	F6	F6
Blank Keyframe	F7	F7
Clear Keyframe	Shift+F6	Shift+F6

Hungry Minds™

For Dummies: Bestselling Book Series for Beginners

TM

References for the Rest of Us!®

BESTSELLING BOOK SERIES

Are you intimidated and confused by computers? Do you find that traditional manuals are overloaded with technical details you'll never use? Do your friends and family always call you to fix simple problems on their PCs? Then the For Dummies® computer book series from Hungry Minds, Inc. is for you.

For Dummies books are written for those frustrated computer users who know they aren't really dumb but find that PC hardware, software, and indeed the unique vocabulary of computing make them feel helpless. For Dummies books use a lighthearted approach, a down-to-earth style, and even cartoons and humorous icons to dispel computer novices' fears and build their confidence. Lighthearted but not lightweight, these books are a perfect survival guide for anyone forced to use a computer.

> *"I like my copy so much I told friends; now they bought copies."*
>
> — Irene C., Orwell, Ohio

> *"Quick, concise, nontechnical, and humorous."*
>
> — Jay A., Elburn, Illinois

> *"Thanks, I needed this book. Now I can sleep at night."*
>
> — Robin F., British Columbia, Canada

Already, millions of satisfied readers agree. They have made For Dummies books the #1 introductory level computer book series and have written asking for more. So, if you're looking for the most fun and easy way to learn about computers, look to For Dummies books to give you a helping hand.

Hungry Minds™

1/01

Macromedia
Flash® MX ActionScript

FOR

DUMMIES®

Macromedia
Flash® MX ActionScript

FOR
DUMMIES®

by Doug Sahlin

Hungry Minds™

Best-Selling Books • Digital Downloads • e-Books • Answer Networks • e-Newsletters • Branded Web Sites • e-Learning

New York, NY ◆ Cleveland, OH ◆ Indianapolis, IN

Macromedia Flash® MX ActionScript For Dummies®

Published by
Hungry Minds, Inc.
909 Third Avenue
New York, NY 10022
www.hungryminds.com
www.dummies.com

Library of Congress Control Number: 2002102448

ISBN: 0-7645-1637-X

Printed in the United States of America

10 9 8 7 6 5 4 3 2 1

1B/QT/QW/QS/IN

Distributed in the United States by Hungry Minds, Inc.

Distributed by CDG Books Canada Inc. for Canada; by Transworld Publishers Limited in the United Kingdom; by IDG Norge Books for Norway; by IDG Sweden Books for Sweden; by IDG Books Australia Publishing Corporation Pty. Ltd. for Australia and New Zealand; by TransQuest Publishers Pte Ltd. for Singapore, Malaysia, Thailand, Indonesia, and Hong Kong; by Gotop Information Inc. for Taiwan; by ICG Muse, Inc. for Japan; by Intersoft for South Africa; by Eyrolles for France; by International Thomson Publishing for Germany, Austria and Switzerland; by Distribuidora Cuspide for Argentina; by LR International for Brazil; by Galileo Libros for Chile; by Ediciones ZETA S.C.R. Ltda. for Peru; by WS Computer Publishing Corporation, Inc., for the Philippines; by Contemporanea de Ediciones for Venezuela; by Express Computer Distributors for the Caribbean and West Indies; by Micronesia Media Distributor, Inc. for Micronesia; by Chips Computadoras S.A. de C.V. for Mexico; by Editorial Norma de Panama S.A. for Panama; by American Bookshops for Finland.

For general information on Hungry Minds' products and services please contact our Customer Care Department within the U.S. at 800-762-2974, outside the U.S. at 317-572-3993 or fax 317-572-4002.

For sales inquiries and reseller information, including discounts, premium and bulk quantity sales, and foreign-language translations, please contact our Customer Care Department at 800-434-3422, fax 317-572-4002, or write to Hungry Minds, Inc., Attn: Customer Care Department, 10475 Crosspoint Boulevard, Indianapolis, IN 46256.

For information on licensing foreign or domestic rights, please contact our Sub-Rights Customer Care Department at 212-884-5000.

For information on using Hungry Minds' products and services in the classroom or for ordering examination copies, please contact our Educational Sales Department at 800-434-2086 or fax 317-572-4005.

For press review copies, author interviews, or other publicity information, please contact our Public Relations Department at 317-572-3168 or fax 317-572-4168.

For authorization to photocopy items for corporate, personal, or educational use, please contact Copyright Clearance Center, 222 Rosewood Drive, Danvers, MA 01923, or fax 978-750-4470.

Hungry Minds™ is a trademark of Hungry Minds, Inc.

About the Author

Doug Sahlin is an author, graphic designer, and Web site designer living in Central Florida. He is the author of *Carrara 1 Bible* (Hungry Minds, Inc.), *Carrara 1 For Dummies* (Hungry Minds, Inc.), *Flash 5 Virtual Classroom* (Osborne/McGraw-Hill), and *Fireworks 4 For Dummies* (Hungry Minds, Inc.). His articles and product reviews have appeared in national publications such as *3D*, *Computer Graphics World*, *Video Systems*, and *Corel Magazine*. His tutorials have been featured at numerous Web sites devoted to graphic design.

Dedication

Dedicated to the memory of George Harrison, the quiet Beatle. All things must pass. . . .

Author's Acknowledgments

This book was a great deal of fun to write, but let's face it — Flash is fun to work with. The work progressed without a hitch thanks to the overwhelming support I received. Thanks to Steve Hayes of Hungry Minds for giving me the opportunity to write this book. Special thanks to Project Editor extraordinaire Andrea Boucher (living proof that blonde-haired people are the smartest on the planet) for her fastidious attention to detail and for being a pleasure to work with. Kudos to Den Laurent, a lovely Web designer living in London town, for doing a thorough job as this book's Technical Editor. Kudos to the tenth power for the dynamic Flash duo of Eric Wittman and Jeremy Clark. This project would not have been possible without your assistance. Many thanks to all of the fine folks at Macromedia for creating such wonderful software and for supporting authors.

I get a warm and fuzzy glow when I think of all the support available in the Flash community. One hand truly does wash the other. You people are terrific. Thank you. While on the subject of the Flash community, I would like to take this opportunity to thank fellow Flash author Bonnie Blake for becoming a member of MLC Productions. Thanks for your help and support, good friend.

A big "muchas gracias" to all the vendors who contributed the fabulous software found on this book's CD. Thanks and a tip of the hat to the dynamic duo from Brainsville, soon to be a triumvirate if Elaine keeps showing up as a co-worker at conferences.

Special thanks to the lovely and talented Margot Maley Hutchinson and her cohort in crime, Sudden Sam. I would also like to take this opportunity to acknowledge the help and support of my friends and family, especially you, Karen, Ted, and Colin.

I'd like to take a moment to say thank you to a very special person in my life, my mother Inez, who'll be in my thoughts always. I wish she were here to read this.

Publisher's Acknowledgments

We're proud of this book; please send us your comments through our Hungry Minds Online Registration Form located at www.dummies.com.

Some of the people who helped bring this book to market include the following:

Acquisitions, Editorial, and Media Development

Project Editor: Andrea C. Boucher

Acquisitions Editor: Steven H. Hayes

Technical Editor: Denise Laurent

Editorial Manager: Constance Carlisle

Permissions Editor: Laura Moss

Media Development Specialist: Marisa Pearman

Media Development Manager: Laura Carpenter VanWinkle

Media Development Supervisor: Richard Graves

Editorial Assistant: Amanda Foxworth

Production

Project Coordinator: Regina Snyder

Layout and Graphics: Joyce Haughey, Stephanie Jumper, Laurie Petrone, Betty Schulte, Julie Trippetti, Mary J. Virgin

Proofreaders: Laura Albert, TECHBOOKS Production Services

Indexer: TECHBOOKS Production Services

General and Administrative

Hungry Minds Technology Publishing Group: Richard Swadley, Vice President and Executive Group Publisher; Bob Ipsen, Vice President and Group Publisher; Joseph Wikert, Vice President and Publisher; Barry Pruett, Vice President and Publisher; Mary Bednarek, Editorial Director; Mary C. Corder, Editorial Director; Andy Cummings, Editorial Director

Hungry Minds Manufacturing: Ivor Parker, Vice President, Manufacturing

Hungry Minds Marketing: John Helmus, Assistant Vice President, Director of Marketing

Hungry Minds Production for Branded Press: Debbie Stailey, Production Director

Hungry Minds Sales: Michael Violano, Vice President, International Sales and Sub Rights

Contents at a Glance

Cartoons at a Glance

By Rich Tennant

"Well, it's not quite done. I've animated the gurgling spit-sink and the rotating Novocaine syringe, but I still have to add the high speed whirring drill audio track."

page 281

"Well, shoot — I know the animation's moving a mite too fast, but dang if I can find a 'mosey' function anywhere in the toolbox!"

page 343

"Is this really the best use of Flash MX ActionScript animation on our e-commerce Web site? A bad wheel on the shopping cart icon that squeaks, wobbles, and pulls to the left?"

page 161

"I can't really explain it, but every time I animate someone swinging a golf club, a little divot of code comes up missing on the home page."

page 7

"Look into my Web site, Ms. Carruthers. Look deep into its rotating, nicely animated spiral, spinning, spinning, pulling you in, deeper... deeper..."

page 71

Cartoon Information:
Fax: 978-546-7747
E-Mail: richtennant@the5thwave.com
World Wide Web: www.the5thwave.com

Table of Contents

Part V: The Part of Tens 343

Chapter 17: Ten Tips for Trouble-Free ActionScript 345

Chapter 18: Ten Internet Resources for ActionScript 353

Appendix: About the CD 357

Introduction

● ●

*W*elcome to *Macromedia Flash MX ActionScript For Dummies*, your road map to creating your very own ActionScript without having to sink your teeth into — or strain your eyes while reading — a dry computer manual that tells you how to but really doesn't *show* you how to. In this book, I show you how to use the most popular ActionScript to create useful-but-not-so-cool, useful-and-way-too-cool, and cool-but-oh-so-frivolous items for your movies. If you find a category I haven't identified, congratulations.

Who Should Buy This Book

The fact that you have this book in your hands, whether you're looking at it in a bookstore, or in the comfort of your own home or office, means you have the need to come up to speed with ActionScript. If you've exhausted all other avenues for coming to grips with ActionScript, or you just need a single course serving of a popular action for a project you're working on, or because your boss said you've got to have x number of actions in your newest Flash movie and . . . by the way, I need the finished project by the end of the week, you've got the right book in your hands. This book can be read from cover to cover, or you can flip to the index, find the topic of need and get the information you need quickly.

My goal while creating this book was to avoid techno-geek-speak like the plague. There's nothing worse than being lulled to sleep by reading words that should make sense but don't. I've written the book in good ol' plain English — my favorite language next to pig Latin — and when appropriate (and when it survived my editor's furrowed brow), I spiced up the reading with a bit of humor.

Foolish Assumptions

Before you rush up to the counter, whip out your favorite charge card — you know, the one with a credit balance left on it — or plunk down your hard-earned coin of the realm for this book, there are a few things you need to get the most out of this book. They are

- ✔ A PC or Macintosh computer with enough resources to run Flash.
- ✔ A copy of Flash MX installed on your computer.

✔ A basic knowledge of how to create a Flash document and publish it as an .SWF movie, along with a basic knowledge of working with the Timeline, creating frame-by-frame animations, tweened animations of the shape and motion variety, as well as a basic knowledge of the Flash interface and how to open all of those adorable little panels that are scattered all over the workspace when you launch Flash for the first time.

✔ An urge to understand and use ActionScript.

✔ A creative mind to use what I show you and put your own spin on it.

How This Book Is Organized

This book is organized. Ahem, it has to be; otherwise the publisher never would have given me the opportunity to write it. But seriously, reader, this book is organized into five sections. Each section is divided into a number of chapters, which are further divided into sections and sub-sections, which are comprised of sentences, which are comprised of words and . . . well, you get the picture. You do not need to read this book as a whole; read as much or as little as you need. I only have one rule; please use an approved bookmark to keep track of where you are. DO NOT, I repeat, DO NOT bend the corner of the page. It not only destroys the aesthetics of the book, it also hurts the feelings of the team that worked so hard to create a book that looks nice in any bookcase, on any computer desk, or on any nightstand.

Now that I have that little bit of housekeeping out of the way, here is a list of the parts and what you can expect to find in each.

✔ **Part I: Demystifying ActionScript:** This section of the book introduces you to ActionScript and what it can be used for. It introduces you to the Actions panel, and you even get to create your very first ActionScript in the first chapter. Now how's that for getting up and running in a hurry?

✔ **Part II: Using Elementary ActionScript, My Dear Watson:** I know, your name's probably not Watson. If it is, then this part's title is an added bonus. I just happen to like Sir Arthur Conan Doyle, his super sleuth Sherlock, and his faithful sidekick Watson. In this section of the book I show you how to use some of the elementary actions and variables in your scripts. I also show you how to manage complex Flash Web sites and create loops for movie sections that you want to play over and over and over and over and. . . .

✔ **Part III: Using Not-So-Elementary ActionScript, My Dear Watson:** Okay, so I really like Sherlock and Watson. In spite of the title redundancy, the section does not have redundant information. In this part I show you how to create objects that do things like read the current time and date from your computer's operating system. I also show you how to create Dynamic text, an object you use to give and receive information in your Flash movies. This part finishes with a chapter on how to exterminate — eek, egads, why isn't my movie working? — bugs in your ActionScript.

✔ **Part IV: Integrating ActionScript Elements in Your Flash Movies:** In this part I show you how to create stuff for your Flash movies. The stuff you'll be creating ranges from oh-so-useful stuff to oh-wow-that-is-so-cool stuff. Each chapter in this section contains exercises that I've created. And by the way, I've also created the graphic elements for the exercises so you can maximize your benefit by working on ActionScript and nothing but ActionScript.

✔ **Part V: The Part of Tens:** Here you get a couple chapters that have ten snippets of valuable tips and Internet resources that you can use to further your career as an ActionScripter.

✔ At the tail end of the book, you get the CD appendix, which tells you all about the goodies on the CD and how to install them on your computer.

✔ Speaking of the CD . . . if you write it, they will print it. At least that's how I always thought it was supposed to be. I wrote. Lots. So much, in fact, it didn't all fit in this book. But hey, that's good for you, reader. You've got a whole bunch of bonus material on the CD-ROM in the way of additional tutorials, three appendices with reference material for the most popular actions, and an entire chapter devoted to inspirational Flash Web sites.

Conventions Used in This Book

Many of the sections in this book are step-by-step instructions on how to create a certain effect or do something with ActionScript. When you see the laws of English grammar bent with a word such as `loadMovie`, you know it's an action written with a `special typeface like this`. ActionScript code is also shown in this manner. When you are instructed to type a value or text within a dialog box, the text you are to type is bold within the text or non-bold within a numbered step.

Whenever you see something like Choose Modify⇨Shape⇨Expand Fill, this is the path to a menu command. In this example , you would click the Modify menu at the top of the Flash workspace, click Shape, and then click Expand Fill.

In Flash MX, there are more actions stuffed in the Actions panel than there are Smiths in the NYC phone book. Well, almost. But speaking of books, these actions are in books. And the books have books and more books and, oh my, that's a lot of books. Rather than telling you to click that book, click this book, and then click this action, I list the path to the action in this manner:

Click Actions⇨Movie Clip Control and then double-click `loadMovie`. This means: click the Actions book icon, click the Movie Clip Control icon, and then double-click `loadMovie`. It saves you from reading the same thing over and over, and it saves me from having to type the same thing over and over. As a bonus, knocking out the superfluous words gives me more pages (1.8 at last count) to show you how to do cool stuff.

People work in different ways. Some people close an actions book immediately after using it while others leave it open. The people who leave actions books open are the same people who don't close cabinet doors after raiding the panty (and you wonder why you always get caught). If you fall into this group, you may still have a book open that happens to have the action you need for the next step. I can't please both types of reader, so you always see the full path to an action.

Icons Used in This Book

Throughout the book, you'll see some tastefully designed icons that were designed by tasteful and artistic Hungry Minds graphic gurus. These icons alert you to certain useful information that I certainly hope you'll find useful. You can almost read the icons in each chapter and use them as stepping-stones to quickly get a grasp of ActionScript. At any rate, if you read from an icon, you'll get a good idea of the information presented in the section the icon is smack dab in the middle of.

Whenever you see this icon, you'll find information that shows you how to perform an ActionScript task quickly, alert you to an ActionScript shortcut, or show you a way to streamline your workflow. These little snippets of wisdom were extracted the hard way, through the blood, sweat, and tears of the author; a nice chap I'm intimately familiar with.

The sole purpose in life — okay in this book — of the Remember icon is to jog your memory about information you already know — or should know. It serves as a reminder without having to present the information again, step-by-step-by-step.

Whenever you see this icon, take heed. It's warning you of a dire outcome that has occurred because the author did not follow the warning presented here. You're free to disregard the sage bits of advice presented with these icons; however if the dire outcome occurs, don't say you weren't warned.

If you're a card-carrying member of the geeks-r-us club and have a monogrammed pocket pal, you'll like the info associated with this icon.

When you see this icon, prepare to copy an exercise file from the book's CD to your hard drive. I've prepared the start of each exercise you'll find in this book. All you have to do is copy the file to your hard drive and follow the steps to create a finished ActionScript movie. The batteries aren't included — cause if you're using a desktop, you use household or office current; and if you're on a laptop, the batteries had better be charged up — but the graphics are.

This icon is your road map to other information about the same topic, or a topic presented with, or alluded to within the section you're reading.

Where To Go From Here

The logical place to go after finishing this book — or as much of this book as you care to or need to finish — is straight to your computer to create your own ActionScript movies. If, however, you need more information about Flash, or incorporating Flash within an HTML document, here are some useful books you might consider purchasing (both published by Hungry Minds, Inc.):

- *HTML 4 For Dummies*, 3rd Edition, by Ed Tittel and Natanya Pitts
- *Macromedia Flash MX For Dummies* by Ellen Finkelstein and Gurdy Leete

Part I

Demystifying ActionScript

The 5th Wave By Rich Tennant

"I can't really explain it, but every time I animate someone swinging a golf club, a little divot of code comes up missing on the home page."

In this part . . .

So, you've got this thing called Flash MX and you already know how to create really cool animations with it, but you want more. Yet at the same time, you quake in your boots — or bedroom slippers if you create Flash documents in your pajamas — at the very mention of the words ActionScript, code, or programming. If that sounds like you, then you'll find a lot of useful information in this part of the book.

In this part, I introduce you to the major players in ActionScript, the actions themselves and the objects you can — and cannot — apply them to. I introduce you to good ActionScript habits by showing you how to plan an ActionScript movie. In Chapter 1, I get you quickly up and running by showing you how to create your first movie with ActionScript. If you've been shying away from ActionScript because the genesis of all ActionScript — the Actions panel — looks pretty darned scary, you'll overcome your trepidations in this part. You'll also know all about syntax and other fascinating ActionScript terms if you check out Chapter 3.

Chapter 1

ActionScript: What It Is and What It Isn't

In This Chapter

▶ Introducing ActionScript

▶ Using Actions in your movies

▶ Planning an interactive movie

▶ Creating your first ActionScript

The fact that you have this book in your hands means that you know how to do some neat stuff with Flash and want to take your movies to the next level by adding ActionScript to them. If you don't know how to do some cool stuff with Flash and you're still at the bookstore, slowly put this book back on the shelf and look for a copy of *Macromedia Flash MX For Dummies,* by Gurdy Leete and Ellen Finkelstein (Hungry Minds, Inc.). Or if you're new to Flash and you have the need to get up to speed quickly, use this book in conjunction with *Macromedia Flash MX For Dummies* as a dynamic duo to get up and running with the latest and greatest version of Flash and some way cool ActionScript.

In this chapter, I familiarize you with the concept of ActionScript and what you can do with it. And believe me, what you can do with it is a lot. Whether it's bells and whistles you want for your Flash movies or useful stuff, like user-response forms and the like, ActionScript has an end for your means. At the end of this chapter, you get your feet wet and create your first ActionScript.

The Actions panel's got lots of books. And some of these books have books within a book. To add some actions to your scripts, you have to click this book icon, then click that book icon, then click another book icon, and so on. Rather than bore you with a lot of words, I'm going to show the path to each action as shown in the following example: Click Actions⇨Movie Control and then double-click goto.

What ActionScript Is — and What You Can Do with It

ActionScript is first and foremost a scripted programming language. Don't let that description scare you away because the designers of Flash have given you all the tools you need to create as much or as little ActionScript as you need. ActionScript is not one long document, like the script of a movie. ActionScript is composed of bits and pieces of code that you use in conjunction with the other elements of your Flash document to create a unique and interesting user experience. You've probably already used some basic ActionScript in your previous Flash documents to control the flow of a movie from one scene to the next or to navigate to a different frame in the movie. In its most basic form, ActionScript is useful. When you start stretching the ActionScript envelope, it becomes downright awesome. After you start using it, you begin to lie awake at night, thinking of new ways to use ActionScript in your movies.

ActionScript turns your basic Flash content into something special and entertaining. For example, I'm sure that you've visited Flash Web sites where the designer gives you something to look at (a *preloader*) while the site is loading. A preloader can be as simple as the word *Loading* flashing on the screen or something more visually exciting, like moving spheres, dancing letters, or the like. With ActionScript, you can take a preloader to the next level by letting the viewer interact with it while waiting for the site to load. Rather than have your Web site visitors watch a group of moving spheres, for example, you can script the spheres so that they follow your visitor's mouse like that woolly little creature that follows Mary.

Understanding Object-Oriented Programming — without Disorienting Yourself

When you decide to create interactive content and add ActionScript to a Flash document, you apply the actions to buttons, movie clips and/or keyframes rather than create a long script and embed it in a document, as is required with some other scripting languages.

A *document* is a Flash file before it's published; after it's published, it's called a *movie*.

So then, rather than worry about creating one long script, you need to figure out to which objects you need to apply actions in order to achieve the wham-bam-socko effect you're after. And if you're using ActionScript to create a not-so-wham-bam-socko effect, you still apply the actions to objects. The objects to which you apply the actions are keyframes, buttons, movie clips, and user-defined components (the movie clip formerly known as Smart Clip).

An action you apply to a keyframe is executed when the movie reaches that frame. Flash executes an action you assign to a button when a user's mouse interacts with the scripted button. When you add actions to a movie clip or user-defined component, Flash executes the action depending on when the event you choose happens. Flash has different event handlers that trigger the action based on what is happening to the object from which the action is being called. For example, when you move your mouse over a button, the event is a rollover. A movie clip loading is also an event. When you program an action to execute when a movie clip loads, the event is logically called Load. And you'll be happy to know that most of the events in ActionScript are logical to a fault, just like that pointy-eared Vulcan on *Star Trek*. I show you how to handle events for movie clips in Chapter 9; buttons are covered in Chapter 11.

Okay, you assign actions to objects. Even *I* knew that when I began creating ActionScripts. But you can also assign objects from the Actions panel to other objects. That may sound like double-talk, but it isn't. The objects on the Actions panel are organized in classes. For example, one of the many classes of objects you find in the Actions panel is named Date (not to be confused with the prune-like fruit); an object in this class that is added to an ActionScript retrieves information about the date and time from the operating system of the host computer (the one playing the Flash movie). In the Actions panel, you also find Sound objects and Movie Clip objects, aptly named critters that you use to modify sounds and movie clips in your Flash productions.

Introducing ActionScript Elements

I like to think of ActionScript as programming for nonprogrammers. If you've ever done any dabbling with JavaScript, you know that it's powerful. You also know that it's complicated. ActionScript, on the other hand, can be as complicated as you want to make it. You don't need to master every single available action in order to get something done. When you decide to add interactivity to a Flash movie, you find out how to use the necessary actions and then apply them. An ActionScript isn't a single document that tells the Flash movie what to do; rather, it's little bits that you add here and there to complete the effect you're after. You attach actions to buttons, keyframes, movie clips, and your powerful user-defined components (the user in this case being you, the creator of the Flash document and little old ActionScript whiz). Listing 1-1 shows a JavaScript used to swap an image when a Web site visitor rolls a mouse over a hot spot.

Listing 1-1   Typical JavaScript

```
<script language="JavaScript">
<!--
function MM_findObj(n, d) { //v3.0
    var p,i,x; if(!d) d=document;
    if((p=n.indexOf("?"))>0&&parent.frames.length) {
    d=parent.frames[n.substring(p+1)].document; n=n.sub-
            string(0,p);}
    if(!(x=d[n])&&d.all) x=d.all[n];
    for (i=0;!x&&i<d.forms.length;i++) x=d.forms[i][n];
    for(i=0;!x&&d.layers&&i<d.layers.length;i++)
            x=MM_findObj(n,d.layers[i].document); return x;
}

    function MM_swapImage() { //v3.0
    var i,j=0,x,a=MM_swapImage.arguments; document.MM_sr=new
            Array;
    for(i=0;i<(a.length-2);i+=3)
    if ((x=MM_findObj(a[i]))!=null){document.MM_sr[j++]=x;
            if(!x.oSrc) x.oSrc=x.src; x.src=a[i+2];}
}

    function MM_preloadImages() { //v3.0
    var d=document; if(d.images){ if(!d.MM_p) d.MM_p=new
            Array();
    var i,j=d.MM_p.length,a=MM_preloadImages.arguments;
            for(i=0; i<a.length; i++)
    if (a[i].indexOf("#")!=0){ d.MM_p[j]=new Image;
            d.MM_p[j++].src=a[i];}}
}
//-->
</script>
```

Whenever you see two forward slashes (//) in an ActionScript, this is a comment. A *comment* is like a note to yourself that explains what's happening in the next line of the script. You'll see comments in listings throughout the book. I've added these to give you an explanations of what's going on.

In case you think that I'm some kind of JavaScript guru, I'm not. I pasted this code from a document I created with a program named Fireworks. If I had to script the preceding mess by myself, I would never have a Web site with swapping images. On the other hand, I did create Listing 1-2 from scratch — with a little help from the Actions panel.

Listing 1-2   Adding Interactivity with ActionScript

```
on (rollOver) {
    _root.aboutus.gotoAndPlay("begin movie");
}
on (rollOut) {
    _root.aboutus.gotoAndStop("end movie");
}
on (press){
    _root.aboutus.gotoAndStop("end movie");
    loadMovieNum ("about.swf", 1);
}
```

This ActionScript causes a button to call a specific frame (begin movie) in a movie clip named aboutus when a user's mouse is rolled over the button. When the mouse rolls off the button, the ActionScript tells Flash to go to a frame called end movie. When the button is clicked, another Flash movie is loaded, giving the Web site visitor more information. For one thing, this script looks much simpler than the cockamamie business in Listing 1-1. This one also took less than a minute or so to script with the Actions panel.

Rather than make you manually enter a bunch of complicated lines of text, like you do in some other scripting languages, the designers of Flash have given you a neat little device known as the Actions panel. I show you how to use the Actions panel in Chapter 2. But if you're chomping at the bit to see what it looks like, click the arrow next to the Actions panel to take a sneak peek, as shown in Figure 1-1. If you happen to be a timid Flash designer and you don't have the Actions panel displayed in the Flash workspace, choose Window⇨Actions.

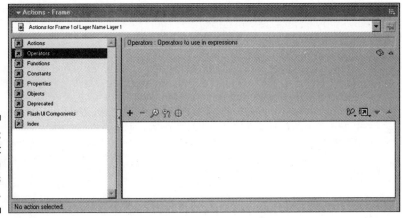

Figure 1-1:
ActionScript begins on the Actions panel.

The Actions panel is an integral part of your arsenal when creating ActionScript. The default Flash MX panel layout docks the Actions panel below the Stage for easy access. I strongly advise you to leave the panel right there so you've got easy access to all the Actions when a blinding flash — or shimmering candle, depending on how good your idea is — of inspiration strikes.

When you first open the Actions panel, you notice a bunch of little icons that look like books with arrows on their covers. Click a book's cover, and it opens to reveal all the actions in that group (book). The first time you click one of these book icons, you may think that you've opened Pandora's box. Some of the books even have subbooks. (Yikes — a book within a book!)

Each one of the books contains like actions, objects, or functions that you can add to your ActionScripts. Elements from the different books can be mixed and matched to achieve the desired result. In the following sections, I give you an overview of the elements of an ActionScript and what they're used for.

Introducing movie clips

Movie clips serve two functions in Flash. They're reusable animations, and they're objects that you can manipulate with ActionScript. A movie clip is a symbol. When you place an instance of it on Stage, you can give that instance a unique name. *Instances* are clones of the original symbol that are identical in all aspects. After you name an instance, you can apply actions to it and get the clip to jump through the hoop, so to speak, by referring to the instance's name in your ActionScript.

If you're experienced in Flash, you're probably used to creating movie clips with many frames. Movie clips have their own, unique timelines that run independently from the main movie's timeline.

When you call a movie clip into action, the movie clip plays frame by frame — unless, of course, you've used actions to stop the movie clip at a certain frame or created a loop using the `goto` action. You can apply actions to the frames within the movie clip to make the movie clip behave the way you want. After you have an instance of the movie clip on Stage, you can use ActionScript to make it do something, such as move from one point to the next, when a button is clicked or become invisible. Movie clips are the heart of Flash interactivity.

Introducing user-defined components

User-defined components are movie clips with brains. *User-defined components* have parameters you can change on the fly to suit your movie or to suit the particular instance of a user-defined component. For example, if you create a user-defined component with a dynamic text field that displays the name of a product, you can quickly change the product name by redefining the component's parameters as you're editing the movie. You can use another instance of the same movie clip to display another product by again changing the clip's parameters. Redefining a clip's parameters is just a right-click (in Windows) or Ctrl+click (on the Macintosh) away. I show you how to convert your basic movie clip into a component with parameters that you define (hence the name user-defined component) in Chapter 9.

Introducing the Actions book

If you haven't peeked inside the Actions panel yet, when you do, I advise you to open the first book — labeled Actions because it's got actions in it — with extreme caution because when you open up this book, it's like one of those old-fashioned encyclopedias with many books. Yup, you guessed it — this is one of those books I forewarned you about. It's got many more books inside.

Within the almighty Actions book, you find books with actions to give you basic control over the flow of a movie, books with actions that control movie clips, books that contain actions you can use to create containers for bits of information you either collect from visitors or dispense to visitors, and a whole lotta other books. For example, you can use a variable to have Flash store a visitor's name, which can then be displayed in a dynamic text box. Oh, my — what power you have when you give Flash a memory with variables. And dear reader, if you're wondering what a variable is, it's an object that can store different bits of information. The content of the information can vary throughout the course of a movie, hence the name variable.

✔ **Movie Control book:** If you need to get control over your movie, here's the first place you should go. In this book you'll find actions to go to a particular frame, play the movie, stop the movie (also known as movie interruptus) and you've even got one to stop all sounds, which effectively silences the lovely strains to the old Simon and Garfunkel song, "Sounds of Silence" should it happen to be playing in the movie when the action is executed.

✔ **Browser/Network book:** Here you find the `loadMovie` action that makes it possible for you to replace the base movie or load another movie on top of the base movie. You can also break a big site into individual movies and then apply the `loadMovie` action to a button that, when clicked, loads a movie. I show you how to break a big site into individual movies in Chapter 5.

✔ **Movie Clip Control book:** This book gives you the power to set properties for an object. If you're thinking that properties are best left in the hands of real estate agents, you're missing some of Flash's power. The type of properties I'm talking about has nothing to do with street addresses, two-story town houses, or the like. The properties you deal with here can change an object's width, height, position, rotation, and visibility, among other things. Other actions in the Movie Clip Control book give you the power to create elements that the user can click and drag around the screen (just like you drag your luggage through an airport, only without the effort).

✔ **Conditions/Loop book:** Using the actions in this book, you can create loops with actions. A *loop* is an action or series of actions that repeats while a certain condition is true; for example, a password-entry field where the Web site visitor has three chances to enter the correct password. After the third try, the ActionScript advances to another part of the script, telling the user that he is not authorized to use the site. I show you in Chapter 5 how to create loops without getting dizzy.

✔ **Printing:** This book has one action: `print`. Hmm, maybe future versions of Flash will have extra printing actions, otherwise, why would they make it a book?

✔ **User Defined Functions:** Flash comes with functions, but if you can't find a functional function for your purpose, you can create your own. You use the actions in this book to define your own functions and call your own functions. And when you call your own functions, chances are good, that the function will respond to you.

✔ **Miscellaneous Actions:** The book that holds actions that don't quite fit in any other book. For example, in this book you'll find the `trace` action, which you use to display a message when a certain part of your ActionScript is executed or to trace a variable. In this book you also find the `evaluate` action, which is used to create an expression, which is expressly why this book is called Miscellaneous Actions; all the actions in this book do something, but they're not related, therefore they must be miscellaneous. Huh?

There are so many actions in the Actions panel, you almost need to sublet a small storage warehouse for them all. Unfortunately, giving a tutorial for each and every action, in each and every book, is beyond the scope of this book and would result in three things: a book the size of a doorstop, an author with a severe case of writer's cramp, and a reader (that's you) wondering why the book is larger than most biblical sagas and, most importantly, when it's all going to end.

Introducing the Operators book

The next book you find in the Actions panel is Operators, which in Flash MX is also divided into sub-books. Operators are used in expressions, which are something you probably remember fondly — or not so fondly, depending on your aptitude for numbers — from your high school math classes. My favorite expression in school is 2+2; it always adds up. You can use operators in expressions to calculate things, like the score in a Flash game you create.

With operators, you can also make comparisons and get Flash to do the math. One comparison you can make is to see whether an object's property matches a certain parameter. For example, you can create an expression that evaluates whether an object's *x* coordinate matches a certain value. This comparison can be useful when you create a Flash game. You can also compare text objects, which are known as *strings* in programmer-speak. For example, you can compare strings to verify whether a password entered by a user is correct.

Introducing the Functions book

The next book in the Actions panel is filled with functions. Functions do things when you add them to your ActionScripts. For example, you can use the `getProperty` function to return an object's property, say, the value of its *x* and *y* coordinates on Stage. And there's this nifty function called `eval` that you use to return the value of a variable or an object's property.

In the book I actually only cover one function, `getProperty`. However, if you have the need to get up to speed with other functions in this book, select the action, and then click the Reference panel icon near the upper-right corner of the Actions panel. What? You say you don't know what the Reference panel is? Hang on, I show you how to use the Reference panel in Chapter 2.

Introducing the Constants book

Constants are always the same, hence the truth in advertising when it comes to their name. Some constants are unique values that you use with *Boolean* expressions. Boolean expressions are either true or false. To put this in perspective, it's either day or night. If it's day, day = true; if it's night, day = false. You have other constants you use with variables; for example, the null constant defines a variable that has nothin' in it, honey, while the undefined constant defines a variable as undefined. (And for you geography buffs, constants are located in the nether regions of Constantinople.)

Introducing the Properties book

The Properties book (conveniently located in the Actions panel) is filled with properties that you won't find on a realtor's wish list. You use the type of properties you find here to change an object's properties, such as visibility, opaqueness, or position. Astute readers may also notice that I mentioned properties in the Movie Clip Control book. Well, you find the same properties here, you just address them differently by referring to the object directly by its target path rather than using the `setProperty` action. When you address a property individually, you can create an expression to change the property. It's just a slightly more efficient way of changing a property.

There are also other properties in this book you don't find in the Movie Clip Control book that refer to properties of the actual movie or a movie clip — stuff like the total number of frames, the number of frames loaded, and so on.

Introducing the Objects book

Here's another Actions panel book that's actually a whole library. When you open the Objects book, you find four additional books. And when you open one of these books, you find more books of actions, each one pertaining to a specific object, such as Date, Color, or Math. Each book is a set of methods you apply to an object. For example, you can create a Date object and then use the object's methods to get the current, day, date, and time from the operating system of the computer playing the Flash movie.

Introducing the Deprecated book

Here's a book full of actions that have been denounced, or as the Macromedia folks refer to them, *deprecated*. Deprecated actions are actions from earlier versions of Flash that while still fully functional, have been relegated to deprecated status because there is a better way of doing it — at least in the eyes of Macromedia. If you want to find out what action Macromedia recommends you use in place of a deprecated action, select a deprecated action and then right-click (Windows) or Ctrl-click (Macintosh) and choose View Reference from the drop-down menu. You'll get a detailed explanation of the action (in four part harmony, notated, and quoted), along with the action you are encouraged to use in its place.

Introducing the Flash UI Components book

Flash UI Components actions make it for you to add UI (user interface) components such as check boxes, lists, radio buttons, scroll boxes, and the like to your documents and then modify their parameters. Incidentally, there's also a library of components. In this library of components you find Flash UI components where all the heavy work has been done by the designers of Flash. All you have to do to make these functional is change the component parameters.

Seeing How an ActionScript Flows

When you create an ActionScript to create an effect, Flash executes the actions beginning at the first line of the script, followed by the second line, and so on, unless you create a condition in the ActionScript that, after being evaluated, causes the script to branch off in another direction. For example, you may create an ActionScript that checks for a user password. If the correct password is entered, the user gains access to the Web site. If the password that's entered is incorrect (or as that quirky little robot from *Lost In Space* would say, "does not compute"), the script branches in another direction — perhaps warning the user that he is not authorized to enter the site. After either of those conditions is met, the script ends.

Another type of ActionScript you can create is a *loop*. When you create a loop, a certain set of actions keeps repeating until the condition is satisfied. For example, if you decide to be generous and give your Web site visitor three chances to enter a correct password, the script resets the password-entry field, giving the user another opportunity to enter the correct password. But after three tries, just like in baseball, he's outta there!

Planning Your ActionScripts

When you make the big move and decide to add lots of interactivity to a Flash movie, you should plan things out ahead of time. A bit of preplanning prevents you from running amuck in code after several hours of hard work.

Before you even create the movie, the first thing you need to know is what you want to accomplish. Oh, you can rush in headlong and noodle around with a few ActionScript elements to see what you can come up with. In fact, that's a good way to discover new things you can accomplish with Flash. Many times, your aimless noodling creates a happy accident that you can save for another Flash project. But if your client or boss has you under a deadline, you need to get cracking straight away.

You should also plan on change, especially if you're creating the project for a client. It has been my experience that you can tell the boss that the change is not possible, but I'll leave this for you to decide. It's always best to get a clear picture of your client's expectations before you begin work, which minimizes the opportunities for change caused by miscommunication.

When you create a complex movie with lots of ActionScript, remember to use symbols for as many of your graphic elements as possible. If a change needs to be made, you edit the symbol, and all instances of the symbol change. As an added bonus, using symbols helps reduce the file size of the published movie. Create as much reusable code as possible. For example, if you have several navigation buttons, the ActionScript for each one probably is similar, which means that you can cut down on your work by using the Actions panel's drop-down menu to copy, cut, or paste lines of code from one keyframe to another or from one object to another.

Putting It Down on Paper

After you have a clear-cut idea of what you want to accomplish, you may be tempted to jump right in and create the ActionScript code. Unless it's a very simple effect, *don't.* Put the desired effect down on paper to get a better idea of the ActionScript elements you need in order to pull off the effect. For example, if you've created a button and you simply want the movie to advance to another frame when the button is clicked, you can create the ActionScript quickly right in the Actions panel by using the code shown in Listing 1-3, which tells the movie to advance to frame 3 when the user releases the mouse button.

Listing 1-3   Creating a Simple ActionScript

```
on (release) {
    gotoAndPlay (3);
}
```

If you want the button to do different things, however, depending on where the user's mouse is (playing a movie clip when the mouse rolls over the button, for example, or stopping the clip immediately when the mouse rolls off the button and then advancing to a different frame in the movie), this process becomes a bit more complex. You have two elements to script: the movie clip and the button. After you get familiar with the way ActionScript is displayed within the Actions panel, you can jot your ideas down on paper before you open the Actions panel. Listing 1-4 is an example of what you may jot down for the preceding scenario.

Listing 1-4 Planning an ActionScript

```
When a mouse rolls over the button
    Play frame one of the movie clip
When a mouse rolls off the button
    Stop the movie clip at its last frame
When the button is clicked
    Go to frame twelve of the main movie
End action
```

After you have an idea of how the script will flow, you can open the Actions panel and create the code. Listing 1-5 shows how the scenario would be scripted within the Actions panel.

Listing 1-5 Following the Plan

```
on (rollOver) {
    with (My_movie_clip){
    gotoAndPlay ("begin");
    //"begin" is a frame label for frame 1 in My_movie_clip
    }
}
on (rollOut) {
    with (My_movie_clip) {
    gotoAndStop ("lastFrame");
    //"lastFrame" is a frame label for the last frame of
            My movie clip
    }
}
on (release) {
    gotoAndPlay ("aboutUs");
    //"aboutUs" is a frame label for the 12th frame in the
            main movie
}

    on (rollOver) {
      with (My_movie_clip) {
        gotoAndPlay("begin");
    //"begin" is a frame label for frame 1 in My_movie_clip
      }
    }
```

As you can see in the preceding scenario, you also have to consider the ActionScript for the movie clip. In this case, rather than refer to frame numbers, the script refers to frame labels that you can christen when you initially plan the script. Jotting down what you want to happen in plain English (or whatever other language you prefer; pig Latin is fun but confusing to co-workers) makes it easier to see how all the bits of ActionScript you create for a movie will *dovetail,* or merge.

Producing Your First ActionScript Movie

If you're chomping at the bit to see what ActionScript can do, follow all the steps in the following sections to successfully produce your first ActionScript. Don't worry if you don't totally understand every step. My goal here is to familiarize you with the Actions panel and the power of ActionScript. In this ActionScript movie, you create a text box in which a visitor to the Web site enters his or her name. After the user presses the button, the Flash Player displays a greeting. Of course, the Flash Player isn't greeting the user — *you* are, vicariously, through your ActionScript wizardry.

Creating a document

Before you can use all the bells and whistles on the Actions panel, you need to create a document, known in previous versions of Flash as a movie. This may seem like Flash 101, but it will serve as a refresher. Plus I need to show you where to get some of the assets (stuff you use to create the movie, like buttons and so on) for this ActionScript.

To create a new document for your first ActionScript:

1. **Launch Flash.**

   Okay. I know. This step is blatantly obvious. I'm just keeping you on your toes. Accept the default document that Flash creates when you launch the program.

2. Choose Modify➪Document.

The Document Properties dialog box opens.

3. Click the Background Color swatch and select a dark blue color.

If you want the background color to perfectly match the finished tutorial, select the color with the hexadecimal value 000066 (it's in the first column of blue colors).

4. Click OK to close the Document Properties dialog box.

5. Choose File➪Open As Library.

The Open As Library dialog box appears.

When you're working with files from a CD, loading them on your hard drive is always a good idea, especially if you're going to modify them in any way. CD files are read-only. If you try to test or publish a Flash file loaded directly from a CD, you get an error message. Use your computer's operating system to remove the read-only attributes from the file, and you can modify the file in Flash.

Copy the file chapter 1.fla from this chapter's folder on this book's CD-ROM to your hard drive. Use your operating system to disable the file's read-only attribute.

6. Navigate to the chapter1.fla file from this book's CD and open the file.

The file's document Library opens.

7. Drag the Enter button symbol on Stage and position it slightly above the bottom.

Don't worry about the exact position right now; just make sure it shows up in the finished movie.

8. Choose Window➪Align.

The Align panel opens.

9. With the button still selected, use the Align panel to center it near the bottom of the Stage.

Flash positions the button near the bottom center of the Stage.

Create input and dynamic text boxes

The next step in creating your ActionScript movie is to create an input text box. Input text accepts — you guessed it — input entered from someone watching your Flash movie. For this movie, you also create a dynamic text box. Dynamic text reads information stored in a variable that you assign to the dynamic text box when you create it. In this case, the information stored in the variable is the name entered in the input text box. To create the input text box:

1. **Select the Text tool and then create a text box on Stage.**

   Click anywhere on Stage and drag the tool to the right. Create a box approximately 50 percent wider than the Enter button.

2. **Open the Property inspector by clicking the arrow to the left of the word Properties.**

   After you open the Property inspector, you have access to the parameters for the text box you just created.

   The Property inspector is a major tool in Flash MX. It's a good idea to have it open at all times. To open the Property inspector, choose Window➪Properties. If you're not familiar with the Property inspector, refer to *Macromedia Flash MX For Dummies,* by Gurdy Leete and Ellen Finkelstein (published by Hungry Minds, Inc.).

3. **In the Property inspector, click the triangle to the right of Static Text and from the drop-down menu, choose Input Text.**

   The text box is now set for input text, which creates a blank text box that accepts text input from the user's keyboard.

4. **Select your favorite Font style, click the inverted triangle to the right of the Font Size field, and drag the slider to 24.**

   In Flash MX, you define all text parameters using the Property inspector.

5. **Select a dark color for the text.**

   To define the text color, click the Text color swatch and choose a color from the pop-up palette.

6. **In the Text Alignment section, click the Center Justify button.**

   This button looks exactly like the Center button in most word processing programs.

7. **In the bottom section of the Properties panel, click the Show Border Around Text button.**

   This option creates a border around the input text box and applies a white background behind the text. (If you don't select this option, nobody will know that the box is there.)

8. In the Var field, type name, **as shown in Figure 1-2.**

Your text box is ready to receive input after the movie is published.

9. Select the text box you just created and choose Edit⇨Copy.

This step copies the text box to your operating system's clipboard.

TIP

You can quickly create an exact duplicate of a selected object on Stage by holding down the Alt key (in Windows) or the Option key (on the Macintosh) while dragging the object to a new position.

Figure 1-2:
You set the parameters for input text with the Property inspector.

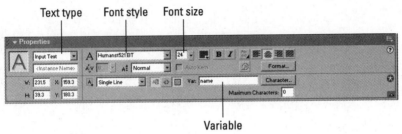

Text type   Font style   Font size

Variable

10. Choose Edit⇨Paste.

The text box is pasted on the Stage. Position it below the original text box. If necessary, use the Align panel to center the boxes relative to each other.

11. In the Property inspector panel, click the triangle to the right of Input Text and choose Dynamic Text from the drop-down menu.

This converts the text field to dynamic text. You use dynamic text boxes to display text from a variable. In this case, the text box displays the information the viewer enters in the input text box you created in the first frame. You can use the same variable name, but you're going to add a bit more interactivity to this text box — you'll be displaying the contents of the input text box and a little more.

12. In the Var field, type welcome.

The dynamic text box is ready to receive information.

Getting interactive with ActionScript

Although it may not seem like it, if you've read the preceding couple of sections, you've already begun using some ActionScript components. Now comes the fun part: putting the whole thing together as a working movie. In this section, you add code to the button:

1. **Using the Arrow tool, select the button.**

2. **Click the arrow to the right of the word Actions to open the Actions panel.**

   The Actions Panel opens. Notice that the panel is listed as Actions-Button. When you add code to a movie clip, the panel is labeled as Actions-Movie Clip; add code to keyframes, the panel is known as Actions-Frame.

3. **Click Actions⇨Variables.**

   The Variables group opens for business.

4. **Double-click the `set variable` action to add it to the list.**

   The `set variable` action appears in the Script pane of the Actions panel window and some text, highlighted in red, that says `Not Set Yet`. This is Flash's way of telling you that it needs more information about the variable: its name and its value. Notice that Flash adds another line of code, `on release`, at the top of the window. This is part of the `on` action and appears whenever you program a button. The `on` action handles a mouse's interaction with a button. In this case, the variable is set when the button is released.

5. **In the Variable field, type the name** welcome.

   This variable is the same one you assigned to the dynamic text box. When the script is executed, the value of the welcome variable is displayed in the dynamic text box.

6. **Type "Hi there," +name in the Value field and click the Expression box.**

   This line of code combines the phrase `"Hi there,"` with the variable name. The phrase is in quotes because it is a text object, or, as it is known in the programming world, a *string*. Remember to leave a space after the comma; otherwise, the phrase and the name will run together, a run-on variable, if you will. The value is an *expression* because Flash is combining the string with a variable.

If variables seem foreign right now, hang in there; they all make sense when you read Chapter 6.

7. Close the Actions panel.

That's it. You're done. Your finished ActionScript for the button should look just like the one shown in Figure 1-3.

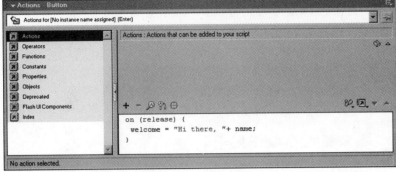

Figure 1-3:
You use the Actions panel to assign actions to objects and frames.

Testing the ActionScript

After you create a movie with ActionScript, it only makes good sense to test it before unleashing it on an unsuspecting public. Testing even the simplest ActionScript can save you from considerable embarrassment — not to mention egg on your face. To test the ActionScript movie you just created:

1. Choose Control➪Test Movie.

Flash publishes the file in .swf format and opens a new window.

2. Click inside the input text box you created.

A flashing vertical bar appears inside the text box, just waiting for you to enter some text.

3. Type your name.

4. Click the Enter button.

If you follow these steps exactly, you see `"Hi there,"` followed by your name. If you see something else, something went awry somewhere, and you have to debug the ActionScript, as explained in the following section.

Debugging your first ActionScript

When you create movies with lots of ActionScript buried in movie clips, buttons, and frames, you can use the Debugger to help keep track of everything. I show you how to use the Debugger in detail in Chapter 13; for right now, I want to give you an idea of what the Debugger keeps track of for you. To debug your first ActionScript:

1. **In the workspace, choose Control⇨Debug Movie.**

   Flash publishes the movie and opens it in another window. A window named Debugger also opens, as shown in Figure 1-4.

Figure 1-4:
You use this rascal to debug your Action-Scripts.

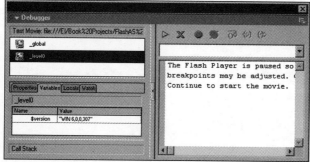

2. **Click the Toggle Breakpoint button that looks like a green fast-forward button.**

   When you first start the Debugger, the Flash movie is paused so the Breakpoints can be adjusted. When you set a breakpoint, you do it at a certain point in a script to stop the movie so you can see what's happening. I show you how to use Breakpoints in Chapter 13.

3. **In the Debugger's Test Movie window, click the level0 button.**

   This button displays the elements used in the main timeline of your movie. In simple movies, you have only one timeline. However, if your movie has movie clips, user-defined components, or movies loaded into other levels, the Debugger displays a button for each timeline.

4. **If it's not already selected, click the Debugger's Variables tab.**

   The Variables section of the Debugger opens. In the Name column, the only variable listed is Version. The Value column shows the version of the Flash Player that your operating system is using to play the movie.

   A variable is not displayed in the Variables section until it has a value.

5. **Click inside the input text box and begin typing.**

   When you begin typing, name is displayed in the variable column, which is the actual name for the variable you assigned to the input text box. In the Value column, you see what you're typing. What's happening is that the Debugger is keeping track of the variable being used, along with its value.

6. **Click the Enter button to finish playing the movie.**

   If the movie played correctly, welcome is displayed in the Debugger's Name column. In the Value column, you should see Hi there followed by the text you entered in the input text box with the variable name. Your Debugger window should look similar to the one shown in Figure 1-5.

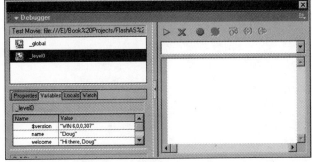

Figure 1-5: The Debugger keeps track of the variables in your movies.

Publishing Your Movie

After creating the ActionScript movie and testing and debugging it, you publish the movie for the entire world to see on the Web — or for a selected audience to see, if you're publishing it for a multimedia format. To publish your movie:

1. **Choose File⇨Publish Settings.**

   The Publish Settings dialog box opens.

2. **Click the Formats tab.**

   The Formats section opens, as shown in Figure 1-6.

3. **Select the format (or formats) in which you want to publish the movie.**

   A tab appears for each format you select. The default formats are Flash and HTML. Select these formats, and Flash publishes the movie in its native .swf format and embeds the movie in an HTML document.

4. Click each format tab you selected and set the parameters for that format.

I spare you the drudgery of going over each and every format. After all, this is a book about ActionScript. If you need a refresher on the Publish Settings command, refer to *Macromedia Flash MX For Dummies,* by Gurdy Leete and Ellen Finkelstein (Hungry Minds, Inc.).

5. After adjusting the publish settings for each selected format, click OK to save the settings or click Publish to publish the movie in each selected format.

6. To publish the movie after saving the settings, choose File⇔Publish.

To preview the movie as it will appear in your system's default Web browser, press Ctrl+F12.

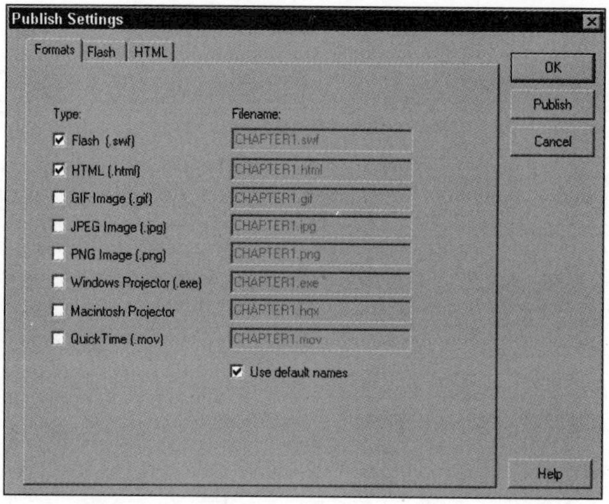

Figure 1-6:
You choose publishing formats with the Publish Settings dialog box.

Chapter 2

Taking Action with ActionScript

· ·

In This Chapter

▶ Using the Actions panel

▶ Using parameter text boxes

▶ Adding Actions to a script

▶ Controlling the flow of an ActionScript

· ·

*I*f this is your first foray into ActionScript, I have some good news for you. You don't have to be a typing wizard and enter every action manually. Thanks to the Actions panel, adding an action to a script is as simple as double-clicking it, dragging and dropping it into the Actions panel's Script pane, or selecting it from a drop-down menu. Of course, whenever you have something sweet, the bitter seems to go along with it. The bitter that accompanies the sweetness of the Actions panel is that the panel has *lots* of actions, all of which are subdivided. The sheer volume of available actions is what makes ActionScript so powerful for you, the designer. Here's another drop of sweetener: You don't have to know how to use each and every action to do some very cool things with Flash.

In this chapter, I show you how to use the foundry that creates every Flash ActionScript: the Actions panel. I also show you how to use the Actions panel to assign actions to objects and frames. I also show you an alternative for Flash's automated method of creating ActionScript: Expert mode.

The Actions panel's got lots of books. And some of these books have books within a book. To add some actions to your scripts, you have to click this book icon, then click that book icon, then click another book icon, and so on. Rather than bore you with a lot of words, I'm going to show the path to each action as shown in the following example: Click Actions⇨Movie Control and then double-click goto.

Exploring the Actions Panel

When you decide to add interactivity to a Flash production by adding actions to a button, keyframe, movie clip, or user-defined component, you start with the Actions panel. You simply have no other way to add actions to your documents. Like everything else in Flash, the Actions panel is versatile and friendly, yet somewhat intimidating — or so it seems when you first open it. After you get the knack of working with the Actions panel and see what it adds to your Flash documents, you begin to regard it as an old friend.

Navigating the Actions panel

Before you can start adding sizzle to your Flash creations with the Actions panel, you have to navigate your way around this multifaceted powerhouse. To begin your journey into the wild and wonderful world of ActionScript, open the Actions panel, as shown in Figure 2-1, by clicking the arrow to the left of the panel's title. Actually, you can click the panel's title also. The Flash programmers decided to give you a bigger target area for those times when you're still slaving away on an ActionScript in the wee hours of the morning and hand-eye-hand-mouse coordination has gone the way of the dodo.

 At first glance, the Actions panel appears fairly innocuous. After all, you have two panes: One is filled with little book icons, tastefully decorated with an angled arrow, and the other pane (the Script pane) is blank. If the Actions panel stays that way, your career as an ActionScripter (and any chance for membership in the hallowed Amalgamated Consortium of ActionScripters) is doomed.

Opening an Actions book

Each of the book icons contains a group of similar actions. Take another look at Figure 2-1 and notice the nine sub-books contained with the Actions book. Each of these sub-books contain actions and, like the degree of difficulty in a gymnastic exercise, the actions get a tad more complicated as you go from top to bottom. And when you get to Index, Flash literally throws the book at you — every action in every book is alphabetized for easy retrieval. For those who know their action ABCs, this is often the quickest way around the Actions panel as some of the actions are buried deep within a book within another book within . . . well, you get the idea. To open one of the action books, click its book icon. The closed-book icon becomes an open book, revealing its contents. Figure 2-2 shows the Actions panel with the Movie Control book open for business.

Actions books

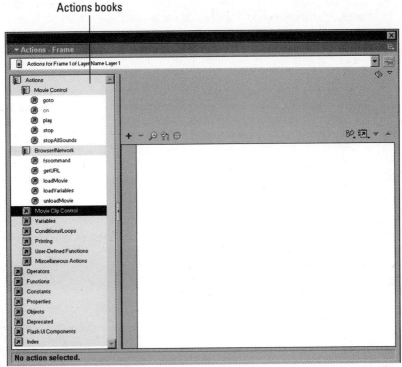

Figure 2-1:
To create
Action-
Script,
you have
to open the
Actions
panel.

Movie Control actions

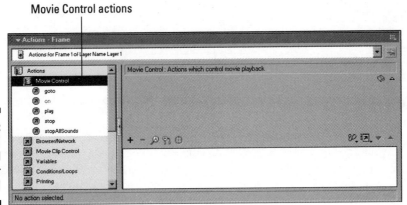

Figure 2-2:
Actions!
Come and
get your
actions!

In Figure 2-2, notice that you can see a circle (again, tastefully decorated with the obligatory arrow) to the left of each listing in the book. The circle icons serve two functions: They're visual references for each action, and you use them to add actions to your scripts. If you like visual references, icons, and the like, this is the way to work with actions.

Some people prefer dealing with the cold, hard logic of the written word. If you're a card-carrying member of that group, the Flash programmers also thought of you when they created the Actions panel. To reveal a drop-down menu of every actions group, click the plus button (+) just above the editing window in the Script pane. To reveal all actions in a group, move your cursor over the group's name. Figure 2-3 shows the Actions panel drop-down menu with the Movie Control group expanded. Notice that each action's shortcut is listed to the right of the action.

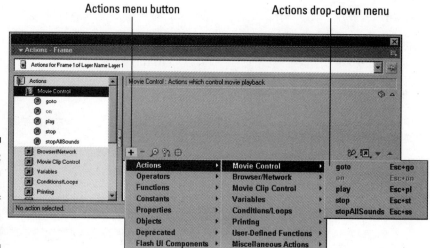

Actions menu button   Actions drop-down menu

Figure 2-3:
You can
open a
group of
actions in
two ways.

Adding Actions to Your Script

After you have the Actions panel open, logic tells you that it's time to put it to use rather than to marvel at its construction. After all, the Actions panel looks good — but it doesn't look that good. You can work with the Actions panel in two ways: Normal mode and Expert mode. When you begin your career as a purveyor of Flash movies with ActionScript, stick to Normal mode; it's much more forgiving. However, if you're experienced in other programming languages, you may find it beneficial to work in Expert mode. I generally find it easier to create complex ActionScript code in Normal mode and fine-tune it in Expert mode.

You can add actions only to buttons, keyframes, movie clips, and user-defined components. If you select anything other than the above, and open the Actions panel, all the actions are dimmed.

For more information on applying ActionScript to buttons, mosey on over to Chapter 11. For more information on working with movie clips and user-defined components (the genius symbol formerly known as smart clip), take a hike to Chapter 9.

Creating ActionScript in Normal mode

The default mode of the Actions panel is Normal mode. When you create a script in Normal mode, you select the action you want to add to the script, and Flash takes care of formatting the ActionScript code properly. After you have the Actions panel open, you can add an action to your script in Normal mode in one of three ways:

- ✔ Click an action group's book icon to open the group, and then double-click the action you want to add to the script. The selected action appears in the Script pane of the Actions panel.

- ✔ Click an action group's book icon to open the group, click an action to select it, and then drag the action into the Script pane of the Actions panel. The action appears, formatted to perfection, in the Script pane of the Actions panel.

- ✔ Click the plus button (+) just above the editing window in the Script pane of the Actions panel, place your cursor over the group you want to open, and click the desired action to add it to the script. The added action is displayed in the Script pane of the Actions panel.

Figure 2-4 shows the Actions panel with several lines of code in it. When you add an action to a script, it appears below the line of code you select when you add the action to the script. Normally, you work in linear fashion from top to bottom, adding an action by using one of the methods just outlined while the last action is still selected.

Notice the window near the top of the Actions panel. There you find a window with a text message that says "Actions for" followed by the description of the currently selected object. To display actions applied to other objects in the selected keyframe, click the triangle to the right of the window and choose an object from the drop-down menu. To display the script for the currently selected object while navigating to other keyframes, or selecting other objects, click the Pin Current Script button as shown in Figure 2-4.

Parameter text boxes

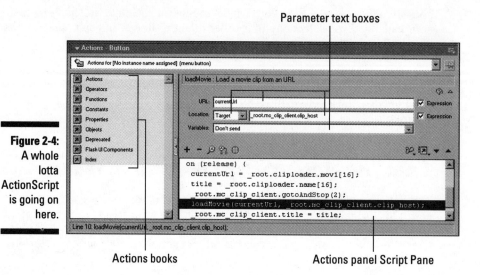

Figure 2-4:
A whole
lotta
ActionScript
is going on
here.

Actions books

Actions panel Script Pane

As you gain more experience with ActionScript, you work with several lines of code in an individual script. When you test a script, you may find that — in spite of your genius ActionScripter status — you've left out an important line of code. To make matters worse, the spot where you need to add the line of code is smack-dab in the middle of the script. Not to worry. To add a line of code in the middle of a script:

1. **Click the line of code just above the spot where you want to insert a new action.**

   The selected line of code is highlighted.

2. **Add the desired action to the script using one of the methods outlined at the start of this section.**

   The new action appears below the line you selected in Step 1.

As you gain experience in ActionScript and create scripts with multiple lines of code, you can keep better track of where you are in the script by clicking the icon in the upper-right corner of the Actions panel and then choosing View Line Numbers from the Action panel's Options menu.

Assigning an action to a keyframe

You assign an action to a keyframe when you want a specific event to occur at that particular point in your Flash movie. Actions you assign to a keyframe can be as simple as a stop action, which halts the movie and awaits further input from the viewer, or they can be complex, multiline codes that define variables and evaluate whether a certain set of conditions is true before advancing to another part of the movie or executing another action. To add an action to a keyframe:

1. **On the timeline, select the keyframe to which you want to assign the action(s).**

   On the timeline, keyframes are frames with black dots in them. To convert an ordinary frame to a keyframe, select the frame and press F6.

2. **Click the arrow to the left of the word Actions to open the Actions panel.**

   The Actions panel opens, as shown in Figure 2-5. Notice that the panel is labeled Actions-Frame.

   When you select an object that actions can be assigned to, the title of the Actions panel changes showing you the type of object selected; for example, when you select a button, the title displayed is Actions-Button. Before you create any ActionScript, it's a good idea to look at the title to make sure you haven't inadvertently selected the wrong object.

Action   Action parameter text boxes

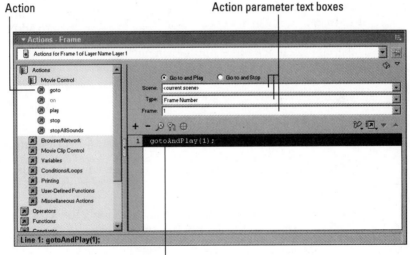

Figure 2-5:
This line of
code has
been
carefully
crafted for a
deserving
keyframe.

Action added to script

3. **Use your favorite method of applying actions to script the keyframe.**

   To reward anyone who is reading this chapter in its entirety, I don't list every possible way to apply an action to a frame. If you're not familiar with assigning actions to a frame or you haven't been reading this chapter in its entirety (you know who you are), please read the earlier section "Creating ActionScript in Normal mode."

4. **Add actions as needed to finish scripting the keyframe. Figure 2-5 shows an ActionScript written for a keyframe.**

When you apply actions to a keyframe, you see a lowercase *a* in the keyframe's position on the timeline.

In Figure 2-5, notice the panel with three windows above the first line of code in the Actions panel. You use these parameter text boxes to modify available parameters for an action. (I discuss the parameter text boxes in detail later in this chapter.) Notice the status line at the bottom of the Actions panel. This indicates the line of the script you are currently working on, along with the code contained in that line.

You can select a regular frame and use any action in the Actions panel. However, the script is not applied to the selected frame; it's applied to the previous keyframe on the selected layer's timeline.

Creating an Actions layer

You can assign an action to any keyframe on any layer in a movie. However, when you have lots of keyframes and lots of layers and you randomly assign actions to keyframes at will, you have a recipe for potential disaster. If you need to go back and modify an ActionScript applied to a particular keyframe, the ActionScript is difficult, if not impossible, to find. And then there's your client to consider. Clients never seem to make up their minds and often have you jump through hoops — by scurrying along the timeline, looking for a particular bit of ActionScript — more than once. Creating a separate layer for actions you apply to keyframes makes your ActionScript easier to edit. (Plus, you have the added advantage of not having to buy any hair-coloring products to hide stress-induced gray hairs.)

I advise you to create an Actions layer whenever you create a movie with ActionScript. To create an Actions layer:

1. **Click the uppermost layer in the Timeline window to select it.**

   The selected layer is highlighted.

2. **Choose Insert⇨Layer or click the Layers icon, the icon that looks like a folded document with a plus sign (+) on it.**

   Flash adds a new layer to the timeline and assigns it the default name Layer, appended by the next available layer number.

3. **Double-click the new layer.**

   The default name is highlighted.

4. **Type Actions and press Enter or Return.**

   The new layer is now called Actions.

After you create the Actions layer, remember to select it whenever you need to create a keyframe to which the ActionScript will be assigned. All the code you assign to keyframes is on the Actions layer and makes your life much easier. Trust me.

Labeling keyframes

When you reference a keyframe in an ActionScript, the Flash Player can locate the frame by the scene the keyframe appears in and the keyframe's number on the timeline. This is all well and good if you're creating simple movies with only a few frames. However, when your movies get more complex and you're dealing with many frames, it's easier to remember a keyframe's label — or name, as some Flash authors who grow attached to their productions prefer to call them. When you assign a label to a keyframe, the label appears on certain drop-down menus in the parameter text boxes. I tell you all about the parameter text boxes later in this chapter, in the section "Modifying an action's parameters." Stay tuned.

Another good reason for labeling frames is that if you add or delete frames from your movie, what was once frame 50 may now be frame 45 or 105, depending on how many frames you added or deleted from the production. If you assigned an action that involves frame 50 and then delete or add a bunch of frames, the Flash Player still goes to frame 50, and your script crumbles like a bad block of Brie. However, if you assign a label to a keyframe, the label reference is retained, no matter how much you mess with the timeline. To label a keyframe:

1. **On the timeline, click the keyframe (a keyframe is filled with a black dot) to select it.**

   The selected frame is highlighted.

2. **Click the triangle to the left of the title Properties to open the Property inspector.**

   The Property inspector, as shown in Figure 2-6, opens.

   You can open any panel by clicking the arrow to the left of the panel's name. However, the *hotspot* (clickable area) for the panel extends all the way to the end of the title bar. The designers of Flash figured you'd get tired after several hours of design and ActionScripting, so they gave you a slightly larger target area when a bad case of the mid-day blahs strikes.

3. **Enter a name for the keyframe in the Frame Label field.**

   You enter a name by clicking inside the <Frame Label> field and then typing the desired name. Choose a meaningful name that reflects what is happening or what will happen in the keyframe.

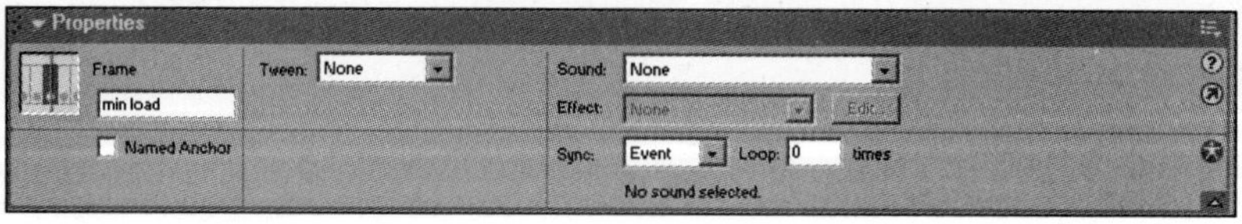

Figure 2-6:
You label a
keyframe
within the
Property
inspector.

4. **Press Enter or Return.**

   Flash assigns the label to the keyframe. The label also appears on the keyframe's position on the timeline and on applicable parameter text box menus, such as the Frame parameter text box when you use the goto action.

Adding comments to frames

The Flash programmers (bless their techno-geek heads) have given you another tool to eliminate confusion and possible panic on your part. This little gem is known as the comment. You can add a comment to any keyframe. *Comments* are little notes to yourself — or other designers working on a project — about what effect or action will occur at a keyframe. Comments come in handy when you work on a project with several designers, set a project aside for several days and then come back to it, or revise an old Flash project for a client. To add a comment to a keyframe:

1. **Select the keyframe to which you want to add a comment.**

   The selected keyframe is highlighted.

2. **Click the triangle to the left of the title Properties to open the Property inspector.**

   The Property inspector makes an appearance.

   If the Property inspector is not visible at the bottom of the workspace, choose Window➪Properties to display the Property inspector. It's a good idea to make the Property inspector a permanent member of your workspace as you use it for a plethora (love that word) of operations in Flash.

3. **In the <Frame Label> field, type two forward slashes (//) followed by the comment.**

   When you precede text in the <Frame Label> field with two forward slashes, you're telling Flash that this is a comment and not a label. When you enter a comment, choose one that has meaning to you and any other Flash authors working on the project, such as ActionScript slider begins here.

4. Press Enter or Return.

The comment is added to the keyframe. You can differentiate comments from labels by noting the green icon on the timeline with two forward slashes before each comment. Figure 2-7 shows a comment that has been added to a keyframe.

Figure 2-7:
Comments are memory joggers — virtual pieces of string tied around your little finger.

Comment added to keyframe

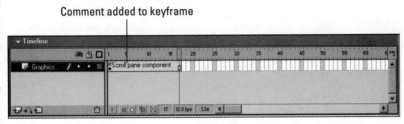

 TIP

If you have a comment or label on a keyframe that is neighbored by several other keyframes, the comment or label display is truncated on the timeline. To reveal the comment or label, hold your cursor over the keyframe until a tooltip appears below the timeline, displaying the comment or label in its entirety. As a bonus, it says `label` or `comment`, which is a dead giveaway to what it is. (These Flash programmers leave no stone unturned.)

Delegating an action to an object

You assign an action to an object when you want it to be an interactive element in your Flash movie; for example, when a button in your movie is clicked or a movie clip is loaded. The only objects you can apply actions to are instances of buttons, movie clips, and user-defined components (high-IQ movie clips) on Stage. To apply ActionScript to an object:

1. Select the object to which you want to apply the action(s).

2. Click the arrow to the left of the word Actions to open the Actions panel.

When you select an object to assign an action to, the type of object selected is displayed with the Actions title. For example, if you select a button, the panel title reads, Actions-Button. Note that if you select a user-defined component, the title reads Actions-Movie Clip, as all user-defined components begin life as a plain-Jane movie clip.

3. **Use your favorite method to assign the desired action(s) to the object.**

   If you inadvertently selected an instance of a graphic symbol or an object on Stage that is not an instance of a button, or movie clip all the actions in the panel are dimmed.

   If you're unsure of exactly how to use the Actions panel to apply actions, mosey on up to the beginning of this chapter and read the earlier section "Creating ActionScript in Normal mode."

Before filling up the Actions panel, take a quick look at the top of the panel. If the panel is labeled Actions-Frame and you think that you're assigning actions to an object (or vice versa), slow down, partner — you've selected the wrong object.

Deleting an action

What the Flash designer giveth, the Flash designer can taketh away. When a script doesn't work out as planned, sometimes you have no choice other than to cut actions until it does. At other times, you may just change your mind and decide to do away with an action. For whatever reason, if you need to delete an action, you can do it easily in the Actions panel. To delete one or more actions:

1. **Select the keyframe or object to which the offending or unwanted actions are assigned.**

2. **Click the arrow to the left of the word Actions.**

   The Actions panel opens, and the actions assigned to the keyframe or object are displayed.

3. **Click a line of code to select it.**

   The selected line of code is highlighted. To add contiguous lines of code to the selection, hold down the Shift key while clicking a line of code.

4. **Click the Delete Selected Actions button that looks like a minus sign (–) in the left corner just above the Script pane in the Actions panel.**

   Consider the code gone.

Controlling the hierarchy of actions

The actions you apply to an object or keyframe are executed in the order you created them. If, in your infinite wisdom (or perhaps because the effect went poof when it was supposed to go pop), you need to rearrange the order in which actions are executed, you can do so easily. To rearrange the order in which actions are performed:

1. **Select the keyframe or object to which the actions you want to rearrange are assigned.**

2. **Click the arrow to the left of the word Actions.**

   The Actions panel opens and displays the actions you assigned to the object or keyframe.

3. **Select the action you need to move up or down in the order.**

   The line of code is highlighted.

4. **To move the line of code up the list, click the Move Selected Actions Up button (the upward-pointing triangle in the right corner above the Script pane).**

   The line of code moves up one position. Click the button again as needed to move the line to the desired position in the order.

5. **To move the selected line down, click the Move Selected Actions Down button (the downward-pointing triangle in the right corner above the Script pane).**

   The selected action moves down one position in the order. Click the button as many times as needed to move the action to the desired position in the order.

Modifying an action's parameters

Certain actions are simple one-liners; in fact, some are only one word. Stop. Yup. That's an action. And it does just as advertised: It stops a movie dead in its tracks. Other actions, like goto, are a tad more complex. For one thing, the Flash Player wants to know where you want it to go; specifically, what scene and what frame. And if you've been a fastidious Flash designer and labeled your keyframes, you specify a specific frame label rather than a frame number. Whenever you add an action that has parameters to your script, the parameter text boxes open for business directly above the Script pane. The number of parameter text boxes that appear is different depending on the action you added to the script. Some parameter text box fields have a button with a triangle icon that, when you click it, opens a drop-down menu of items relating to the action you choose. Other parameter text boxes are plain-Jane text fields you use to enter data, such as the contents of a variable. Figure 2-8 shows the parameter text boxes that appear when you add the goto action to your script. In later chapters, I show you more about the parameter text boxes as they pertain to specific actions. Right now, I want you to make a note of them and how they work.

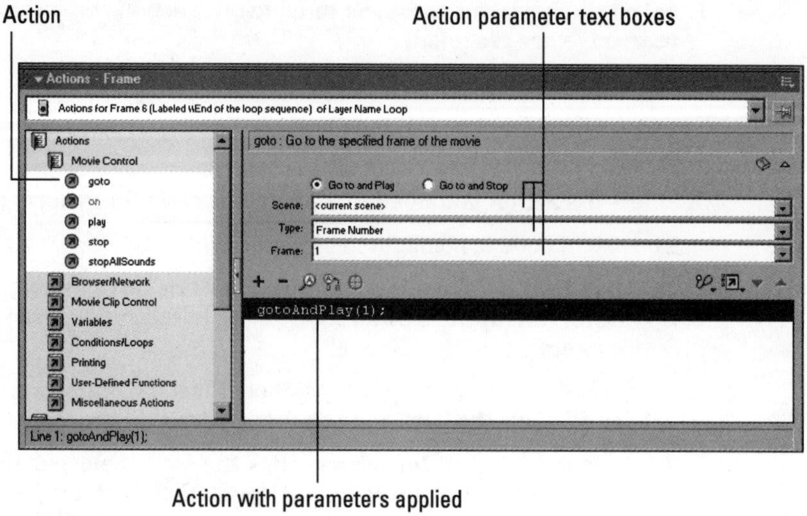

Action
Action parameter text boxes

Figure 2-8:
You use
parameter
text boxes
to set the
parameters
for an
action.

Action with parameters applied

Using the Actions panel's Options menu

In the upper-right corner of the Actions panel is an icon that looks like three small squares and dashes with a downward-pointing triangle. Click this icon to reveal the Actions panel's Options menu, as shown in Figure 2-9. As you can see, the Options menu gives you several options (give the Flash programmers an A+ for logical names) that you can use when creating ActionScript. To select an option, click it.

I know — you're wondering what all the hoopla is about options and why you need them. Here's what they do:

- **Normal Mode:** The default mode for creating ActionScript.

- **Expert Mode:** Lets you use the Actions panel like a text editor. I show you how to use Expert mode in the upcoming section "Creating ActionScript in Expert Mode."

- **Goto Line:** Opens a dialog box that you use to go to a specific line of code in the Actions panel.

- **Find:** Opens a dialog box that you use to find a text value in your script. You cannot use the option to find text within a command — only to find text used to create a variable name or text that describes a variable's contents. This option works in a manner similar to the Find command in most word processing programs. After finding your query, Flash highlights the line the text is found in. You can also find text in your script by clicking the Find button (looks like a magnifying glass), conveniently located above the Script pane.

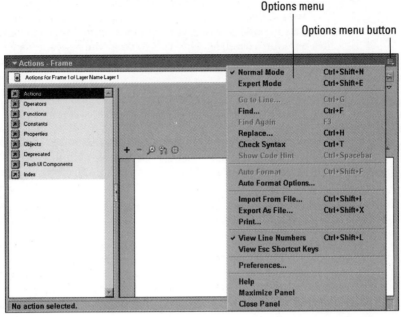

Options menu

Options menu button

Figure 2-9:
You say
you want
options?
The Actions
panel has
them.

✔ **Find Again:** Finds the next instance of the word that was last entered in the Find dialog box.

✔ **Replace:** Opens a dialog box that you use to replace text in your ActionScript. The Replace option doesn't replace text used in actions — only text used to create variable names or values. Lo and behold, there's a button for this command, too. It's the smaller of the two magnifying glasses, directly above the Script pane.

✔ **Check Syntax:** Checks your script for syntax errors. I tell you everything you need to know about syntax in Chapter 3. You can also check your script's syntax by clicking the Check Syntax button above the Script pane.

✔ **Show Code Hint:** When working in Expert mode, this option gives you a hint on how to properly format code for a given action. To make doubly sure you'd be able to get a hint when you need it, the Flash designers included a Show Code Hint button directly above the Script pane.

✔ **Auto Format:** When you work in Expert mode, choosing this option automatically adds necessary formatting to your script such as a semi-colon after a line of code. You choose this command after writing a line of code. Flash displays a warning dialog box if your script is in error, telling you to correct the errors prior to auto-formatting. The quicker way to achieve auto-formatting is by clicking the Auto-Format button above Script pane.

✔ **Import from File:** Lets you import an ActionScript saved in the .as format.

✔ **Export as File:** Lets you export a particularly useful (or brilliant, if you're Wile E. Coyote) bit of code. When you choose this option, Flash opens a dialog box that lets you specify a name for the file and select a folder on your hard drive in which to store the script. Every line of code in the Actions panel is exported. ActionScript files are saved with an .as extension.

If you create ActionScript with many lines of code, you may find it handy to edit the code in a word processing program. You won't feel quite so hemmed in — the Script pane is big, but it's not that big. To use this technique, export your multi-line code and then open the file up in your favorite word processor. After you're done editing the code, save the file and then use the Import from File option from the Actions panel's Options menu.

✔ **Print:** Lets you print a hard copy of the code in the Actions panel on your computer's default printer.

✔ **View Line Numbers:** When this option is selected, Flash displays a line number to the left of each line of code, which makes it easier for you to find a specific spot in a lengthy ActionScript. You also find line numbers beneficial when you set breakpoints, a task I show you how to do in Chapter 13.

✔ **View Escape Shortcut Keys:** When this option is selected, Flash displays each action's keyboard shortcut to the left of its name in the Actions panel.

✔ **Preferences:** Opens the ActionScript Preferences dialog box. Within this dialog box are options you can modify to change the way your scripts are displayed in the Script pane.

✔ **Help:** Launches Flash and ActionScript online help.

✔ **Maximize:** Minimizes other panels that are currently open in the same pane so you can view more of your code.

✔ **Close Panel:** Closes the Actions panel.

You can also increase the size of the Actions panel by clicking the top bar and dragging up. As you drag up, the Stage window is resized so you can see more of the Actions panel, which is helpful when you're dealing with a whole lotta code.

Using the Context menus

If you've been playing around with ActionScript, you've probably already deleted a line of code or two and (with your best Homer Simpson "D'oh!") slapped yourself on the forehead when you realized that you needed the deleted code after all. When this happens and you choose the Undo command from the Edit menu, you don't undo the Delete — rather, you undo every action you just entered in the Actions panel. Fear not, intrepid ActionScript debutante: The Actions panel has its own Context menu that you use to edit ActionScript. To open the Context menu shown in Figure 2-10, right-click (in Windows) or Ctrl+click (on the Macintosh).

Context menu

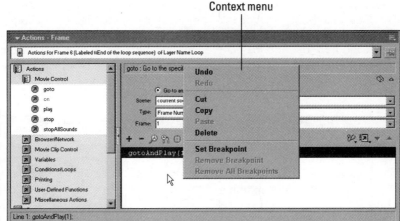

Figure 2-10:
The Actions panel has its own contextual menu.

Dealing with deprecated actions

When an action is *deprecated,* it means that the Flash programmers have built something that does the same thing, only better. Think of this concept as your better mousetrap at work. Deprecated actions are listed in their own book (complete with sub-books) and work just fine in Flash MX; however, they won't work, and may not be available, in future versions of Flash, so the Flash programmers strongly suggest you not use deprecated actions. If you want the latest and greatest bells and whistles, use the favored action in place of the deprecated action. To find out which action to substitute for a deprecated action, refer to the *Flash ActionScript Reference Guide,* which shipped with the program, or click the Reference panel icon and read all about it from within Flash. Remember, what you see in the Reference panel is the same as what you get when you read the Flash ActionScript Reference Guide.

Keeping Track of Your Script with Line Numbers

When you become proficient in ActionScript, you'll be stretching the envelope. When you stretch the ActionScript envelope, you're liable to end up with ActionScript code that extends beyond the boundaries of the Script pane. One solution for this dilemma is to drag the boundary of the Actions panel to see more lines of script. However, it's still possible to create an ActionScript so cool that you end up having to scroll to see every line of code you've created. This is kind of like trying to read a book that's on a continuous scroll of paper. Without some kind of reference, you have no idea of where you are. To get your ActionScript back into perspective, click the Options menu icon in the upper-right corner of the Actions panel and choose View Line Numbers. Voilà — your lines of code are neatly numbered, just as shown in Figure 2-11. As an added bonus, you can use the Goto Line command from the Actions panel's Options menu to go directly to a desired line number. Works just like a book's table of contents, except your fingers don't get that book-page smell when you thumb to a chapter.

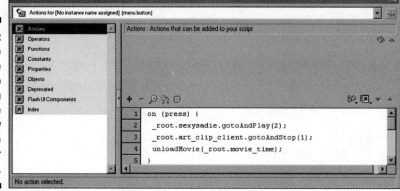

Figure 2-11: Your code will be easier to track when you choose the View Line Number option.

Looking Up Actions in the ActionScript Reference Panel

Every single action that you use is stored in Actions books. When you read a book in the comfort of your own living room — or in your windswept cabana for those of you fortunate enough to live on a tropical island — and come across a word you're not familiar with, you look it up in a dictionary. Well, there are lots of words in the Actions books, and symbols, too. Some of it may seem like gibberish written in an alien tongue. When you run across an action that's foreign to you, you can decipher what the heck all those funny symbols and words mean by opening the ActionScript Reference panel. All you need to do to open up the panel is click the little book icon with a question mark on its cover, which opens the panel shown in Figure 2-12. After the Reference panel appears:

1. **Click an Actions book to open it.**

   Flash expands the selected book and displays every action in the group.

2. **Click the action you want to find out about.**

   The information about the selected action is displayed (see Figure 2-12).

When working in Normal mode, you can have a brief description of every action you select displayed in a window above the Script pane by clicking the inverted triangle to the right of the ActionScript Reference panel icon.

Selected action   Reference Dictionary listing

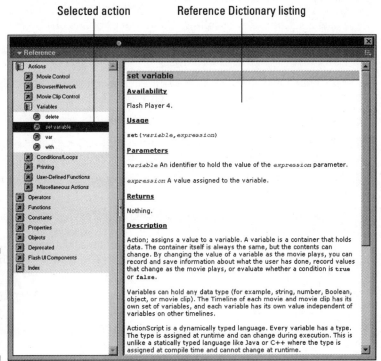

Figure 2-12: When in doubt, look it up in the Reference panel.

Changing ActionScript Preferences

Everyone is different, and that's what makes being a human being so much fun. And every human works a little differently, a fact that even geeks who design computer programs seem to understand. So if for any reason the ActionScript panel isn't your cup of tea, you can easily change the preferences by doing the following:

1. **Click the Options menu icon in the upper corner of the Actions panel and choose Preferences from the Options menu.**

   Flash opens the Preferences dialog box shown in Figure 2-13.

2. **To disable Automatic Indention, click the check box to remove the checkmark.**

   Automatic indentation is enabled by default. This option indents actions within curly braces (an ActionScript staple I show you in Chapter 3) to make a script easier to follow. When this option is disabled, every line of script lines up with the left border of the Script pane.

3. **Enter a value in the Indent box.**

   This parameter determines how far each line indents. The default is 4 pixels. Choose any value between 1 and 64.

4. **To disable Code Hints, click the check box to remove the checkmark.**

   When you create ActionScript in Expert mode, Code Hints display the parameters you need to supply Flash in order for the action to execute.

5. **Drag the Delay slider to the right to increase the amount of time before Flash displays a code hint.**

   The default delay time is 0 seconds (or slightly longer if your system's resources are being heavily taxed). Increase the delay when you become better at ActionScript and don't need as much assistance from Flash. Note that if you disable code hints, the slider is deader than the proverbial doornail.

6. **In the Text section, click the arrow to the right of the Text field and choose an option from the drop-down menu.**

   After you click the arrow, Flash displays all fonts currently installed on your system. The default font is Courier New, a font that programmer geeks are especially fond of. But if you're a right brain kind of person and like to do things differently, choose any font your heart desires. For comic relief when dealing with heavy ActionScript, I recommend Comic Sans MS.

7. **Click the triangle to the right of the Font Size field and choose an option from the drop-down menu.**

The default font size is 10 points, but you can choose a font as small as 8 points or as large as 72 points if you so desire.

8. **In the Syntax Coloring section, disable syntax coloring (selected by default) by clicking the check box to remove the checkmark.**

   Syntax coloring gives you a visual reference of keywords, variables, actions and other ActionScript elements by color-coding them in the Script pane. Syntax coloring is covered in detail in Chapter 3.

9. **To change the color of a syntax element, click the color swatch to the right of its name and choose a color from the pop-up palette.**

   If you disable Syntax Coloring, only the Foreground and Background color swatches are active.

10. **To restore ActionScript preferences to their defaults, click the Reset to Defaults button.**

    Quicker than you can say, "All the king's horses and all the king's men," Flash resets the preferences to their default.

11. **Click OK.**

    Flash sets up the ActionScript editor according to your preferences.

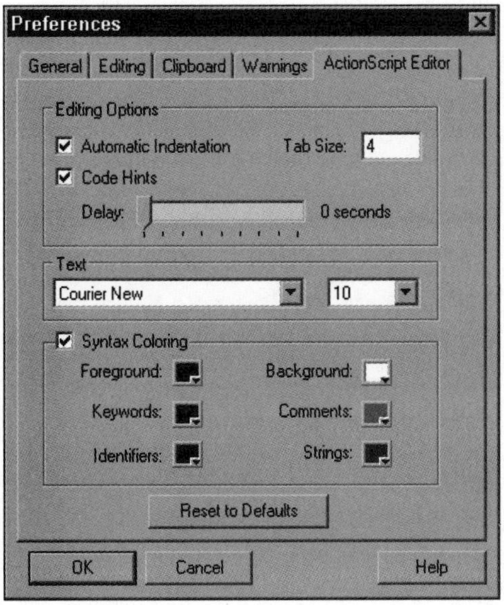

Figure 2-13:
Use this
dialog box
to modify
the way
your scripts
are
displayed.

Creating ActionScript in Expert Mode

When you think that you've reached the genius (or near genius or even adventurous) stage in your ActionScript career, you can create your ActionScript by typing lines of code into the Script pane of the Actions panel. It works like your friendly word processing program. I find it convenient to switch back and forth between Normal and Expert modes, especially when dealing with movie clips on different timelines. But I'm getting ahead of myself here. Don't worry — I show you how to work with movie clips on different timelines many times during the course of this book.

For now, I want you to be aware that Flash has an Expert mode. To switch to Expert mode, click the icon in the upper-right corner of the Actions panel and choose Expert from the Options menu. When you switch to Expert mode, you find the following differences:

✔ You no longer have the parameter text boxes as reference. When you select Expert mode, Flash thinks you ought to be smart enough to figure out the parameters on your own.

✔ You can still add an action to your script by double-clicking it from one of the Actions books or by selecting it from the drop-down menu.

✔ When you add an action to your script from one of the groups, the action is inserted at the cursor's position in the Script pane of the Actions panel.

✔ The up and down arrows you use to rearrange the order of actions are disabled.

✔ The Delete Selected Actions button is no longer displayed.

While working in Expert mode, you can select text that is no longer needed in your code and then press Delete to give it the old heave-ho. You can also drag and drop selected text to a different position in the Script pane.

 You can switch between Normal and Expert mode by clicking the View Options button and choosing the desired mode from the menu. You can also select an option to view line numbers from this menu.

When you create ActionScript in Expert mode, Flash assumes that you're an expert and doesn't throw up any red flags if you enter a line of code with errors. However, if you try to switch back to Normal mode after typing a line or two of ActionScript code with errors, Flash displays the warning dialog box shown in Figure 2-14.

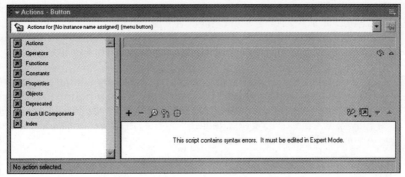

Figure 2-14:
When you
goof in
Expert mode
and try go
back to
Normal
mode, this
is what
you get.

Using Code Hints

Even though Flash assumes you're a high IQ ActionScript guru when you
choose Expert mode, you can still get some help. By default, code hints are
enabled unless you change this by modifying ActionScript preferences. When
code hints are enabled and you choose add an action to the script, Flash displays the necessary parameters you need to supply in order for the action to
correctly execute (see Figure 2-15).

Code hint

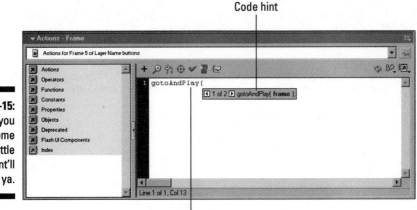

Figure 2-15:
When you
need some
help, a little
code hint'll
do ya.

Partially written code

If you switch to another line of code before filling in the blanks, the code hint disappears. However, you can get the hint back again by placing your cursor inside the parameter holder (brackets or curly braces, devices you'll learn all about in Chapter 3) and then clicking the Code Hint button.

 You can also get Flash to auto-format your code by adding the proper syntax. Write a line of code and then click the Auto Format button in the Script pane — Flash takes care of the formatting for you. If your script is in error, Flash displays a warning dialog box, telling you the script cannot be formatted. Fix the errors and try again.

Generating ActionScripts for Earlier Versions of Flash

Sometimes the Internet takes a while to catch up with the latest and greatest technology. Web browsers are no exception. The Flash Player is standard equipment with most major Web browsers and operating systems. However, when a new version of Flash is released, it takes the browser dudes and dudettes (programmers) a while to catch up. The latest version of the Flash Player can be downloaded for free from Macromedia. If you're relatively sure that the intended audience for your Flash movie is likely not to have the latest version of the Flash Player and is not the type of Web surfer who takes the time to download the player, you can publish your Flash movie in an earlier version. Of course, when you do this, the latest and greatest Flash actions do not work.

If you're going to publish your movie in an earlier version of Flash, follow these steps before you create the first line of ActionScript:

1. **Choose File⇨Publish Settings.**

   The Publish Settings dialog box appears.

2. **Click the Flash tab.**

   The Flash section of the Publish Settings dialog box opens.

    Alternately you can use the Property inspector to change the version of Flash you want to publish the movie in. Click the Publish button to open the Publish Settings dialog box.

3. **Click the triangle to the right of the Version field.**

   A drop-down menu appears.

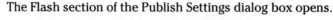

4. Select the version of Flash in which you want to publish the movie.

While you're at it, you may as well finalize all your publish settings. I don't bore you with the details. If you're not sure how to set the rest of the publish settings, refer to *Macromedia Flash MX For Dummies,* by Gurdy Leete and Ellen Finkelstein (Hungry Minds, Inc.).

5. Click OK.

The Publish Settings dialog box closes, and Flash saves the Publish Settings options you selected.

You're probably wondering why I have you set up the publish settings before you create any ActionScript. By doing this task, you don't inadvertently select an action that doesn't work in the version of Flash in which you're publishing the movie; these actions are highlighted in yellow.

Chapter 3

ActionScript: Programming for Non-Programmers

● ●

In This Chapter

▶ Understanding ActionScript terms

▶ Using the Actions groups

▶ Exploring a finished ActionScript

● ●

*A*ctionScript is a scripting language that you use to make things happen in Flash. Like any language, ActionScript has some basic formatting rules you need to follow. Of course, Flash takes care of much of the formatting for you. To branch out and get the most from ActionScript, however, you need to understand the lingo, especially if you're going to create any ActionScript in Expert mode. In this chapter, I decipher the basic components of the ActionScript language. Last, but not least, I dissect a typical ActionScript for you to show you how the pieces of this ActionScript puzzle fit together.

The Actions panel's got lots of books. And some of these books have books within a book. To add some actions to your scripts, you have to click this book icon, then click that book icon, then click another book icon, and so on. Rather than bore you with a lot of words, I'm going to show the path to each action as shown in the following example: Click Actions⇨Movie Control and then double-click goto.

Using ActionScript Lingo without a Dictionary

Just like the language I use to write this book, ActionScript has some basic rules for grammar and punctuation. When I write a sentence, a period ends it. When you create a line of ActionScript, a semicolon (;) ends it. If you've ever worked with JavaScript, you may notice some similarities with Flash ActionScript grammar. In this section, I show you some basic elements used in Flash ActionScript.

Many of the ActionScript elements described in the following sections are created automatically by Flash. However, to exploit the full power of ActionScript, you may find that mastering some of these concepts is useful so that you can create your own ActionScript in Expert mode.

Understanding commands, arguments, and properties

An *action* is a command that Flash Player executes when a frame is reached, a button is clicked, or a movie clip is loaded. A *command* can be a simple one-word action, such as `stop`, or a command may have an argument attached. An *argument* is something that modifies a command; for example, if you're an on-the-road salesperson and your boss calls you on your cell phone to tell you to meet him at the office. That's a command. If the company you work for has only one office, the command doesn't need to be modified with an argument. If however, you have more than one office, your boss needs to modify the command with an argument, which specifies in which office he wants you to meet him. If you show up late or at the wrong office, an argument of a different type takes place. Personally, I don't like the word *argument* because arguments often have to be settled in court, where truth is stranger than fiction. I prefer to think of anything that modifies a statement as a parameter. Incidentally, in the Actions panel you add an argument to a statement using the parameter text boxes.

You're probably wondering what constitutes a command in Flash and what a command and an argument look like. When you add the line of code `stop ();` to an ActionScript, Flash knows exactly what to do — it stops the movie. The `stop` action's counterpart, play, is the same thing; when Flash sees this command, it knows to play the movie. However, if you add the goto action to a script, Flash doesn't know how to complete this command because you haven't told Flash where to go. In this case, you need to add an argument to the command; for example, `gotoAndPlay (beginmovie)` instructs Flash to advance the movie to a frame labeled `beginmovie`. In this case, `gotoAndPlay` is the command; `(beginmovie)` is the argument.

A *property* is a certain parameter of an object: its size, color, or location. For example, if your boss is making you drive to the office on 27th Street, 27th Street is a property (the location) of the object office. A whole section of properties is in the Actions panel.

Using the dot syntax

In ActionScript, a dot (.) is used to signify certain properties relating to an object or movie clip. You also use a dot to signify the path of a movie clip.

This feature makes it possible to communicate with a movie clip from the main timeline or vice versa. Remember that a movie clip is a unique entity that has its own timeline. When you write an expression with dot syntax, the expression begins with the name of the object or movie clip followed by a dot, which is then followed by the property, method, or variable you want to address. For example, `myclip._x=50` positions a movie clip instance named `myclip` at the *x* coordinate, 50, on Stage. An object's coordinate is its position on Stage.

Another example of the dot at work is `myclip.play ()`, which instructs the movie clip named `myclip` to play.

I show you how to work with movie clips, targets, and paths in Chapter 9.

Using the slash syntax

The dot syntax was introduced to Flash ActionScript with Version 5. If you need to publish your movies in Flash 3 or Flash 4 format, dots won't work. If you publish your work as Flash 3 or Flash 4 movies, rather than using the dot syntax, you have to slash it. Variables are also handled differently in Flash 3 or Flash 4; a colon precedes them.

For example, in the following line of code, a movie clip named `aboutus` calls a variable named `text` that is found in another movie clip named `textlayer`:

```
aboutus.textlayer.text
```

To rewrite this code for Flash 3 or Flash 4, you would write

```
aboutus/textlayer:text
```

If you download some interesting tutorials from the Internet with ActionScript formatted in earlier versions of Flash, you can open the .fla files, and Flash converts any ActionScript to the current version.

What the heck are curly braces?

Curly braces are neither orthodontic devices nor, for that matter, props for an ailing Stooge. *Curly braces* group together a set of statements. The lines of code in Listing 3-1 are from an ActionScript that advances the movie to a frame labeled "beginMovie" in Scene 1. The Curly Braces surround the `goto` statement and the comment that follows it.

Listing 3-1   Grouping Statements Together with Curly Braces

```
on (release) {
gotoAndPlay ("Scene 1", "beginMovie");
//when the button is released, movie advances to a frame
          labeled, "beginMovie" in Scene 1

}
```

Ending a statement with a semicolon

Every good statement must come to an end, even an ActionScript statement. I know that I'm always happy whenever my bank statement ends with a positive balance. In ActionScript, you terminate a statement with a semicolon, which makes everything neat and tidy. If you get a case of the "forgets" while working in Expert mode and you forget to include a semicolon, Flash still runs the script — provided you've got everything else right.

Using ActionScript to direct Flash Player

When you create a line of code with the Actions panel, you're giving Flash Player a direct command to do something. You can throw many different types of commands at Flash Player, but they all fall into a category. Listed below, in plain non-technobabble English, are the different categories of commands you can use in ActionScript and an example of a line of code from Flash.

- ✔ **Execute this command.** This is the simplest action you can throw at Flash. It's a no-brainer. When Flash sees a line of code that says `play ()` ;, it knows only one thing to do — play the movie.

- ✔ **Execute this command with this parameter** (or *argument,* for those of you who like technospeak). When you choose an action in this category, you need to provide Flash with more detailed information (parameters) so that Flash Player can do its job. An example of this type of action is `getURL ("http://www.mypage.com", "_self", "POST")`;. This action (`getURL`) is directing Flash Player to a Web page. The parameter you provide is the site's URL (`www.mypage.com`).

Highlighting and checking syntax

By default, the Actions panel highlights the syntax of code you enter. That's a good thing. The colors give you a visual reference to what the bits of your

ActionScript code actually do. If part of the code isn't the right color, it's a dead giveaway to a potential bug that you can exterminate before leaving the Actions panel. For example, if you were working in Expert mode and typed `Gotoandplay` (bad syntax) rather than `gotoAndPlay` (using the proper syntax), the code would be colored black rather than highlighted in blue.

Decoding syntax colors

When the Syntax Coloring option is enabled through the Preferences dialog box, syntax is highlighted after you enter a line of code or after you select an action and let Flash format the code. Syntax is highlighted as follows:

- ✔ Keywords and actions (such as `goto`, `stop`, `_root`) are highlighted in blue.

- ✔ Paths are highlighted in blue.

- ✔ Properties are highlighted in blue.

- ✔ Comments (notes to yourself in the Actions panel) are highlighted in light gray.

- ✔ Strings (text) surrounded by quotation marks are highlighted in light green.

Disabling syntax coloring

If for some reason you decide to work without the safety net of highlighted syntax, click the Options button in the upper-right corner of the Actions panel and choose Preferences to open the Preferences dialog box; then deselect Syntax Coloring. After you turn the option off, all lines of code in the Actions panel are jet black. To enable highlighted syntax, click the Options button in the upper-right corner of the Actions panel, choose preferences, and when the Preferences dialog box opens, choose Syntax Coloring.

Modifying syntax colors

When Syntax Coloring is enabled, Flash uses the default colors listed in the previous Decoding Syntax Colors section. You can modify the colors to whatever color suits your fancy — my favorite color is red, especially when it's painted on a Ferrari — by choosing Preferences from the Actions panel Options menu. After the Preference dialog box opens, click the color swatches in the Syntax Coloring panel and choose a color that floats your boat.

Checking syntax

To check your syntax for errors, click the Options button near the upper-right corner of the Actions panel and choose Check Syntax from the drop-down menu. Or if you like to take the easy way out — and who doesn't? — click the Check Syntax button above the Script pane. Note that the Check

Syntax button is only available in Expert mode, 'cause when you're working in Normal mode, Flash assumes it has entered all the code and of course Flash thinks it is infallible with it comes to coloring syntax.

Decoding syntax errors

When you make a mistake — and you will — in a line of ActionScript code, Flash highlights the boo-boo with a solid red background. To get a clue to where you went wrong, move your mouse over the incorrect syntax. A tooltip appears, telling you what Flash expected. The error message appears in the status window at the bottom of the panel as well. Figure 3-1 shows a line of code with an error in it and the tooltip. In Figure 3-1, the chosen name for the variable is in error because it's a reserved keyword, a useful subject that I discuss in the next section.

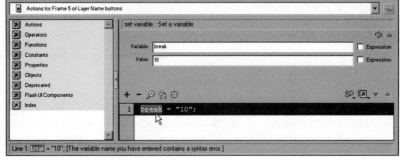

Figure 3-1:
When you
make an
ActionScript
mistake,
Flash comes
to the
rescue.

Reserved keywords

Remember when you were a kid and your parents told you not to say certain words? Oh, you knew the words all right, but dire things happened if you uttered them in the presence of an adult. Now that you're grown up, you can say the words whenever you want — and probably cause those within earshot to raise an eyebrow — even though you probably shouldn't. ActionScript has words that you can't use when you're creating variables, functions, or label names. If you use one of these words, Flash doesn't wash your mouth out with soap, but it does raise a red flag — literally. For example, if you use a reserved keyword in a variable name, the reserved keyword is highlighted in red with the error message `The variable name you have entered contains an error`, as shown in Figure 3-1. Table 3-1 shows every reserved ActionScript keyword.

Table 3-1		Reserved Keywords	
break	for	new	var
continue	function	return	void
delete	if	this	while
else	in	typeof	with
instanceof	case	default	switch

Using comments to make sense of it all

ActionScript can get pretty hairy at times, especially when you're cramming lots of actions onto one frame or one object. After you get the code to work as you have envisioned and wear out your best shirt from slapping yourself on the back, you move on to bigger and better things, like finishing the movie or taking a well-deserved coffee break. Then you come back to your complex ActionScript later and need to make a few changes. As you look at the script, you forget why you did what you did.

This used to happen to me all the time. Fortunately, I started using the Flash ActionScript device known as the comment. It's an instant memory jogger. You add comments to a script in the Actions panel. To add a comment to your ActionScript:

1. **Click the line of code before the spot where you want the comment to appear.**

   The selected line is highlighted. Some Flash designers prefer to add comments after the line(s) of code they want to comment on; others add comments before the code. After you work with ActionScript for a while, you know which method works best for you.

2. **Click Actions⇨Miscellaneous Actions.**

   The Miscellaneous Actions book displays all of its hardware.

3. **Double-click the** comment **action.**

   Two forward slashes (//) appear in the Script pane of the Actions panel. A text field named Comment opens in a parameter text box just above the Script pane.

4. **Place your cursor inside the Comment field and enter the comment. Figure 3-2 shows a comment being used in a script.**

As you type, the comment is added after the two forward slashes. All comments are colored light gray. Use as much text as you need, and make sure that the comment is something you and any other Flash author will understand. After all, you never know: You may get promoted to the exalted position of Chief-Mucky-Muck-In-Charge-Of-Really-Cool-ActionScript. Then you can create the heavy ActionScript and delegate the rest of the project to another designer while you do something important, like getting caught up on yesterday's sports scores.

Comment in script

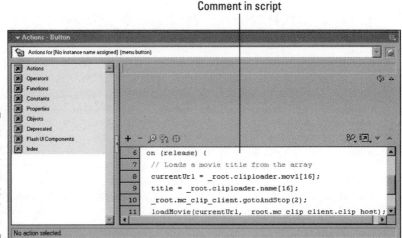

Figure 3-2: Comments are your virtual ActionScript memory joggers.

When you add a long comment to an ActionScript that exceeds the boundary of the Actions panel, the comment doesn't wrap to the next line. Flash adds a scroll bar at the bottom of the right pane of the Actions panel, which you drag to reveal a lengthy comment. To prevent against this occurring, end the comment at the right border of the Script pane, and then invoke the `comment` action again to finish the comment on another line.

Dissecting a Typical ActionScript

Imitation — as long as it doesn't break any copyright law — is the sincerest form of flattery, and Flash designers are no exception to this rule. You can download complete .fla files that feature some snazzy effects created with ActionScript from lots of places on the Internet. Unfortunately, many of these files are undocumented or poorly documented, sometimes by design. After all, when you become the next ActionScript guru who creates an effect that is all the rage, you want to strut your stuff and show it to the world, but you don't want to give all of your secrets away.

To follow along with this exercise, locate the file named enter.fla. It's in the Chapter 3 folder of the CD that comes with this book. Copy the file to your hard drive, and use your computer's operating system to disable this file's read-only attributes.

After opening a .fla file in Flash, you can often decipher how the effect was achieved by looking at each element in the movie and the code that was used to create the effect. To dissect the ActionScript used in the enter.fla file:

1. **Launch Flash and choose File⇨Open.**

   The Open dialog box appears.

2. **Locate the enter.fla file and open it.**

   Flash loads the file, as shown in Figure 3-3.

If you look at Figure 3-3, the whole thing looks pretty simple. Only three items are on Stage: a block of text, a white rectangle, and an Enter button. You can see two layers: one for Objects and one for Actions. Notice the two instances of lowercase *a* in each of the Actions layer's keyframes. They tell you that ActionScript is lurking behind each frame.

Figure 3-3:
To crack an ActionScript code, you have to open the file.

Before you start poking around under the hood, take a look at the final effect:

1. **Choose Control⇨Test Movie.**

   Flash publishes the movie and opens it in another window.

2. **Click inside the white rectangle, type your name, and click the Enter button.**

   Flash Player advances the movie to frame 2. You see another white rectangle with your name in it, preceded by a greeting that reflects what time of the day it is.

When you play the movie, the whole effect seems fairly simple until you realize that the greeting changes depending on what time of the day it is. If the computer's clock reads between 12:00 midnight and 12:00 noon, the greeting is Good morning. If the time is between noon and 6:00 p.m., the greeting reads Good afternoon. During the only remaining time (between 6:00 p.m. and midnight), the greeting reads Good evening. So how did the Flash designer script the movie so that the greeting changes with the time of day? You have a little better idea when you look at the components used to create the movie.

✔ The white rectangle in the first frame is an input text box. *Input text boxes* are used to accept — you guessed it — input. A variable called name is assigned to the text box. *Variables* are containers that hold values; in this case, the names of the visitors to the Web site.

✔ The Enter button in the first frame is programmed to send the movie to the second frame when the button is clicked.

✔ The white rectangle in frame 2 is a dynamic text box. *Dynamic text* can accept information from a variable of the same name. In this case, the variable assigned to the dynamic text box is welcome.

✔ The only remaining elements of the movie are the actions assigned to the keyframes in the Actions layer.

Now that you know the components involved, examine each one a little more closely. Figure 3-4 shows the parameters for the input text box used in the first keyframe as displayed in the Properties panel. If it seems a little foreign right now, hang in there: I get down to the business of input text boxes and dynamic text boxes in Chapter 10. At this point, I want you to notice the Var (short for variable) field. The input text box accepts the data the user enters and stores it in the name variable. The dynamic text box in the second key-frame displays data that has been assigned to the variable named welcome.

Now that you know what's going on with the text boxes, all you need to know to replicate the effect is what ActionScript is used to get from alpha to omega. The first bit of business is to look at the actions assigned to the first frame. If you're following along with the exercise file on your computer:

1. Click the first frame on the Actions layer to select it.

The frame is highlighted.

2. Click the arrow next to the word Actions.

The Actions panel opens, and the actions assigned to the keyframe are displayed.

Figure 3-4:
Input text boxes are used to accept data.

Input Text properties   Input text box variable name

Hmm, not much going on, is there? For those of you not following along with the file, `stop()` is the only code listed. Without this simple action, Flash Player would skip right past the first frame, and the visitor would never have the chance to enter his or her name in the input text box.

Now that you know what makes the first frame tick (or should I say stop?), look at the action that's executed when the button is clicked. Figure 3-5 shows the simple line of code assigned to the button. The first part of the code `on release` is known as the event handler. An *event handler* is the event that must occur for the next part of the script to be handled, or executed. In this case, Flash Player waits for the mouse button to be released. When the button is released, Flash Player goes to frame 2 and stops.

You're almost there. Now comes the big leap — adding the script that changes the greeting based on the time of day. If you're following along with the Flash file, do the following:

1. Click the second frame on the Actions layer to select it.

The frame is highlighted.

2. Open the Actions panel.

For those of you who have been skipping the previous gems of wisdom in this section (shame on you), you open the Actions panel by clicking the arrow to the left of its title.

The Actions panel opens, and the actions assigned to the keyframe are displayed. If you're not following along with the Flash file — caught ya — see Figure 3-6.

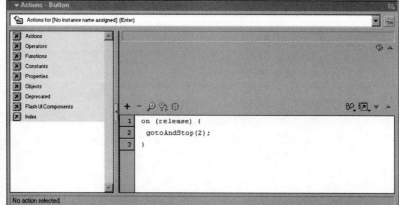

Figure 3-5:
You add
interactivity
to a button
with
Action-
Script.

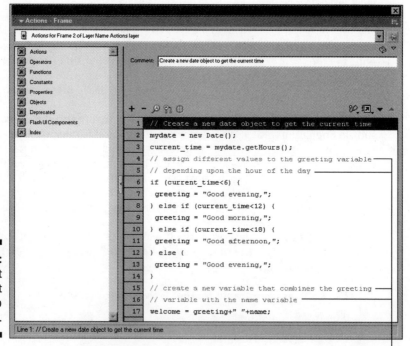

Figure 3-6:
ActionScript
is smart
enough to
tell time.

Comments

Take a look at each line separately to see what it does. But before you do that, notice the text following the two forward slashes. Those are comments I added so that I would remember what I did when it came time to write this section. I strongly advise you to get in the habit of adding comments to any ActionScript other than the simplest lines of code.

If you're ever working with another Flash author's code, comments help you figure out how the designer achieved the effect.

The first line of code after the initial comments `mydate = new Date();` creates a new Date object. An *object* is a collection of methods. The various Date object methods used retrieve the time of day or date from your computer's clock. In this case, the only method used for this script is the current hour.

The second line of code `current_time = mydate.getHours();` creates a variable named `current time`. The variable's value is equal to the current time that the date object retrieves from the computer's operating system using the `getHours()` method of the Date object.

The next two lines in the script are comments — for which I may be awarded the ActionScript Good Scriptkeeping Award. Immediately after the comments are lines of code that Flash Player uses to make a decision based on the contents of the `current_time` variable. Before examining each of these decision makers, it's important to know that the Date object uses the 24-hour military clock. I show you in Chapter 8 how to add interactivity to your scripts with objects.

The decision-making lines of this script use the `if`, `else if`, and `else` actions. These actions are used in conditional statements, a subject I discuss in great detail in Chapter 12. To break down a conditional statement into simple English: If one condition is true, this happens; else, this happens. The `else if` action is used if more than two possible outcomes exist. Now it's time for you to see how these actions determine the value of a variable named `greeting`, which changes the display in the dynamic text box in frame 2. Listing 3-2 shows the decision-making code used in frame 2.

Listing 3-2 Decisions, Decisions

```
if (current_time<6) {
                greeting = "Good evening," ;
} else if (current_time<12) {
    greeting = "Good morning,";
} else if (current_time<18) {
    greeting = "Good afternoon,";
} else {
    greeting = "Good evening,";
};
```

Confusing? Maybe. I break it down into English for you in Listing 3-3.

Listing 3-3   ActionScript in Plain English

```
If the time is between midnight and 6:00 AM,
    the visitor receives the greeting "Good evening"
If the time is between 6:00 AM and 12:00 noon,
    the visitor receives the greeting "Good morning"
If the time is between 12:00 noon and 6:00 PM,
    the visitor receives the greeting "Good afternoon"
If the time is other than any of the above,
    The visitor receives the greeting, "Good evening"
```

Compare Listing 3-2 and Listing 3-3; ActionScript isn't that difficult after you decipher the language.

ActionScript is merely another way of saying something. In this case, it's a set of instructions combined with other elements to achieve the final outcome — the greeting to the visitor who enters her name and clicks the button. To finish up the ActionScript for frame 2, another variable, named welcome, is created. The line welcome = greeting+" "+name; declares the variable and sets its value equal to the greeting determined by the decision-making lines of code and the name the user entered before clicking the button. Of course, the user could "fake out" Flash by entering something other than her real name, but that's a whole 'nother kettle of fish.

Part II
Using Elementary ActionScript, My Dear Watson

The 5th Wave   By Rich Tennant

"Look into my Web site, Ms. Carruthers. Look deep into its rotating, nicely animated spiral, spinning, spinning, pulling you in, deeper... deeper..."

In this part . . .

*I*f you've ever had the hankering to actually create something with the Actions panel, this is the part for you. In this part you'll begin to understand how to use your favorite actions — and not so favorite if you've never used them successfully before — to get Flash MX to do something. First, I show you how to make your Flash movies take a fork in the road — or not — by assigning actions with keyframes and objects. Then I show you how to manage a really-really-big Flash movie by cutting it into bite-sized — or for you techno-geeks in the crowd, *byte-sized* — chunks. I also show you how to give Flash a brain — or as they say in some parts of the country, smarts — by using variables. And last but not least, I show you how to use properties to make an object look or behave differently. And if you've ever been thrown for a loop and would like to get even, there's a special section on creating loops in Chapter 5.

Chapter 4

Directing a Movie

· ·

In This Chapter

▶ Advancing a movie to different frames

▶ Advancing a movie to a different scene

▶ Stopping a movie

▶ Using the `getURL` action

· ·

*O*ne of the more basic — but extremely beneficial — uses of ActionScript is controlling the flow of a movie. When you add frames and keyframes to the timeline and publish the movie, the Flash Player runs the movie, beginning at frame 1 until it concludes — unless, of course, you do something to change it. Why would you want to change the flow of the movie? For one thing, no two viewers are alike. And, if your movie is a full-fledged Web site, perhaps your viewers don't want to see all of it. If it's a large site, viewers will probably lose interest the minute they see something they don't like. Then, quicker than you can blink an eye, they're clicking the Back button to get outta Dodge, which is a bad thing because they may miss some of the cool effects you created with ActionScript in the parts of the site they may want to view.

To keep viewers interested, give them a choice. Create a menu or some buttons for the different parts of the site. When viewers click the button, the attached ActionScript that you so skillfully crafted transports them to what they want to see. That's interactivity with a capital *I*.

The Actions panel's got lots of books. And some of these books have books within a book. To add some actions to your scripts, you have to click this book icon, then click that book icon, then click another book icon, and so on. Rather than bore you with a lot of words, I'm going to show the path to each action as shown in the following example: Click Actions⇨Movie Control and then double-click `goto`.

Using the Stop Action without a Crossing Guard

The first and most obvious action is to stop a movie. You can add a `stop` action to the main timeline or to a movie clip's timeline. For example, you stop the movie when you want viewers to read a large block of important information. At least, it had better be important, or else you'll lose viewers. After they read the block of text, they click a button to resume the movie.

You use the `stop` action in a movie clip's timeline, also. Suppose that a movie clip on the timeline displays a message when a site visitor rolls his or her mouse over a button. But the movie clip is always on Stage, so you don't want the clip to play when the movie loads — only when the clip is summoned from a button. To do this, you put the `stop` action in the movie clip's first frame, which is blank, and put the text message and other content in consecutive frames. When the movie loads, a visitor never sees the movie clip until he rolls his mouse over the proper button. When you call a movie clip from the main timeline, you specify the path so that Flash knows where to look for it.

I show you how to work with movie clips and target paths in Chapter 9.

Adding a Stop Action to a Timeline

The `stop` action halts a movie at the keyframe to which you add the action. A perfect use for a `stop` action is to prevent a movie clip from looping continuously. The `stop` action has no parameters, or, if you prefer program-speak, arguments. To add a `stop` action to a timeline:

1. **Select the keyframe where you want the movie to stop.**

   Click a keyframe to select it. If the frame you selected isn't a keyframe, convert it to one by pressing F6. Flash lets you apply an action to a frame; however, it's assigned to the preceding keyframe on the timeline.

2. **Click the arrow to the left of the word Actions.**

   The Actions panel opens.

3. **Click Actions➪Movie Control, and then double-click the `stop` action. Or if you prefer, click the plus button (+) to the upper left of the Script pane and choose Actions➪Movie Control➪stop.**

   The `stop` action is added to the selected keyframe. Figure 4-1 shows a `stop` action being added to a keyframe.

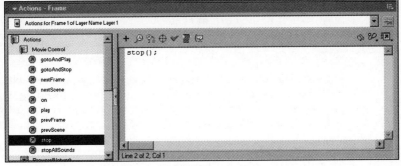

Figure 4-1:
Adding a
stop action
to a timeline
is a virtual
cease-and-
desist order.

Using the goto Action without a Road Map

Another useful action is the goto action. With it, you can advance the movie to a specific scene or specific frame. You add the goto action to a keyframe on the main timeline or to a movie clip's timeline, or you can add the action to a button to advance the movie based on a user's interaction with the button. A goto action is typically used when you're creating a preloader. You want the movie to go to the beginning frame of the preloader until the movie has loaded.

Adding the goto action to a timeline

When the need arises to add interactivity to your movie, or if you just feel like putting a fork in the middle of the road, you can do it with the goto action. But before your movie can be viewed with a forked road, you need to add the goto action to the timeline, as shown in the following steps:

1. **Click the keyframe to which you want to apply the action.**

   If the frame isn't already a keyframe, press F6 to convert it.

2. **Click the arrow to the left of the word Actions, or for that matter, click the title bar.**

   The Actions panel opens for business.

3. **Click Actions➪Movie Control to open the group.**

   The Movie Control group is ready to rock and roll.

4. **Double-click goto.**

   Flash adds the line of code gotoAndPlay (1) to your script, and the parameter text boxes, as shown in Figure 4-2, makes an appearance. The default parameters for the goto action tell the Flash Player to "go to and play frame 1 in the current scene."

5. **To have the Flash Player go to a specific frame and stop, select the GoTo and Stop option, which you find directly above the Script pane.**

   With this option selected, the Flash Player goes to the specified frame and stops, awaiting further instructions before proceeding to another part of the movie. You specify whether to Go to and Play or Go to and Stop by clicking the proper radio button directly above the Script pane.

You can also add the goto action to a button or movie clip. I show you how to work with movie clips in Chapter 9; with buttons, in Chapter 11.

Figure 4-2: You use the goto action to advance the movie to a different frame.

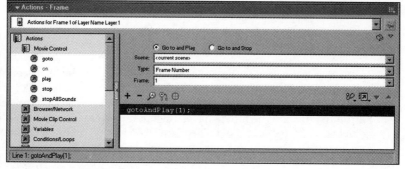

Navigating to a scene

I know what you're thinking: "What good is the action if it goes to frame 1 only in the current scene?" Well, there's more. Take another look at Figure 4-2, and you see a couple of parameter text boxes. The Scene text box is the first one you come across. You use it to advance to a specific scene in your movie. If you have more than one scene in a movie, they play in succession — until you tell the Flash Player to act differently with the goto action. To navigate to a specific scene in your movie:

1. **Select the frame or button you want to trigger the scene change.**

2. **Click the arrow to the left of the word Actions.**

   The Actions panel opens.

   By default, the Actions panel is docked at the bottom of the workspace. If for some reason you've moved it or closed it, you can return it to its hallowed position by choosing Window⇨Actions.

3. **Add the `goto` action to your script.**

   If you've been reading this chapter from the beginning, you already know how to do this; you get one gold star. If you don't know how to add the `goto` action to your script, please read the preceding section, "Adding the goto action to a timeline."

4. **Click the triangle to the right of the Scene field.**

   The drop-down menu shown in Figure 4-3 appears.

5. **Click the scene to which you want the movie to advance.**

   Flash adds the selected scene to the `goto` action, and a new line of code appears in the right side of the Actions panel; for example, `gotoAndPlay (Main_movie, 1)`. The line of code in the example advances the movie to frame 1 of a scene named Main_movie. The Main_movie scene plays when the frame containing the `goto` action is reached. To stop the movie when the frame is reached, select the Go to and Stop option directly above the Script pane.

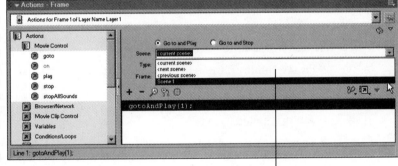

Figure 4-3: You also use the `goto` action to advance to a different scene in the movie.

Scene drop-down menu

Navigating to a specific frame

The ability to have Flash go to and play a specific frame is useful when you're creating games or interactive movies where you give viewers the choice of what part of the movie they want to see. For example, you can create a button with a `goto` action that addresses a specific frame on a movie clip. When the button is clicked, the movie advances to the specified frame on the movie clip and either plays or stops, depending on the choice you make in the parameter text boxes. To advance a movie to a specific frame:

1. **Select the keyframe or object to which you want to assign the action.**

   Remember that you can assign actions only to keyframes, buttons, or movie clips. A keyframe is filled with a solid dot. If you select a regular frame, you can convert it to a keyframe by pressing F6.

2. **Click the arrow to the left of the word Actions.**

   You can also open the Actions panel by clicking the Actions title bar.

   The Actions panel opens for business.

3. **Add the** `goto` **action to your script.**

   Flash adds the default line of code, `gotoAndPlay (1)`. If you skipped right to this section without reading the carefully crafted text in the previous sections, you may not know how to apply the `goto` action. If this is the case, or if you need a refresher course, read the earlier section "Adding the goto action to a timeline."

4. **When you use the** `goto` **action to navigate to a specific frame, you first need to choose whether you want the movie to go to a frame number or a frame label. To specify which one, click the triangle to the right of the Type field.**

   A drop-down menu appears.

5. **Select one of the following options:**

   • **Frame Number:** Choose this option (it's the default setting) when you're referring to the target keyframe by its number.

   • **Frame Label:** Choose this option when you're targeting a keyframe you've labeled.

   • **Expression:** Choose this option if you're using a variable to refer to the target frame. You can also create an expression, that when evaluated, advances the movie to a specific frame.

   • **Next Frame:** Choose this option when you want the movie to advance to the next frame when the action is executed.

   • **Previous Frame:** Choose this option to have the Flash Player advance to the previous frame when the action is executed.

6. **In the Frame field, do one of the following:**

   • Enter a number in the field to advance the movie to a known frame number when the action is executed.

   • Click the triangle to the right of the Frame field and choose a labeled frame from the drop-down menu shown in Figure 4-4. Every frame in the scene you've labeled appears on this menu. If you select a different scene in the Scene field, the frames you've labeled in that scene appear on the menu.

   • If you chose the Expression option in Step 5, type the name of the variable or the expression you want Flash to evaluate.

I strongly advise you to get in the habit of labeling every keyframe in your movie. If you reference a frame number in an action and then add or delete frames, you have to remember to change the frame number in your ActionScript as well; otherwise, the action isn't executed properly. If you reference a frame label, the action is still executed correctly, no matter how much you alter the timeline.

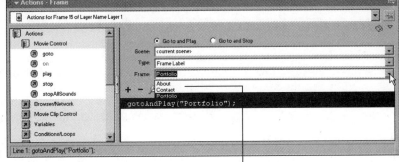

Figure 4-4: Navigate to a labeled frame with ease using this drop-down menu.

Drop-down menu of labeled keyframes in scene

Using ActionScript to Play It Again, Sam

Another useful action you use within a movie is not so much for navigation as it is to get things going again after you've stopped a movie. The action is play. Think of it as the Flash green light to continue the movie with reckless abandon — or at a slightly less frenetic pace if an older audience will view your movie. You can use the play action with a button that, when clicked, calls in the Flash medics to perform CPR and restart a stopped movie. Another way you can use the play action is to assign it to a keyframe and use the action to play a movie clip that has been lying dormant on Stage, just waiting for the keyframe to be reached so that the movie clip can have its 15 minutes (err, seconds is more like it . . . a 15-minute movie clip would be humongous) of fame.

To add the play action to a script:

1. **Click the keyframe or object to which you want to apply the action.**

2. **Click the arrow to the left of the word Actions.**

   I know, you may think I'm getting redundant, but some people don't read these books from start to finish, and they need to know how to open the panel. If you've read every word of this chapter, I apologize for the redundancy. For those who haven't read every word (I'm speechless), clicking this arrow opens the Actions panel.

3. **Click Actions⇨Movie Control.**

The Movie Control actions are ready for you to take control of them.

4. **Double-click the play action to add it to the script.**

Flash adds the action to your script. When the action is executed, the movie plays.

Creating an Interactive Animation

To see how the goto, play, and stop actions can be combined to create interactivity, you create an animation to be controlled by a button. The object you animate is a ball. I don't show you how to set up the scene; you already know how to do that. The purpose of this section is to show you how to create the ActionScript code that causes the animation to play on demand.

To follow along in this section, copy the chapter_4_start.fla file to your hard drive and use your computer's operating system to disable the file's read-only attributes.

Creating the animation

1. **Launch Flash and choose File⇨Open.**

2. **Navigate to the folder where you stored the chapter_4_start.fla file and open the file.**

Flash loads the file. Notice that you have a button symbol and a ball symbol in your movie. Two layers are also set up: one for the button and one for the ball animation. See? As I promised, you don't have to create the scene.

3. **Select frame 12 on both layers and press F5.**

Flash adds 11 frames to both layers.

4. **Select frame 12 on the ball layer and press F6.**

The frame is converted to a keyframe.

5. **On the ball layer, click any frame and choose Insert⇨Create Motion Tween.**

An arrow connects the beginning and ending keyframes. The frame's background is tinted purple.

6. **On the ball layer, select frame 6 and press F6.**

Flash converts the frame to a keyframe.

7. **With frame 6 still selected, click the ball to select it.**

8. **Choose Window⇨Align.**

   The Align panel opens.

9. **Click the To Stage button and then click the Align Vertical Center button.**

   The ball moves to the vertical center of the movie.

10. **Move the playhead to frame 1 and press Enter or Return to preview the movie.**

    If you've set up your motion tween correctly, the ball moves smoothly from the top of the Stage to center Stage and back again. If you were to publish this movie, it would play as an endless loop; the ball would keep moving up and down like a virtual yo-yo, which may cause you or any pet or fellow office worker within viewing distance to experience vertigo. To control the motion — and prevent a possible bout with vertigo — you add ActionScript to the frames and to the button.

Adding actions to the timeline

The first step to adding interactivity and control to the animation is to add actions to the timeline. The actions you add to the timeline work in conjunction with the action you add to the button to create motion on demand. To add the actions to the timeline:

1. **Click the ball layer to select it and then choose Insert⇨Layer.**

   Flash inserts a new layer at the top of the stack.

2. **Label the layer** `actions`.

   Always create a separate layer for timeline actions. Editing a complex movie with lots of ActionScript is much easier if you have all your actions in a single layer. (Consider this process as getting your virtual ducks in a row.)

3. **Create a keyframe at Frames 1, 6, and 12.**

   Notice that these frames are the same ones you converted to keyframes for the ball animation. Do you see a pattern emerging here?

4. **Click the arrow to the left of the word Actions.**

   The Actions panel opens.

5. **Click Actions⇨Movie Control.**

   The Movie Control group opens.

6. **Select frame 1 and double-click the** `stop` **action. Or, if you prefer to work with menus, click the plus button (+) near the upper-right corner of the Actions panel and choose Actions⇨Movie Control⇨stop.**

You can also painlessly (pun intended) add an action to your script by dragging and dropping it from the Actions panel's left pane into the Script pane.

A new line of code, `stop ()`, appears in the right pane of the Actions panel. A lowercase *a* appears in the selected frame.

7. **Repeat Steps 5 and 6 to add the** `stop` **action to frame 6.**

The Actions panel stays open like a barn door in a hurricane breeze unless you close it. It's a good idea to close the panel after finishing your scripting so you can gain back valuable workspace. It also saves you from having to scroll past a couple hundred actions.

8. **Select frame 12 and add the** `goto` **action to the script.**

Flash adds the default `gotoAndPlay (1)` code to the script.

9. **In the parameter text box area above the Script pane, select the GoTo and Stop option and accept the default frame number 1.**

The line of code is modified to read `gotoAndStop (1)`, as shown in Figure 4-5. This line of code recycles the animation to frame 1 when frame 12 is reached.

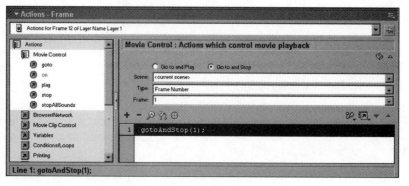

Figure 4-5:
To create interactive animation, you add actions to keyframes.

Programming the button

If you're following along throughout this chapter (which is the best way to do it in this case), I could have had you test the animation in the preceding section. Of course, nothing would happen because a `stop` action on the first frame grinds everything to a halt before it can begin. To get the movie to play, you must add the `play` action to the button that has been wondering when you're going to give it some attention. To program the button:

1. **Select the button.**

2. **Click the arrow to the left of the word Actions.**

   The Actions panel opens.

3. **Click Actions⇨Movie Control, and then double-click the play action.**

   Flash generates a new line of code, as shown in Figure 4-6. Accept the default event settings and close the Actions panel.

That's all there is to it. You've successfully created the code for an interactive animation. You may be wondering why Flash added on (release) to your play action. That, my friend, is known as an *event handler*. The event handler added to this script tells the Flash Player to play the movie (handle the action) when the button is released (the event occurs). You get an event handler whenever you add an action to a button or movie clip. I show you how to work with movie clip event handlers in Chapter 9; button clip event handlers are in Chapter 11.

Figure 4-6:
When the button is clicked, the movie plays.

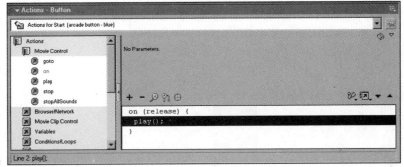

Testing the animation

If you've followed this entire exercise from the beginning, you may want to wander off recklessly in search of entertainment, refreshment, or a sofa for a well-deserved nap. But before you do, I want you to test the animation so that you can get a handle on what all those lines of code actually do. Before you exit Flash and close the book, do the following:

1. **Choose Control⇨Test Movie.**

   Flash publishes the movie and opens another window. If you followed the steps exactly, all you see are the button and the ball at the top of the movie.

2. **Click the button.**

   The ball moves smoothly to the center of the movie.

3. Click the button.

The ball moves to its initial position at the top of the movie, just like the proverbial tortoise popping back into its shell.

If you've got a bit of the old Sherlock Holmes in your makeup, you've probably already deduced exactly what happened here. If you're like Holmes's counterpart, Watson, I make it all elementary for you. When the movie started playing, nothing happened because of the `stop` action in frame 1. When you clicked the button, control was passed to the button, and the `play` action took over, advancing the movie to frame 6, when it came to another grinding halt — can't you smell the burning rubber? — thanks to the `stop` action you added to this frame. After the button was clicked a second time, the `play` action again came into play, and the movie advanced to frame 12. Frame 12's `goto` action took over and advanced the movie back to frame 1, where it stops and waits for the button to be clicked again, which starts the cycle again. Now that you know how it works, it may seem rather elementary, but this interactive animation is the basis of a cool item you can add to your Flash movies: a pop-up menu. I show you how to program a pop-up menu in Chapter 16.

If your interactive animation didn't work correctly, compare your code to the chapter_4_complete.fla file that is in this chapter's folder on this book's CD.

Opening Another Web Page with the getURL Action

Sometimes, in spite of your best efforts to tantalize a client with your Flash wizardry, the client gets a severe case of frugalitis when you submit a proposal to create a complete Flash site. At this point in the negotiating process, you realize that a bird in the hand is better than two in the bush, so you revise your proposal to include a cool Flash intro — with ActionScript, of course — followed by a cool but slightly less interactive HTML site. After your client signs on the dotted line, you need to get from Flash to HTML. The easiest way to do that is with the `getURL` action. When you add the `getURL` action to a keyframe, Flash opens the URL specified in the viewer's default Web browser.

You can also use the `getURL` action to open HTML elements with embedded goodies such as QuickTime videos from your Flash movie in addition to other elements, such as blank e-mail windows already formatted with your e-mail address. You can add the `getURL` action to a button or a keyframe. To open a Web page using the `getURL` action:

1. **Select the object or keyframe to which you want to apply the action.**

2. **Click the arrow to the left of the word Actions.**

   The Actions panel opens.

3. **Click Actions⇨Browser/Network Control.**

   The Browser/Network Control group of actions invites you to browse their menu of goodies.

4. **Double-click the** `getURL` **action.**

   Flash adds the action to your script, and the parameter text boxes open.

5. **In the URL field, type the address of the Web page you want to open, as shown in Figure 4-7.**

   Be sure to use the proper syntax; for example, `http://www.myworldandyerwelcome2it.com`.

   To open a blank e-mail form, type **mailto:myemail@myISP.com** in the URL field, using your real e-mail address after the `mailto:` part. For example, `mailto:das001@earthlink.net` is the code needed to open a blank e-mail form with my e-mail address. When the action is executed, a blank e-mail composition page pops up.

6. **By default, Flash opens the URL in the same window. To open the URL in another window, click the triangle to the right of the Window field and choose one of the following:**

   - **_blank** opens the linked document in a brand-new, unnamed browser window.

   - **_parent** loads the linked document in the window of the frame that contains the link. If the frame isn't nested, the linked document loads in the full browser window.

   - **_self** loads the linked document in the same frame or window as the link.

   - **_top** loads the document in the full browser window, removing all frames.

7. **In the Variables field, accept the default option Don't Send or click the triangle to the right of the field and choose either Send Using Get or Send Using Post.**

   You can send variables to another Web page using the Send Using Get option or forward the variables used in a form to an e-mail address using the Send Using Post option in combination with a CGI script.

8. **Close the Actions panel to apply the script.**

   When the movie is published and the action is executed, the movie loads to the desired URL.

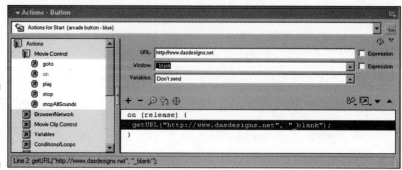

Figure 4-7:
`GetURL`,
whoever
he is.

Opening a URL in a Different-Size Window

When it comes to JavaScript, I'm a devout coward. However, I've memorized one or two neat little lines of code that I use with my Flash movies. One of the code lines uses JavaScript to open an URL in a different-size window. That capability comes in handy when you want your visitor to view another Web page and still have access to your Flash movie. To open an URL in another window:

1. **Select the object or frame to which you want to apply the code.**

   In most cases, you use a button to open the window.

2. **Click the arrow to the left of the word Actions.**

   The Actions panel pops open for business.

3. **Click Actions⇨Browser/Network Control.**

   The Browser/Network Control group opens for action.

4. **Double-click the `getURL` action.**

   The `getURL` action is added to your script, and the parameter text boxes make an appearance

5. **In the URL field, type** Javascript:newwin1 ().

   The piece of code tells Flash to reference JavaScript within the main HTML document. The URL for the site you're going to open is in a piece of JavaScript that you enter into the HTML document in which the Flash movie is embedded.

That's all you need to do in Flash to open the URL in a different-size window. If you have more than one URL you're going to open in a different window, you use the same set of steps on another button, except that the JavaScript you enter in Step 5 is Javascript:newin2 (), Javascript:newin3 (), and so on. To finish the effect, after you publish the movie in the Flash and HTML formats, you open the HTML page in an HTML editor (or a friendly word processor) and enter between the <head> and </head> tags the code shown in Listing 4-1.

Listing 4-1   JavaScript to Go

```
<script language="Javascript">
function newwin1() {


            window.open('http://www.mysite.com.allaboutme.htm
            ', 'links'
            ,'scrollbars=yes,width=640,height=480')


}
</script>
```

Enter different values in the width and height fields to open the URL in the window size of your choice. If you don't want the window to have scroll bars, change scrollbars=yes to scrollbars=no. And, of course, you replace mysite.com with the actual page you want to open when the button is clicked (unless you really want to open a site named www.mysite.com).

I have a tendency to forget this bit of JavaScript because I don't use it every day. If you're like me, create a document in your word processor and copy into it this code and any notes you need to jog your memory. When you need the code, open the document, copy the lines of code, and then paste them between the beginning head tag (<head>) and ending head tag (</head>) of your HTML document.

Chapter 5

Managing a Movie

· ·

· ·

*B*y nature, Flash movies are tiny critters. Due to the nature of the Flash SWF (small Web file) format, you can pack lots of action into a tiny package. Sometimes, though, when you use lots of bitmaps in your movies, they can become quite large, even though they're smaller than sites using other media to achieve similar results. When that happens, you must manage the movie. After all, who wants to sit around, minute after minute, waiting for a site — even a cool one like your Flash movie — to download? Certainly not I.

In this chapter, I show you how to manage a site with ActionScript. I also show you how to create loops. *Loops* handle repetitive actions while a certain condition is true. I also show you how to control the movie's final output in the Flash Player by using the `FSCommand` action.

The Actions panel's got lots of books. And some of these books have books within a book. To add some actions to your scripts, you have to click this book icon, then click that book icon, then click another book icon, and so on. Rather than bore you with a lot of words, I'm going to show the path to each action as shown in the following example: Click Actions➪Movie Control and then double-click `goto`.

Breaking a Really Big Movie into Byte-Size Chunks

Until you get your handprints plastered into the Flash movie ActionScript guru's Sidewalk of Fame, not many people — except for a few close friends and your relatives, of course — bother to wait for a big Flash movie to download, no matter how good it is.

Suppose that you have a client who wants you to create an interactive Flash movie showing his catalog of goods. If the client's catalog is extensive, you end up with a very large movie. The answer is to create one movie that is the main interface and then break down the client's catalog into individual movies that are linked to buttons in the main movie. When clicked, each button loads an individual part of the site on top of the main movie. The solution enables your client to display the entire catalog of goods without chasing away site traffic because of lengthy downloads.

When you decide that your Flash content is too large for one movie, the first thing to do is figure out how you're going to break the site down. If you're confronted with a problem like the catalog scenario in the preceding paragraph, break the site down into a main movie that contains all the main elements of the site, such as a banner and the navigation menu. The navigation menu breaks the catalog offering down into like groups of products. The next step is to create individual movies for each group of products. Remember to use the same dimensions for each movie. If you don't, the Flash Player resizes any movies you load to match the main movie. Publish each movie in .swf format and save the original file in .fla format for any future editing.

Creating individual movies for a large Web site

The easiest way to create several movies that link together is to create the main movie first. When you create the main movie, visualize where you want the content to be placed. You can do this task directly in Flash by creating a rectangle using the Rectangle tool and positioning the rectangle where you want the loaded content to be placed. Choose a fill color that contrasts well with the document background color. Create the elements for the main movie around the rectangle, as shown in Figure 5-1.

Save the main file and then use the Save As command to save the file as template.fla. The second file is the template for the movies you create that load into the main movie. To create a template for the movies you load into the main site:

1. **Delete all the interface elements, such as buttons and banners, leaving only the rectangle that designates the content boundary of the movies you'll load into the main site.**

2. **Select Layer 1 in the timeline.**

    At this point, you have only one layer.

3. **Choose Insert⇨Layer.**

    Flash adds another layer to the movie.

4. **Right-click (in Windows) or Ctrl+click (on the Macintosh) the first layer and choose Guide from the drop-down menu.**

   Flash converts the layer to a Guide layer. You may consider naming the layer Guide so that you know its role in your Flash movie.

5. **Select the rectangle on the bottom layer and then choose Edit⇨Cut.**

   Flash copies the rectangle to the clipboard.

6. **Select the first frame in the Guide layer and then choose Edit⇨Paste in Place.**

   The rectangle is pasted into the same position it occupied before you cut it. Now you have a guide to work with when you're positioning elements that will be created for a movie that loads into another movie. The rectangle on the guide layer isn't visible when the movie is published.

7. **Lock the guide layer, as shown in Figure 5-2.**

   When you use the template to create movies you load into the main movie, create layers above the guide layer for the elements in the new movie.

Figure 5-1:
Create the elements for the main site first.

Guide layer

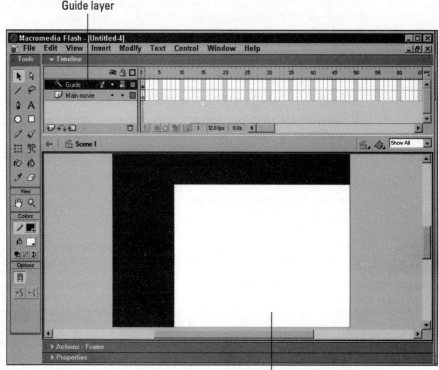

Figure 5-2:
Create a
template for
the movies
you load
into the
main movie.

Place graphics within rectangular guide

Creating a template with a guide layer makes it easy to precisely position the content for the movies you load into the main movie. As long as you don't exceed the boundaries of the rectangle, the published movie loads into the main movie without blocking any of the main movie's content. You also need to be sure to load the movie into the right level. I know — I haven't said anything about levels. They're covered in the next section, where I show you how to load and unload movies.

Loading and unloading movies without a forklift

When you break a large site into component movies, you use ActionScript to load them and unload them as needed. You use the loadMovie action to load movies and the unloadMovie action to unload movies. Logical, isn't it? And simple, too. But it's not quite that simple. You also need to be concerned with levels. *Levels* are like floors in an apartment building. The main level of a movie is like the bottom floor of a multistory apartment building, which means that you have only one way to go: up.

Understanding levels

It may help for you to think of the different levels of a Flash movie as you think of layers on the timeline. The bottom layer of the timeline is like the bottom level of the movie. Any objects in movies that you load into levels above the main movie eclipse objects directly beneath them on the main layer.

The main movie's level is Level 0. You can have up to 99 levels in a movie. Think of the multistory apartment scenario again. Level 0 (the main movie) is the ground floor. When nothing is happening on the ground floor, all you see is the movie's background color. When action occurs on the timeline, the background color is eclipsed by the action. When you load a movie into Level 1, it's similar to getting neighbors on the second floor. But the floor for the second level isn't visible. When action occurs on Level 1 and one of the objects moves over an object in Level 0, the object on the lower level is hidden. If, however, you load a movie into Level 0, it's a new group of tenants moving into the apartment on the first floor; the new stuff replaces the old.

Using the loadMovie action

You use the loadMovie action to load a published Flash movie. In most cases, you assign the loadMovie action to a keyframe or a button. The action has two parameters that you use to specify the destination for the movie you're loading and whether any variables will be sent from the loaded movie. To add the loadMovie action to a script:

1. **Select the object or keyframe to which you want to assign the action.**

2. **Click the arrow to the right of the word Actions.**

   The Actions panel opens.

3. **Click Actions⇨Browser/Network Control.**

   The Browser/Network Control group gets ready to rumble.

4. **Double-click loadMovie.**

   Flash adds the action to the script, and the parameter text boxes appear above the Script pane.

5. **In the URL parameter text box, type the path and title to the movie you're loading.**

   Enter the directory where the movie can be found, along with the movie's title (mymovie.swf). If you've assigned the movie's path to a variable, enter the variable's name and check the Expression box.

Upload all of your Flash movies into the Web site's root directory. Then, when you use the `loadMovie` action, all you need to concern yourself with is the movie's title.

6. In the Location field, choose one of the following:

> **Level:** Choose the default setting when you're loading the movie into a level in the main movie.

> **Target:** Choose this option when you're loading the movie into a target movie clip within the movie. I show you how to load movies into a target movie clip in Chapter 9.

7. In the blank field to the right of the Location field, enter the number of the level or the path in which you're loading the movie.

Remember that if you load the movie into Level 0, you erase the base movie. Choose any level from 0 to 99. Figure 5-3 shows the ActionScript for loading a movie into Level 1.

8. Click the triangle to the right of the Variables field and choose one of the following:

> **Don't send:** Choose this setting (the default) if no variables are associated with the movie you're loading.

> **Send using GET:** Choose this option when you have a small number of variables to work with. The option appends the variables to the end of the URL.

> **Send using POST:** Choose this option if you have lots of variables.

In Flash MX, you can now load a JPEG image using the `loadMovie` action. All you have to do is enter the filename for the image in the URL field, complete with extension, for example: `myImage.jpg`. Make sure you load the image into a target that is the same size as the image. I show you how to create targets in Chapter 9.

Figure 5-3:
You use the
`loadMovie`
action to
serve up
another
movie.

Using the UnloadMovie action

When you load a new movie into the same level where one is playing, the new movie replaces the old movie. When movies are playing on multiple levels and you're loading new content, you need to use the `unloadMovie` action to clear the deck. To assign the `unloadMovie` action to a keyframe or object:

1. **Select the object or keyframe to which you want to apply the action.**

2. **Click the arrow to the left of the word Actions.**

   The Actions panel opens.

3. **Click Actions⇨Browser/Network Control.**

   The Browser/Network Control actions group assembles, waiting for you to make a choice.

4. **Double-click** `unloadMovie`**.**

   The `unloadMovie` action is added to your script, and the parameter text boxes appear.

5. **Click the triangle to the right of the Location parameter text box and choose one of the following:**

   Level: Choose the default option if the movie you want to unload is loaded into a level.

   Target: Choose this option if the movie you've unloaded is loaded in a target.

6. **In the field to the right of the Location field, depending on the option you chose in Step 5, enter either the number of the level in which the movie is loaded or the target path to the loaded movie.**

Breaking a movie into scenes

Another convenient way to control the flow of a movie is to break it into scenes. Suppose that you have a client who hoodwinks you into creating a bandwidth-heavy site with bitmap images of the board of directors and an exiting trailer. First and foremost, the beast takes a while to load, which means that you need to create a preloader. Second, dealing with actions spread across hundreds of frames can become a logistical nightmare. The solution is to break the movie into scenes.

Adding a scene to a movie

You can add a scene to a movie at any time. If you planned the movie ahead of time, create all of your scenes before you begin adding objects and actions to the movie:

1. **Choose Window➪Scene.**

   The Scene panel (as shown in Figure 5-4) opens and displays all the scenes that are in the movie.

2. **To add a scene to the movie, click the Add Scene button at the bottom of the panel.**

   Flash adds the new scene to the panel and names it Scene, appended by the next available scene number.

3. **Double-click the scene name.**

   The default scene name is highlighted.

4. **Enter a new scene name.**

   I strongly advise you to get in the habit of naming all your scenes. Choose a name that's meaningful to you and any other designers working on the project. Naming a scene is especially important when you use ActionScript. The scene name appears on drop-down menus in the parameter text boxes when you choose an action that can target a specific scene and frame. Remembering a scene name is easier than remembering a scene number, especially if you juggle the order in which the scenes play or if another developer is working on the movie with you.

Scenes play in the order in which they were created; however, you can make your site interactive by giving users the option of viewing a different scene. You can easily do this by assigning the goto action to a navigation button.

You can change the order in which scenes play by opening the Scene panel, clicking a scene's title, and then dragging the title to a different position in the panel. You can delete an unwanted scene by clicking the Delete Scene button in the Scene panel.

Figure 5-4:
You use the
Scene panel
to create
a scene of
the virtual
variety.

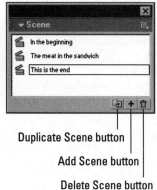

Duplicate Scene button

Add Scene button

Delete Scene button

Making Loops: Doing the ActionScript Loop-de-Loop

Flash uses two kinds of loops. With the first type of loop, a number of frames play and then start over again. A preloader is a good example of this type of loop. It cycles back and forth between a given number of frames. This type of loop can be an endless loop; the frames just keep playing and playing, or it can terminate if a certain condition is met. A preloader's loop terminates when the movie is loaded. You can also create a frame-based loop that recycles an animation over and over and over and. . . .

The second type of loop takes place within a single frame. This type of loop is used to perform a line or several lines of code when a certain condition is true. Four types of loops fall into this category:

✔ **Do While:** A do while loop will *do* a certain function *while* a condition is true, which explains why the Flash technodudes and dudettes created the do while action. When the condition is no longer true, the loop terminates, and the next action in the script takes over.

✔ **While:** With this loop, *while* a certain condition is true, another set of actions is being performed. In this type of loop, the condition takes precedence over the action being executed.

✔ **For:** This loop is set to run *for* a predetermined set of iterations. After the specified number of loops has been run, the next action in the script is performed.

✔ **Endless:** An endless loop performed on a single frame is a no-no in Flash. All loops you create on a single frame must be executed before the movie can advance to the next scene. If your movie is set up with the default frame rate of 12 FPS (frames per second), the loop must be executed in $\frac{1}{12}$th of a second. If a do while or while loop is scripted improperly, the loop may not be executed within a single frame. When you create such a monster and use the Test Movie command to test your script, the warning dialog box shown in Figure 5-5 appears. I strongly advise you to click the Yes button and abort the script. Otherwise, your computer may lock up, and you lose your current edits in the movie you're working on.

Figure 5-5:
If you create
a loop
that isn't
executed on
a single
frame, Flash
lets you
know
about it.

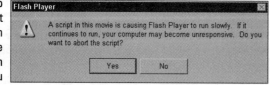

Creating a while loop

To show the power of a single frame loop, create an animation using the while action. The animation creates a field of spinning stars against a black background.

To follow along with this section, copy to your hard drive the file named starburst_begin.fla from the Chapter 5 folder on this book's CD. Use your operating system to disable the file's read-only attribute.

1. **Launch Flash and choose File⇨Open.**

2. **Navigate to the directory where you stored the starburst_begin.fla file, and open it.**

   Notice that you have a nice, black background and nothing else.

3. **Choose Window⇨Library.**

   The document Library opens. I've created two items for this movie. These items and ActionScript are all you need. The dark_star movie clip already has some actions assigned to it. If you're curious, double-click the movie clip icon and look at the actions I've assigned to each keyframe or just go to the next step. The actions I used on the movie clip are presented in detail in Chapter 7.

4. **Drag an instance of the dark_star symbol from the Library to the Stage.**

   It doesn't matter where you put the star, ActionScript soon has it cloning itself and moving randomly about the Stage.

5. **Click the arrow to the left of the word Properties.**

   The Property inspector opens.

6. **In the <Instance Name> field, type starBurst and press Enter or Return.**

7. **Click the Graphics layer, choose Insert⇨Layer, and name the new layer** *Actions.*

   Remember to put your actions on a separate layer, even in a simple one-frame animation.

8. **Select the first frame on the Actions layer and click the arrow to the left of the word Actions.**

   The Actions panel opens.

9. **Click Actions⇨Variables.**

   The Variables group opens.

10. **Double-click the** `set variable` **action.**

    Flash adds the action to the script, and the parameter text boxes opens.

11. **In the Variable field, type** increment; **in the Value field, type** 0. **Be sure to check the Expression box.**

    I know — I haven't shown you how to use variables. Consider this your baptism by fire. I tell you everything you want to know about variables in Chapter 6.

12. **In the left pane of the Actions panel, click Conditions/Loops and then double-click** `while`.

    The action is added to the script, and a lone parameter text box named Condition opens. In this field, you enter the condition that must be true for the loop to continue.

13. **In the Condition text box, type** increment<=30.

    In this case, the next action in the script repeats as long as the variable named `increment` is less than or equal to 30.

14. **On the left side of the Actions panel, click Movie Clip Control and then double-click** `duplicateMovieClip`.

    Yes, this is another action you probably don't know about. You get a better understanding of the `duplicateMovieClip` action in Chapter 9. For now, please just follow along.

15. **In the parameter text box area, fill in each field as follows:**

    - **Target:** starBurst
    - **New Name:** "starBurst"+increment
    - **Depth:** increment

    Be sure to check the Expression box to the right of the New Name field. All you're telling Flash to do is duplicate the instance of a movie clip named `starburst`. Each duplicate is named `starburst`, appended by the current value of the variable increment. The Depth value tells Flash how many duplicates to make; in this case, the final value of `increment`, which is 30.

16. **On the left side of the Actions panel, click Actions➪Variables and then double-click** `set variable`.

    The action is added to the script. Yep, the parameter text boxes open.

17. **Fill in the parameter text boxes as follow:**

    - **Variable:** increment

    - **Value:** ++increment

    You may recognize the friendly `increment` variable from Step 11. This line of code changes the value of the variable. The code you enter in the value field is an ActionScript math shortcut. Whenever two plus signs (+) follow a variable, they increase the value of variable by 1. It's the same thing as saying `increment + 1`; it's just quicker to hit the plus key (+) twice. Be sure that you check the Expression box to the right of value. After all, it's a mathematical expression.

18. **Move your cursor over the curly brace under the last line of code you entered.**

19. **Click Actions➪Movie Control and then double-click** `stop`.

    Flash adds the action to the script. Your finished ActionScript for frame 1 should look exactly like the one shown in Figure 5-6.

20. **Close the Actions panel and then choose Control➪Test Movie.**

    Flash publishes the movie and opens another window. You should see an expanding field of rotating stars.

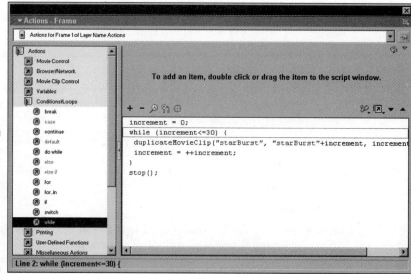

Figure 5-6: The `while` action loops the frame while a certain condition is true.

If your movie didn't create a field of rotating stars, locate the file starburst_final. fla in this chapter's folder on this book's CD. Load the file and compare the finished code to what you just created.

Okay, let me break the loop you created in frame 1 into common English. Listing 5-1 follows the ActionScript line for line.

Listing 5-1   Looping in Plain English

```
Create a variable named increment that has a value of 0;
While the value of increment is less than or equal to 30;
    Duplicate the starburst movie clip 30 times
    Increase the value of increment by 1
When 30 duplicates have spawned, stop the script
```

Of course the movie keeps playing because there's only one frame. When the value of increment reaches 30, the script recycles itself by resetting the value of increment to 0, and the loop plays again.

Using the for action

You use the for action when you know how many iterations you need within a loop sequence. For example, if you need to change four answers in a quiz, rather than write a separate line of code to reset each answer, you can write a single line of code and have it loop four times. This type of loop comes in handy when you store data in arrays. I know — another new term. Don't worry. I show you how to use arrays in Chapter 6.

You can also use the for action to create a for loop when you need to make changes to several movie clips at one time.

To apply the changes without giving yourself carpal tunnel syndrome from typing a zillion lines of code, you set up a for loop with the same number of loops as you have movie clips and then type the code once. Now that you know what a for loop can do, take a look at Figure 5-7 to see what one looks like.

Creating a loop with the for action is not as tricky as it looks if you break it down into its component parts. The for action initializes the loop in the first line. Notice that the for action is broken into three parts, neatly separated by semicolons and surrounded by parentheses. The first part of the code shown in Figure 5-7 sets the value of a variable named i equal to 0. After the semicolon is the condition that must be true in order for the loop to continue; in this case, for the loop to continue, the value of i must be less than or equal to 4. The last part of the statement sets the increment of each loop. In this case, the value of i increases by 1 with each loop. The ++ after i is simply shorthand that increases the value by 1. (Tuck this one in your hip pocket. It makes more sense after you read Chapter 12.) The line of code surrounded by the curly braces is the action that occurs while the loop is running. You can have more than one action execute within a loop, as long as you need the additional actions to execute the same number of times as the loop. The action that executes five times in the scenario shown in Figure 5-7 changes the *x* scale and *y* scale of each movie clip to 50 percent of its original value. The movie clip instances are named sphere0, sphere1, sphere2, and so on. Rather than write a separate line of code for each movie clip, you write a single line of code and let the for loop execute it five times. This concept may seem a bit odd as the loop stops when i=4, but the loop starts counting at 0, which is the initial value of i.

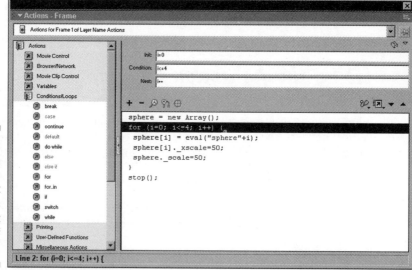

Figure 5-7:
You use
a for loop
to repeat
the same
action a set
number of
times.

Creating a loop with the for action

When you create a loop with the for action, you're saving yourself lots of time. If you hopped straight to this section before checking out anything else in this chapter, check out the preceding section to see the power of this tool. To add a for loop to a script, do the following:

1. **Select the keyframe to which you want to apply the action.**

   If the frame you've selected isn't already a keyframe, convert it to one by pressing F6.

2. **Click the arrow to the left of the word Actions.**

   The Actions panel opens.

3. **Click Actions⟹Conditions/Loops.**

   The Conditions/Loops group opens.

4. **Locate the for action and double-click it.**

   Flash adds the action to the Script pane of the Actions panel, and three parameter text boxes appear.

5. **In the Init parameter text box, enter the name of the variable and its initial value.**

   You can enter any name (except a reserved name) for the variable. It has been accepted practice among programmers to use i, j, or k for variables in a loop. This practice dates back to the days when computers with the power of your desktop PC were the size of a small apartment. Follow the variable name with an equal sign (=) and the beginning value. If the loop you're creating is counting up, begin with the lowest value. Normally, it's 1 or, if you're reading variables from an array, 0. However, in some cases, you could start with a different number; for instance, if you have ten movie clips and want the action to be applied to clips 5 through 10, your initial value is 5. If the loop you're creating is counting down, begin with the highest value.

   For a refresher course on reserved names, bookmark this page and ditty-bop over to Chapter 3.

6. **In the Condition field, enter the condition that must be true for the loop to continue.**

   If you're creating a loop that you want to run five times and the variable you were using in the loop is named i, the condition is i<=5. In other words, while the value of i is less than or equal to 5, the loop continues.

7. **In the Next parameter text box, enter the value by which you want the loop to increment (or decrement, if you're counting down).**

   You can use any increment (or decrement) to suit the action you need to duplicate. For example, if you're applying the action to every other instance of a movie clip, you use an increment (or decrement) of 2; every fifth instance, an increment of 5; and so on. The actual instance that is affected by the action depends on the beginning value. If i=1 and the increment is 2, the loop goes 1, 3, 5, 6, and so on, until the condition for the loop to continue is met or exceeded. If you want the loop to increase in increments of 1 and the variable is i, type **i++** in the Next field. If the loop is counting down by a value of 1, type **i--** in the Next field.

8. **With the last line of code still selected, add the desired action to the script, as shown in Figure 5-8.**

The action(s) you add depend on what you want to happen while the conditions for continuing the loop are true. The code in Figure 5-8 introduces you to an action named `trace`, which is something you use to trace a value when a script is running.

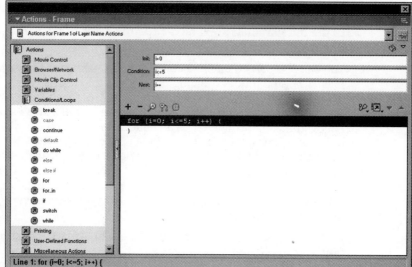

Figure 5-8: This `for` loop loops five times.

Creating a Preloader

In previous versions of Flash, you use the `ifFrameLoaded` action to test whether a specific frame is loaded. In Flash MX, the action has been *deprecated,* a fancy word that means the designers think you should use their better mousetrap. In this case, the better mousetrap is the `framesLoaded` action, which tests to see if a specific number of frames have been loaded. To create the preloader, you create a scene with a preload loop, which is a set of frames that play over and over again until the designated frames have loaded. To evaluate how many frames have loaded, you need to create a statement. In plain English the statement says, "If the designated number of frames have loaded, go to the main movie."

I generally prefer to build a preload loop after the rest of the movie has been created. That technique does two things: First, you know whether you need a preload loop; second, you know exactly how many frames you're working with.

Testing to see whether you need a preloader

If you've been working with Flash for a bit, you know that it does a wonderful job of compressing movies into a compact package. However, sometimes the file size can get large, especially if you have lots of bitmap images in your movie. In reality, what happens is that if your movie exceeds a user's bandwidth (the number of kilobytes per second that she can download at her connection speed), the movie stops playing while it waits for additional frames to load. With a preloader, you prevent interruptus bandwithicus (a term I just created) by loading all the essential elements while the preload loop plays. To see whether you need a preloader for your movie, run the following test:

1. **After you've finished creating your Flash masterpiece, choose Control➪Test Movie.**

   Flash publishes the movie and plays it in another window.

2. **Choose Debug and then select a connection speed from the drop-down menu.**

   I generally test my movies at the 28.8 setting. Testing at this setting ensures that even viewers with slow connections can view your movie without interruption. If you're relatively sure that your viewing audience accesses the Internet at a different connection speed, change the setting nearest to that connection speed.

   You can also create a custom setting if your viewers access the Internet with a cable modem or ISDN. Choose Debug➪Customize and modify any or all the user settings to suit your needs.

3. **Choose View➪Show Streaming. While you're looking at this menu section, make sure that you also have the Bandwidth Profiler option selected.**

   Flash begins playing the movie as it will load at the connection speed you selected in Step 2. As the movie plays, a green bar scrolls across the timeline at the top of the window. A downward-pointing arrow indicates the frame being played. Watch the arrow as the movie plays. If it catches up with the scrolling green bar and stops, that's a bad thing. It means that your movie will be interrupted while additional frames load. When this happens, you need a preloader.

To follow along with the next section, copy the file preloader.fla from the Chapter 5 folder in the CD that came with this book. Use your operating system to disable the file's read-only attribute.

Building the preloader

After you decide that a viewer's bandwidth may not be up to speed, you build a preloader. The most primitive preloader is shown in this set of steps. The preloader displays Loading, which can get rather hypnotic because it plays over and over until the movie loads. To build the preloader:

1. **Launch Flash, choose File⇨Open, navigate to the folder where you copied the preloader.fla file, and open the file.**

   Flash opens the file, and you see the main scene of the movie. I've already created the content and a preloader scene for you.

2. **Click the Edit Scene button near the upper-right corner of the workspace and choose Preloader from the drop-down menu.**

   The Preloader scene opens. Notice that three layers of content are already set up. The first two layers contain the elements that keep your viewers entertained while the site loads.

3. **Click the first frame in the Actions layer to select it.**

4. **Click the arrow to the left of the word Properties.**

   The Property inspector opens.

5. **In the <Frame Label> field, type preloadLoop and press Enter or Return.**

   Flash labels the frame.

6. **Select the eleventh frame on the Actions layer and convert to a keyframe by pressing F6.**

   A new keyframe is created.

7. **Click the arrow to the left of the word Actions.**

   The Actions panel opens.

8. **Click Actions⇨Conditions/Loops and then double-click the if action.**

   The action appears in the Script pane and the Condition parameter text box opens.

9. **Place your cursor inside the Conditions field, and in the left pane of the Actions panel, click Properties.**

   The Properties group of actions is at your beck and call.

10. **Double-click the framesLoaded action.**

    The property appears in the Conditions field and is added to your script. Your cursor should be blinking in the Conditions field. Don't touch it.

11. **Enter the following: >=.**

This may look familiar from your high school math. Yup, it's your basic greater than or equal to math operand. Don't move that cursor yet.

12. **In the left pane of the Actions panel, click Properties and then double-click** totalframes.

Okay, now you've got part of the task accomplished. In layman's terms, the statement you just created is checking to see if the frames loaded are greater than or equal to the total number of frames in the movie. Now you need to tell Flash what will happen when this condition is true. If your head is spinning right now, don't worry, I show you the nitty-gritty about conditional statements in Chapter 12.

13. **Click Actions⇨Movie Control and then double-click** goto.

Flash adds the goto action and opens up some parameter text boxes for you. Oh joy.

When you add an action to a script in Normal mode, make sure that the preceding action is still selected; otherwise, your code won't be formatted properly.

14. **To finish the code for this keyframe, click the triangle to the right of each field in the parameters text area, and do the following:**

   • **Scene:** Choose Mainmovie from the drop-down menu.

   • **Type:** Choose Frame Label from the drop-down menu.

   • **Label:** Choose beginmovie from the drop-down menu.

Your Actions panel should look like the one shown in Figure 5-9.

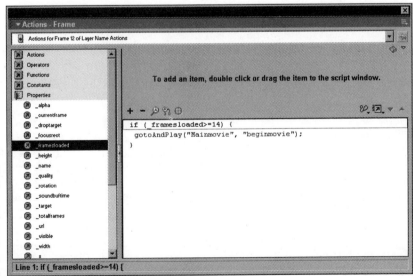

Figure 5-9: You use the frames-Loaded action in a preload loop.

15. **To finish creating the preloader, select frame 12 and press F6 to convert it to a keyframe.**

    A new keyframe is born.

16. **Click the arrow to the left of the word Actions.**

    The Actions panel opens.

17. **Click Actions⇨Movie Control and then double-click** goto.

    The action appears in the Script pane of the Actions panel, and the parameter text boxes for this action appear.

18. **Accept the default Go to and Play option, click the triangle to the right of each parameter field, and do the following:**

    • **Scene:** Choose Preloader from the drop-down menu.

    • **Type:** Choose Frame Label from the drop-down menu.

    • **Label:** Choose preloadLoop from the drop-down menu.

19. **To test the preloader, choose Control⇨Test Movie.**

    Flash publishes the movie and plays it in another window. Whoa! What happened to the preloader? The preloader appeared only momentarily because the movie loaded at light speed from your hard drive. To test the preloader, you need to stream the movie as it would download from the Internet.

20. **Choose View⇨Show Streaming.**

    If you followed these steps correctly, you see Loading flashing on the screen, followed by three small dots. When the final frame is loaded, the movie begins.

The heart of the preloader is frame 11. The conditional statement tests to see if all the frames of the movie have loaded. If they haven't, the next frame of the Preloader scene plays, which goes back to the frame labeled preloadLoop and starts the cycle again. If all the frames of the movie have loaded, the next action on frame 11 is executed, and the movie begins.

In this movie, all the frames are needed to load in order for the movie to play without interruption. If you test a movie as outlined in the previous section and notice that the movie begins playing before the green bar reaches the last frame, you can modify your conditional statement to reflect that. For example, If framesloaded>=50 executes the next action as soon as frame 50 is loaded, which, if you follow my example, plays the first frame of the movie's main scene.

If your preloader didn't come up to snuff, locate the preloader_final.fla file in this chapter's folder on the CD that comes with this book. Open the file in Flash and compare the code to what you've just created.

Chapter 6

Giving and Getting Information with Variables

*I*f you've ever seen the classic *Wizard of Oz* movie, you remember that the scarecrow's quest was for a brain. The scarecrow without a brain is much like Flash without variables: It can't remember anything. In this chapter, I show you how to give Flash brains by creating variables that can store and dispense various bits of data as needed. Variables are like brain cells, and the lines of ActionScript you create are the synapses that fire to trigger a specific brain cell. In the scarecrow's case, the synapses were straw, which would have caused the poor scarecrow all sorts of maladies if they were to actually *fire*.

The Actions panel's got lots of books. And some of these books have books within a book. To add some actions to your scripts, you have to click this book icon, then click that book icon, then click another book icon, and so on. Rather than bore you with a lot of words, I'm going to show the path to each action as shown in the following example: Click Actions⇨Movie Control and then double-click `goto`.

"So What Are Variables, and Why Do I Need Them?"

Variables make it possible for you to do all sorts of things in Flash. When you add variables to a movie, you have the power to collect data from the viewer and use it later in the movie. You can personalize a movie for a viewer by collecting his or her name at the start of the movie and using it throughout the movie. For example, if you create a Flash quiz, you can personalize the congratulatory message when a question is answered correctly by accessing the variable that holds the viewer's name.

You also have the power to display data you've assigned to variables within your ActionScript. If you take a close look at the word *variable,* you notice the similarity to two words in the English language: *vary* and *able.* That's right — the content of a variable is able to vary; in other words, it can change. For example, if you start a movie with a `name` variable and the data stored within `name` is named `Bill`, you can use ActionScript to change the data in the variable from `Bill` to `Jill`. That's where the power of variables comes into play.

Another common use for a variable is to create (or *declare,* in programmer-speak) a variable with nothing in it. This is known as a *null* variable. You vary the content of the null variable throughout the movie by plucking data from other variables or from data you've accumulated through the use of objects, such as the Date object. You can also combine data from two other variables and fill the null variable with it.

Understanding Data Types without a Ph.D.

When you create a variable, it can hold one of three types of data: text (or *strings,* in programmer-speak), numbers, or Boolean, which is pronounced exactly like you're trying to scare someone named Leanne ("Boo, Leanne!"). Here's the rundown:

- **Strings** are variables that are made up of characters, such as a letters or other alphanumeric data. You can create a string of any length, from a single character to an entire sentence or, for that matter, *several* sentences; it's sort of your mini novel within a variable. When you use a number in a string, the number cannot be evaluated with a mathematical expression. Here are a few examples of strings: `John`, `Mary`, `Mary123`, and `Today is a great day to be alive`.

- ✔ **Number** variables can be used to change the characteristics of an object, such as its position, rotation, and size. When you assign a number to a variable that is evaluated, you specify it as an expression. To find out more about expressions, read the "Working with numbers" section later in this chapter. Examples of variables you use to evaluate an expression are 27, 621, and 3.14156.

- ✔ **Boolean** variables can have only two possible values: true or false. Boolean variables are covered in detail in the "Working with Booleans" section, which I serve up before the end of this chapter.

The neat thing about variables in ActionScript is that they can hold different types of data at different times. In most programming languages, you need to declare the type of value the variable holds. ActionScript is more forgiving. When you change the type of data a variable contains, Flash deals with it on the fly.

Understanding the Difference between String Data and Numeric Data

When you call on a variable to hold string data, you're using a literal value. A *literal value* can be any combination of alphanumeric characters, including spaces and punctuation. When a string variable contains text data, it's known as a *string literal*. A string variable with numeric data is known as a *numeric literal*.

When you create a variable with numeric data that is used to change the characteristics of an object in your movie, you specify that the value of the variable is an expression. An *expression* is something that Flash can evaluate and use to return an actual value.

Understanding literal values

You use literal values to get information from people who view your ActionScript movies. You can also use literal values to display information to people who view your movie. For example, if you create a Flash movie for an e-commerce site, you can use literal values to get a visitor's contact information and respond to a request for further information and then use another variable to display information about a product.

Suppose that you want to create a variable for the title of this book. This is a string literal. In ActionScript, a variable for the title of this book may look like this: `title="Flash MX ActionScript For Dummies"`. Whenever you see quotation marks surrounding a variable's value, it's a dead giveaway that the variable's value is string data.

A numeric literal is also designated with quotation marks around the variable's value. For example, a variable for a street address in ActionScript may look something like this: `streetAddress= "126"`.

You can combine variables that contain literal values. Suppose that you have a variable named `streetAddress` and a variable named `streetName`. You can create a new variable named `physicalAddress` that combines these two variables, as shown in Listing 6-1.

Listing 6-1   Combining Literal Values

```
streetAddress="126"
streetName="Lover's Lane"
physicalAddress=streetAddress+ " " +streetName
```

Notice that the `physicalAddress` variable isn't surrounded by quotes. That's because you want Flash to add the value of `streetAddress` and `streetName` to create the value of the variable `physicalAddress`. In other words, this is an expression in which Flash adds the two literal values together. If you display the value of this variable in a movie, you see 126 Lover's Lane. Notice another literal value between `streetAddress` and `streetName`: a space surrounded by quotation marks. Without the addition of this value, the two variables would run together, and you would have 126Lover's Lane.

Before you graduate to working with full-fledged mathematical expressions, you need to understand what happens when you combine two numeric literals with an expression. Suppose that you have a numeric literal variable that is equal to 2 and a second numeric literal variable that is equal to 3. When you combine the two variables in an expression, as shown in Listing 6-2, you expect the result to be 5. But the result of this expression is actually 23 because you've asked Flash to combine two numeric literals, and it took you literally.

Listing 6-2   Combining Numeric Literals

```
a="2"
b="3"
c=a+b
```

In the next section, I show you how to create variables that Flash can evaluate. Please read on.

Understanding expressions

When you create a variable that you want Flash to use in evaluating some property of an object, the value of the variable must be an expression. For example, if you want to specify the *x* position of an object named Harvey on Stage, you create a variable that looks something like this: `Harvey_.x=250`. I know — that looks pretty scary. It did to me, too, when I first started using ActionScript. In plain English, all this line of code is doing is creating a variable for the *x* position of an object named `Harvey`, whose value is 250. The value of the variable isn't surrounded by quotation marks, so you know that it's an expression Flash can use to evaluate the *x* position of Harvey. If, later in the movie, you need to move Harvey to a different *x* position, you simply change the value of the variable.

You can also combine variables that contain expressions. Listing 6-3 shows the same code that's in Listing 6-2, with two important exceptions: The values of the variables `a` and `b` aren't surrounded by quotation marks, which means that they're expressions. The value of variable `c` is an expression that combines variable `a + b`. In this case, however, you're combining two expressions, not two numeric literals. The value Flash returns for `c` in this case is 5, the same as it was when I added 2 and 3 in grade school. Whew! It's nice to know that some things don't change.

Listing 6-3   Combining Expressions

```
a=2
b=3
c=a+b
```

The power of combining expressions becomes more apparent as you delve deeper into ActionScript. For example, you can combine expressions to keep score in games. At the beginning of the game, you create a variable named `score` and set its value equal to 0. For every correct answer, the value of `score` is increased by a set number of points.

Creating Variables for Your ActionScripts

You add a variable to a movie whenever you need to capture some data entered by someone viewing your movie or to store data in the movie that is displayed on demand or used in conjunction with other elements of your movie. For example, if you create a quiz game, you create one string variable for a correct answer and one for an incorrect answer. The variable that is displayed depends on the answer entered by the movie's viewer.

Similar to everything else in life, variables have a certain set of guidelines that must be adhered to in order for ActionScript to perform as originally planned. If you didn't plan, shame on you. Lack of planning is the reason that most ActionScripts fail. But I digress.

Naming a variable

I start this section with a fact that is blindingly obvious: Every variable needs a name. The variable's name is the link to the data that is stored within. Naming a variable is easy — much easier than trying to choose a name for a baby. For one thing, you know what the variable is going to do in the movie. When you're trying to figure out what to name your child, you don't always know what gender the little tyke will be or whether you'll be surprised parents and end up with quintuplets (instant family — just add names).

As a parent, you can rely on a book to get a name for your baby. With variables, no such book exists, and you can name a variable just about anything you want, as long as you don't give it a name that confuses Flash. The following elements *cannot* be included in a variable name:

- **Reserved words and commands that Flash may mistake as part of an action:** Don't use break, case, continue, date, default, delete, else, for, function, if, in, instanceof, new, on, return, switch, this, typeof, var, void, while, or with as a variable name. You can, however, have one of these reserved words as part of a variable name; for example, the name breakDance doesn't cause the script to run improperly.

- **Punctuation:** You also give Flash — and yourself, for that matter — a migraine if you use any of the following ActionScript punctuation: { }, ; , or ( ). If you precede a variable name with two forward slashes (//), Flash thinks your variable is a comment.

- **Mathematical operators:** If you use +,-, *, or / as part of a variable name, Flash thinks that you're trying to do math.

- **Spaces:** No spaces allowed. For example, bills password isn't acceptable. If you need to separate two names in a variable, use an underscore, as in bills_password, or capitalize the second word in the variable, as in billsPassword.

- **Numbers:** Numbers cannot precede a variable. A variable name of 7level doesn't work; level7 does.

When you create a name for a variable, it should be displayed in black in the Actions panel. If you make any sort of mistake in naming the variable, Flash lets you know in a heartbeat by highlighting the variable in red with the message The variable name you have entered contains a syntax error. As smart as Flash is, it doesn't tell you what the syntax error is. I suggest that you reread the preceding bulleted list and embed it into your memory. It can save you lots of frustration in the future.

Another thing to remember about variable names is case sensitivity. When you create lines of code in Expert mode, Flash is very sensitive to case. If you enter geturl rather than getURL, Flash is flummoxed (I love that word) and doesn't execute the action. However, if you create a variable named billspassword and later refer to it as BILLSPASSWORD, Flash thinks that they're the same thing.

If you're working with values on different timelines, you need to add the path to the variable name. For example, if you're working with a variable named title in a movie clip named movie_time on the main timeline, the full name of the variable is _root.movie_time.title.

I discuss paths in detail in Chapter 9.

Another thing to note about variable names is that you can assign the same variable name to a different timeline, and Flash recognizes it as a different variable. For example, if you have another movie clip in which you want to use a variable named title, Flash will differentiate between the two, even though you may not.

Declaring a variable

When you decide to give Flash a memory by creating a variable, you have to *declare* the variable — which reminds me of a wild story I heard about how the variable was invented. It happened in the Deep South, during the antebellum period. A gentleman was sitting on a porch during a hot summer's day, sipping a mint julep. A thunderstorm suddenly erupted; the gentlemen put down his drink, stroked his beard, and said, "I do declare; this is a variable kind of day." Of course, the word *declare* just snapped me back into the present and reminded me what this section is about — declaring a variable. To do so:

1. **Select the object or keyframe where you first want to declare the variable.**

   If you're going to use a variable throughout a movie, it's a good idea to declare it on the first frame in the movie. If, for example, you declare a variable for an input text box, declare the variable in the first frame but don't enter a value for it. When you do this, Flash recognizes the variable but assigns no value to it. The content of the variable is filled when a user enters a value in the input text box.

2. **Click the arrow to the left of the word Actions.**

   The Actions panel opens.

3. **Click Actions⇨Variables.**

   The Actions group opens.

4. **Locate the set variable action and double-click it.**

Flash adds the action to the script, and the parameter text boxes appear above the Script pane.

5. In the Variable field, enter a name for the variable.

Choose a name that describes the data the variable will hold and remember not to break any of the variable-naming conventions. If you don't know how to correctly name a variable, I declare — you've probably jumped directly to this section. Before proceeding to Step 6, please take a moment to read the preceding section, "Naming a variable."

6. In the Value field, enter the value you're assigning to the variable, as shown in Figure 6-1.

If the value will be evaluated, make sure that you check the Expression box.

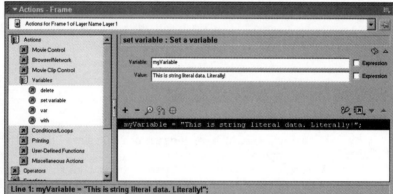

Figure 6-1:
I do declare —
the contents of a variable can vary.

Passing a variable to other objects

When you've got a variable in a Flash movie, you can pass the buck, so to speak. That is, you can take the content from one variable and pass it to another variable. This process is kind of like going to your friendly drive-up banking window, whipping out your ATM card, taking money from your bank account (a variable that stores your money whose value constantly varies, depending on your income and outgo), and putting it into your wallet or purse (another variable because it stores money, too).

To pass the contents of one variable to another, you simply equate the value of the new variable to the value of the old variable. Figure 6-2 shows a line of code that passes the contents of one variable to another. Notice that the value of the new variable is actually an expression. If the new variable's value was not an expression, the value of the new variable would be equal to the name you entered in the Value field, not the desired contents of the variable.

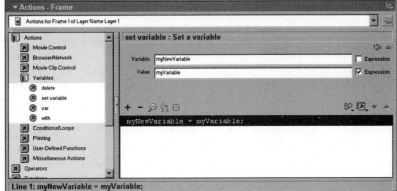

Figure 6-2:
One variable
passes the
baton to
another.

You can also create a new variable and set its value equal to the content of two or more variables already used in your movie. Suppose that you create a user feedback form in Flash. Earlier in the movie, if you asked the user to enter his or her first name and stored it in one variable called firstName and then asked for his or her last name and stored it in a second variable called lastName, you can create a new variable named fullName that combines the variable firstName and lastName. Figure 6-3 shows the ActionScript code to create the fullName variable. Notice the quotation marks between the two variables. You may have trouble seeing it in the figure, but there's a space between the quotation marks. Without the space, the first name and last name would run together.

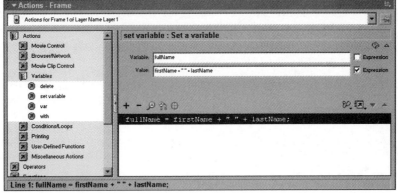

Figure 6-3:
You can
combine the
contents of
two or more
variables to
create a
new
variable.

Resetting a variable

If you're using a variable several times within a Flash movie, you may have to reset the variable. For example, if you've created a variable whose contents change based on user input, you need to reset the variable to a null (empty) value; otherwise, the user sees his or her last input when the input text box appears again. To reset an existing variable:

1. **Select the object or keyframe you want to use to reset the variable.**

   If you're working with an input text box, select a keyframe before the input text box appears again or assign the variable to a button that, when clicked, advances the movie to the frame the input text box appears on.

2. **Click the arrow to the left of the word Actions.**

   The Actions panel opens.

3. **Click Actions⇨Variables.**

   The Variables group opens.

4. **Locate the `set variable` action and double-click it.**

   The action appears in the Script pane of the Actions panel, and the parameter text boxes strut their stuff.

5. **In the Variable field, enter the name of the variable you want to reset.**

   Enter the name exactly as it appeared when you first declared the variable. Even though variables aren't case sensitive, entering the variable the same way you wrote it the first time is a good idea. This practice makes matters less confusing for you when you need to edit the movie later, and it makes life much easier if other designers are working with you on the project.

6. **Leave the Value field blank.**

   The content of the variable is blank until new data is passed to it.

Working with Different Variable Data Types

You add variables to a movie to store data within your movie. What you can do with the variable depends on the type of data that is held by the variable. Remember that the type of data held within a variable can change throughout the course of a movie.

Working with strings

String data can be text or numbers or both. If numbers are included within string data, they are evaluated as alphanumeric data. In other words, even though they're numbers, Flash doesn't do the math. You can use variables with string data to display information in dynamic text boxes when necessary. You can also create a null (empty) string variable in an input text box from which to collect data.

I show you in Chapter 10 everything you may want to know about dynamic text and input text.

The uses for variables with string data are almost unlimited. You can use them in games, to inform and to collect data. Use your imagination to come up with new and exciting ways to use variables with string data.

Evaluating strings

You can do more with string data than just display it: You can evaluate the content of strings. For example, if you create a field for a user to input his or her name, you can use the length property of the String object to evaluate how many letters are entered. If a user gets heavy-handed on the keyboard and enters more letters than you want, you can create additional lines of code to reset the value of the input box to null (empty) and tell the user to enter the information with less than a zillion letters, or something like that. You can also use ActionScript to return the value of a character at a certain position in the string; for example, the third letter. This action is useful when you're creating a guessing-word game.

Some people type only lowercase letters, and others type with the Caps Lock key on, and then you have people who work with words for a living — like your friendly author — who use both uppercase and lowercase letters. If you're creating a movie that evaluates text the viewer enters, you can use the String objects to convert the text to lowercase.

You can evaluate a variable with string data from a keyframe or an object. To evaluate data in a string variable:

1. **Select the object or keyframe where you want Flash to evaluate the variable with string data.**

2. **Click the arrow to the left of the word Actions.**

   The Actions panel opens.

(I know the preceding instruction may seem like a blatant case of redundancy. But I don't mind typing it for readers who haven't read the whole book and don't know how to open the Actions panel. If you have read the book from word one (bless you, my friend), you may remember that the Actions panel is docked at the bottom of the workspace by default. If for some reason you've closed it, choose Window⇨Actions to return the panel to its rightful home.)

3. Click Actions⇨Variables.

The Variables group opens.

4. Locate the `set variable` action and double-click it.

Flash adds the action to the Script pane of the Actions panel, and those pesky parameter text boxes open.

5. In the Variable field, enter a name for the variable.

The variable you're creating stores the results of the evaluation performed on the string data.

6. In the Value field, enter the name of the string variable you want to evaluate.

The variable name is added to the script.

7. In the left pane of the Actions panel, click Objects⇨Core⇨String⇨ Methods⇨Properties.

The Methods and Properties of the String object are displayed, as shown in Figure 6-4.

I know, that's a whole lotta button clicks. After you get more familiar with ActionScript and know the actual method or property you need to evaluate a string, click the Index icon and scroll down until you find what you want.

8. Click the method or property you want to use to evaluate the string.

For example, to return the number of characters in a string, including spaces, choose `length`; to transform all characters to lowercase, choose `toLowerCase`. Many string methods are rarely used, so I don't waste your time by explaining each one. To see what each string method does, open the Actions panel, click Objects⇨Core⇨String⇨Methods, and roll your mouse over each String method's name. A tooltip appears, telling what the string object does.

Before you rush off to the next section, double-click a method or property to display it in the Script pane. Notice the dot (.) before the method or property. In order to evaluate the string, you need to include the target path so the method or property is properly affixed to the string, a sticky subject I show you in Chapter 9.

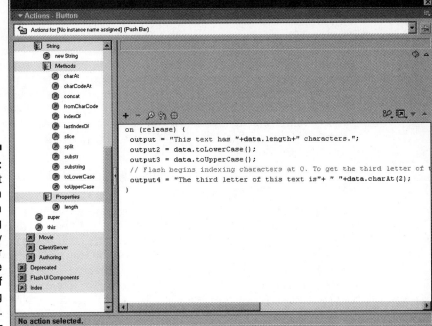

Figure 6-4:
You get information about a string variable by using one or more methods of the String object.

In this chapter's folder on this book's CD is a file named evaluate_strings.fla. To get an idea of what you can use string objects for, copy the file to your hard drive and use your computer's operating system to disable the file's read-only attribute. Launch Flash and open the file. To play the movie, choose Control➪Test Movie. If you want to see the actions used to evaluate the string data, select the button and open the Actions panel.

Working with numbers

Flash has all the tools and operators you need to perform mathematical calculations in your Flash movies. In fact, if you want, you can even create a calculator that your viewers can play with or use to balance their checkbooks while watching your movie. In this section, I give you a brief introduction to the power of numbers in Flash. In Chapter 12, I show you how to use the most popular operators and methods of the Math object.

The following steps use Flash to create a simple adding machine. To follow along with these steps, locate the Flash_add.fla file in this chapter's folder on the *Macromedia Flash MX ActionScript For Dummies* CD. Copy the file to your computer's hard drive and use your operating system to disable the file's read-only attributes. To get Flash to do the math:

1. **Launch Flash, choose File⇨Open, locate the Flash_add.fla file you copied to your hard drive, and open the file.**

   Notice that I've already set up the main movie for you. The movie consists of three text boxes. The top two boxes are input text boxes, which are used to accept data from people who view your movie. The bottom text box is a dynamic text box, used to display data that is stored in a variable. In this movie, you use the dynamic text box to display the adding machine's answer. You may have already dabbled briefly with input and dynamic text boxes. If you haven't, don't worry; just follow along with these steps. I show you how to set up dynamic text boxes and input text boxes in Chapter 10.

2. **Click the top input text box to select it and then click the arrow to the left of the word Properties.**

   The Property inspector (Or PI if you prefer) opens, as shown in Figure 6-5. Notice that I've already set the parameters for the text. I've named the variable `data1`. The information entered into this text box is stored in a variable named `data1`. I clicked to Character button and in the Character dialog box, I clicked the Only radio button, selected the Numerals (0-9) option, and added a decimal point in the blank field to the right of the Fonts section. This action limits the data that is accepted to numeric data with a single decimal point.

Figure 6-5:
To create a Flash adding machine, you need text boxes to accept and display the numbers.

3. **Click the next input text box.**

   The Property inspector should already be open. If it isn't, click the arrow to the left of the word Properties. Notice that this input text box has been assigned the variable name `data 2` and that the parameters of the text box allow only numeric data to be accepted.

4. **With the Property inspector still open, click the text box below the Enter button.**

   This text box has been set to dynamic text that displays the contents of a variable named answer.

   You can close the Property inspector now. If you don't, the workspace will be a tad crowded when you do the next step.

5. **Click the button on Stage and then click the arrow to the left of the word Actions.**

   The Actions panel opens. Before you wildly enter code into the Actions panel, examine the pieces you have to work with. You have three variables: data1, data 2, and answer. To have Flash compute the result of adding data1 and data2, create a variable named answer in the dynamic text box and set its value equal to the result of adding data1 to data2. But you must consider one other important factor here: When Flash looks at the data entered in the two input text boxes, it recognizes them as numeric literal data until you tell Flash otherwise. If the variables from the two input text boxes are read as numeric literals, Flash looks at the variable's values literally and just combines the two numbers instead of adding them. For example, 2+3 is displayed as 23 rather than as 5, as you would expect in a functional adding machine.

6. **In the left pane of the Actions panel, click Actions⇨Variables.**

   The Variables group opens for business.

7. **Locate the set variable action and double-click it.**

   Flash adds the action to the Script pane of the Actions panel along with the code on(release). This bit of code is an event handler that tells Flash Player to execute the action when the mouse button is released.

   I show you how to use mouse event handlers in Chapter 11.

8. **In the Variable field, type data1.**

   This is the same variable assigned to the first input text box. In the next step, you add a function that tells Flash that this variable is mathematical or numeric data.

9. **Click inside the Value field; then in the left pane of the Actions panel, click Functions⇨Conversion Functions to open the group, locate the Number function, and double-click it.**

   The Number function is added to the script and a single parameter text box appears with the word *Number* and your cursor highlighted between two parentheses. That's the Flash way of telling you that it expects you to enter an expression for the Number function.

You use the Number function so Flash reads a value as a number and not text or, in programmer-speak, numeric literal data. Even though a viewer enters a number in an input text box, Flash will read it as text unless you specify otherwise with the Number function.

10. **With your cursor positioned between the parentheses, type** data1 **and click the Expression box.**

   The finished line of code reads data1=Number(data1) ;. When this line of code is executed, the contents of the variable data1 are converted to numeric data.

11. **Repeat Steps 7 – 10 for the variable** data2.

   You end up with a line of code that reads data2=Number(data2);. This line of code converts the contents of the variable data2 from numeric literal data to actual numeric data that Flash can do some math with.

12. **Click Actions⇨Variables and then double-click the** set variable **action.**

   Another line of code is added to the script.

13. **In the Variable field, type** answer.

   This is the same variable assigned to the dynamic text box.

14. **In the Value field, type** data1+data2 **and click the Expression box.**

   That's it. Your finished ActionScript should look just like the one shown in Figure 6-6. But don't take my word for it. After you're done comparing your ActionScript to Figure 6-6, jump to Step 15 to test the movie.

15. **Choose Control⇨Test Movie.**

   Flash publishes the movie in a different window.

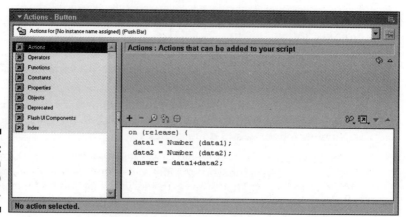

Figure 6-6:
Now Flash
can do
the math.

16. **Place your cursor inside the first text box, enter any number you want, follow suit in the second text box, and press the Enter button.**

Flash does the math.

If you're in a playful mood and you feel like exploring a bit, close the Test Movie window. When you're back in movie-editing mode, select the button and then open the Actions panel. Click the last line of code to select it, and in the Value field do any of the following:

- To have Flash subtract `data2` from `data1`, change the value to `data1-data2`.

- To have Flash multiply `data1` by `data2`, change the value to `data1*data2`.

- To have Flash divide `data1` by `data2`, change the value to `data1/data2` .

If your movie didn't add the two numbers, review this exercise or locate the Flash_add_final file in this chapter's file on this book's CD; then compare the code in it to what you've created.

Working with Booleans

When you or I make a decision, it's generally based on a number of parameters. For example, what to pack in the car when you leave for work in the morning depends on a number of conditions. Are you eating at the office or going out for lunch? Are you stopping at the bank during your lunch hour? Are you driving straight home after work? If not, are you going to the gym? The beach? For a romantic interlude with your significant other? When a computer looks at a situation, it can have only two possible outcomes: true or false. In a computer's eyes, it either is or it isn't. For those of you who know a bit about how a computer operates, it's based on the binary system, which is made up of two primary components: 0 and 1. Granted, a computer is powerful enough to make several true and false decisions in a millisecond, but it makes them only one at a time, and the outcome is always the same — false or true or in binary format, 0 or 1 .

You may be wondering where to work Boolean expressions into your ActionScript repertoire. You can use a Boolean expression to perform one set of actions if the result is true and perform another if the result is false. You can also use logical operators to compare two Boolean expressions. Logical operators make much more sense if you read Chapter 12. Listing 6-4 shows two Boolean expressions at work.

Listing 6-4   Booleans at Work and Play

```
if (lives>0) {
     gotoAndPlay (gamePlay);
} else {
     gotoAndPlay (gameOver);
}


if (username=="BIll" && password=="Enter") {
     gotoAndPlay ("enterSite");
} else {
  warning = "You are not authorized to enter.";
}
```

The Boolean expression in the first statement is (lives>0). As long as this condition is true (the player has more than zero lives), the movie goes to a frame labeled gamePlay. As soon as the condition is false (lives=0), the movie goes to the frame labeled gameOver. The second statement is comparing two Boolean expressions with the and (&&) logical operator. If the first Boolean expression is true and the second Boolean expression is true, the movie jumps to a frame labeled enterSite. If either expression is false (the username is not Bill or the password is not Enter), a variable named warning is set equal to a string literal value of You are not authorized to enter. If the ActionScript in Listing 6-4 had been created for an actual Flash movie, the Flash author would create a dynamic text box with the variable name warning, which of course would display the warning.

Dynamic text and his friend input text are covered with some informative text I created especially for this topic, which you find in Chapter 10. I show you how to work with logical operators in Chapter 12.

Working with Arrays

You create an array when you need to store a large amount of data that's similar but different. Variables are containers for data. When you create a new array, you're actually creating a number of variables with the same name but a different location, or, as they're known in the programming world, *elements*. A kitchen with five cabinets is like an array. Each cabinet is a place where you put kitchen stuff. The stuff in your kitchen cabinets is all used in the kitchen, but slightly different items are in each cabinet.

If you wanted to refer to the contents of your five kitchen cabinets in a Flash movie, you could create a variable for each cabinet, and it would look something like Listing 6-5.

Listing 6-5   To Array or Not to Array?

```
Overhead_left_Cabinet=cups and saucers
Overhead_center_Cabinet=platters and dishes
Overhead_right_Cabinet=fancy china
Lower_left_Cabinet=pots and pans
Lower_right_Cabinet=mixer and bread maker
```

I got tired just typing all that. Can you imagine what it would be like in a Flash movie, where you've got lots of variables that are similar? If you were to create an array named `cabinet`, the location of the cabinets would be

```
Cabinet[0]
Cabinet[1]
Cabinet[2]
Cabinet[3]
Cabinet[4]
```

In Flash, the location of an array (also known as the *offset*) is surrounded by square brackets. The first location of an array is always 0.

The beauty of arrays is the amount of time they save. Rather than type a variable for each kitchen cabinet, as in the hypothetical code in Listing 6-5, you would create an array that does the same thing with one line of code, as shown in Figure 6-7. Please note, for the purpose of showing this figure, I collapsed the left pane of the Actions panel in order to view the entire array.

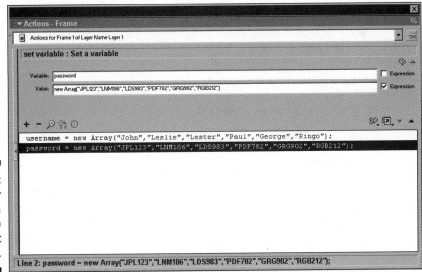

Figure 6-7: An array stores data that's the same, but different.

You can also use the elements from two arrays in a movie and combine them in a single variable. Suppose that you have a movie that generates quotes. You create a separate array that contains the name of the person who said the words of wisdom and then another array for the quotes. The location of the speaker's array corresponds to the same location in the quote array. This process is known as *cross-indexing,* which reminds me of hot cross buns, an oxymoron if there ever was one because the buns aren't hot when you buy them. At any rate, the cross-indexed array for speakers and their quotes would look like Table 6-1.

Table 6-1	An Example of a Cross-Indexed Array
Speaker Array	*Quote Array*
Speaker[0]	Quote[0]
Speaker[1]	Quote[1]
Speaker[3]	Quote[3]
Speaker[4]	Quote[4]

To see an example of a cross-indexed array, navigate to the Chapter 6 folder of the CD that accompanies this book and copy the quotes.fla file to your hard drive. Use your computer's operating system to disable the read-only attribute of this file, and open it in Flash. Choose Control⇨Test Movie to see the movie play. Click the button to generate a random quote. To explore the ActionScript, click the arrow to the left of the word Actions to open the lovable little panel and select the first frame on the Actions layer to see the code used to create the array. Select the button to see the code used to generate and display the random quote.

Creating an array

After you decide that you need an array in your movie, you need to create it. An array begins rather humbly: It starts out life as a variable until you super-charge the variable by setting the variable's value equal to a new array. Here's how:

1. Select the keyframe where you want to create the array.

You can create the array at any point on the timeline before you actually call for some data from the array. To make matters simple, I always like to create my arrays at the beginning of a movie. As always, make sure that you create the array on a layer you've created for actions in your movie.

2. Click the arrow to the left of the word Actions.

The Actions panel opens.

3. Click Actions⇨Variables.

The Variables group opens, waiting for you to choose an action.

4. Locate the `set variable` **action and double-click it.**

The action appears in the Script pane of the Actions panel, and the parameter text boxes for the action open.

5. In the Variable field, enter a name for the variable.

Choose a name that relates to the data you're going to store in the array. Remember that if you have an array with 20 elements in it, for example, you may be referring to the variable name 20 times, so don't create a long variable name. (Remember KISS: Keep It Short, Simple.)

6. Place your cursor inside the Value field and click Objects⇨Core⇨Array.

The Array objects are at your beck and call.

7. Locate `new Array` **and double-click it.**

In the Value field, `new Array()` appears.

8. Check the Expression box.

An *array* is an expression that Flash evaluates when you call for data from the array. If the Expression box is left unchecked, Flash thinks that the value you have entered is a text string and displays it as such.

Figure 6-8 shows the Actions panel after setting a variable equal to a new array. After you supercharge a variable by setting its value equal to a new array, you need to populate the array with data. I show you how to create the elements for your newborn array in the next section, "Creating elements for the array."

Figure 6-8:
Before you can populate an array, you have to create it.

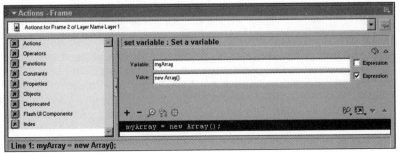

Creating elements for the array

After you create an array, you need to create the elements for it. The elements can be string (text) elements that you display or numeric elements that Flash uses to change the properties of an object, such as its position or rotation. When you create an array with string data, individual elements are separated by commas and surrounded by quotation marks; arrays with numeric data have individual elements separated by commas with no quotation marks. The absence of quotes around the numeric data informs Flash that each element can be evaluated in an expression. If each number were surrounded by quotation marks, Flash would know that each element is a numeric literal and to evaluate each element literally. To create elements for an array:

1. **Create an array, as outlined in Steps 1 – 8 in the section "Creating an array," which, for your reading pleasure and convenience, is directly before this section.**

2. **In the Value field, position your cursor between the parentheses that follow the** newArray **action.**

3. **Enter the data that will be stored in the array.**

   If you're working with string literal data or numeric literal data, surround each element with quotation marks. If you're working with numeric data, quotation marks aren't necessary. Before adding another element to the array, enter a comma. Commas are what separate each element in the array.

If you've got lots of data to enter in the array, the Actions panel is somewhat limiting because of its layout. Create the data for the array in a word processing program, making sure that you place commas between each element and add quotes to string literal or numeric literal data. Also make sure that your word processor doesn't have smart quotes. In smart quotes the quote characters are curved ("") instead of straight (""). If you paste data with smart quotes into the Script pane or one of the parameter text boxes, your script will not execute properly because the Actions panel is too dumb to recognize smart quotes as quotes. After you've typed all the elements for the array, copy them to the clipboard and then paste them between the parentheses in the newly created array. You can either paste them between the parentheses in the Value field or switch to editing in Expert mode and then paste them between the commas in the Actions panel's Script pane. As a bonus, when you create a large array in a word processing program, you can spell-check your work before pasting it into Flash. There is nothing worse than creating a movie for a client and then misspelling a word in an array. Talk about embarrassing.

Getting data from an array

The neat thing about storing data in an array is that you can use another variable to access the data. All you need to do is create a new variable and set its value equal to the element of the array where the needed data is stored. For example, if you have an array named prices that stores the price data of shoes for sale in an e-commerce Flash movie and you want the price of a shoe displayed when its image is clicked, create an intermediate variable called i. You can choose any name for the intermediate variable; i, j, and k are programmer's favorites when creating intermediate variables because they're near each other on the keyboard; a single letter is easier to remember, also. The intermediate variable for each shoe is equal to the array position (offset) of the shoe's pricing information. If you have five shoes in the catalog, you code the ActionScript so that the variable i is equal to element 0 in the array when the first shoe is clicked, element 1 when the second shoe is clicked, and so on. The value of the first shoe is set to 0 because the default array numbering system sets the *offset* (the position of an element in an array) of the first element to 0. You create another variable named displayPrice that is equal to prices[i]. Listing 6-6 shows the ActionScript code that you would create for the first shoe, which is a symbol with the button behavior assigned to it.

Listing 6-6   Getting Data from an Array

```
on (release) {
    i = 0;

    displayPrice = prices[i];
}
```

Table 6-2 shows the relationship between the shoe, the intermediate variable, and the array data.

Table 6-2	Getting Data from an Array	
Item	*Intermediate Variable*	*Array Element*
Shoe1	i=0	prices[0]
Shoe2	i=1	prices[1]
Shoe3	i=2	prices[2]
Shoe4	i=3	prices[3]
Shoe5	i=4	prices[4]

Creating an associative array

You can also use an array to accept data and later display it. This is known as an *associative* array; the data of each element of the array is associated with another variable, or variables, in your movie. Suppose that you want to create a Flash questionnaire. You begin the movie by creating an array equal to the number of questions you ask the viewer, but leave each element of the array empty. When a question is answered, the data from that variable is passed on to a corresponding element in the array. To create an associative array:

1. **Select the keyframe where you want to create the associative array.**

   It's generally a good idea to declare any global variables in the first frame of a movie.

2. **Click the arrow to the left of the word Actions.**

   The Actions panel opens.

3. **Click Actions⇨Variables book icon and then double-click the** set variable **action.**

   The action is added to the script, and the parameter text boxes open.

4. **In the Variable field, enter a name for the variable.**

   Remember to adhere to the variable-naming conventions. If you don't know what they are, read the "Naming a variable" section at the start of this chapter.

5. **Click anywhere in the Value field. In the left pane of the Actions panel, click the Objects⇨Core⇨Array, and then double-click** new Array.

   The line of code newArray() is added to the script. To complete setting up the array, you need to enter the number of elements between the parentheses.

6. **Enter a value between the parentheses for the number of elements you need in the array.**

   Remember that Flash begins array offsets at 0. If you're creating an array with five elements, you enter **4** between the parentheses.

7. **Close the Actions panel.**

   The associative array is set up and ready to receive data. Listing 6-7 shows the code for an array that stores data from a questionnaire with five questions.

Listing 6-7   Creating an Associative Array

```
results = "new Array(4)";
```

To populate the array, you create a variable and set it equal to the corresponding element in the new array. If you're using the results array in Listing 6-7 to store the answers for a questionnaire, you create a variable for the answer to each question. When the user clicks a button to submit the answer, the variable is passed on to an element in the results array. Listing 6-8 shows code for passing the results of a variable named `answer1` to an array element named `results` with an offset of 0.

Listing 6-8   Passing Variable Data to an Associative Array

```
on (release) {
  answer1 = results[0];
}

29
```

Chapter 7

Creating Object Makeovers with Properties and Functions

· ·

· ·

*F*lash has some potent tools for animating instances and changing the properties of symbols on the timeline. You can create some impressive movies, animating instances of symbols with tweening and changing the way objects look by using one of the effects in the Property inspector. But you take your movies to another level when you animate objects and change their properties with ActionScript. With ActionScript, you can have objects randomly darting around the screen like asteroids being sucked into a black hole rather than using the predictable motion created with tweening or a motion path. All it takes is a little imagination and a few (or several, depending on the level of coolness you want in your movie) lines of ActionScript. You can also use ActionScript to hide, move, rotate, or scale an object.

In this chapter, I show you how to create objects and then change their properties. Then I show you how to work with functions. *Functions* are reusable bits of ActionScript that perform tasks in your movies, such as scrolling a block of text or getting the movie's timer. You can use ready-built Flash functions or create your own.

The Actions panel's got lots of books. And some of these books have books within a book. To add some actions to your scripts, you have to click this book icon, then click that book icon, then click another book icon, and so on. Rather than bore you with a lot of words, I'm going to show the path to each action as shown in the following example: Click Actions⇔Movie Control and then double-click goto.

Creating the Object of ActionScript Desire: The Movie Clip

When you change the properties of an item with ActionScript, you change the properties of a movie clip. You cannot change the properties of a graphic symbol or button with ActionScript — unless you nest them inside a movie clip. Before you began using ActionScript, you may have used movie clips as reusable bits of animation. That's still true with ActionScript, but you can also create a movie clip with just a single frame and a single graphic and get the movie clip to jump through your hoop, so to speak, with ActionScript. To create a movie clip:

1. **Choose Insert⇨New Symbol.**

   The Create New Symbol dialog box appears.

2. **Enter a name for the movie clip.**

   Flash assigns all symbols the default name `symbol` followed by the next available symbol number. I strongly advise you to give each symbol a unique name, a name by which you and any other Flash authors working on the project can identify the clip's contents.

3. **Select the Movie Clip behavior and click OK.**

   Flash enters symbol-editing mode. Note that the Create New Symbol dialog box has a memory. Instead of reverting back to the movie clip behavior as it did in Flash 5, the dialog box remembers the last symbol type you created and sticks with it until you make a different choice.

4. **Create or import the graphical elements of the movie clip.**

   If you have already created a graphic symbol that resembles an element you need for a movie clip, locate the symbol in the document Library and drag it on Stage. You can then rescale the symbol as needed. Using symbols rather than creating new graphic elements helps reduce the file size of the published movie.

5. **Click the Back button or the current scene name to return to movie-editing mode.**

   Flash adds the movie clip to the document Library.

Creating an Instance of a Movie Clip

To apply your ActionScript wizardry to a movie clip object, you need to create an instance of it and give it a unique name. If you don't name an instance, no matter how sharp you are at ActionScript, you'll never get an unnamed instance of a movie clip to undergo a makeover — a movie clip without a name has no personality and you can't do a thing with it. Flash also needs to know the path to the movie clip that you want to target the action; part of the path is the instance's name. To create an instance of a movie clip:

1. **Choose Window⇨Library.**

   The document Library opens.

2. **Select the keyframe in which you want the movie clip to appear.**

   If you select a frame rather than a keyframe, the movie clip appears in the nearest keyframe before the frame you select. To convert a normal frame to a keyframe, press F6.

3. **Select the desired movie clip symbol from the Library, drag the clip on Stage, and position it.**

   An instance of the original movie clip symbol is created.

4. **Click the arrow to the left of the word Properties.**

   The Property inspector opens.

5. **In the <Instance Name> field, enter a name for the movie clip.**

   Enter a name that enables you and any other designers working on the project to readily identify the clip and its purpose by name alone.

For the ultimate reference on movie clips and target paths, let your fingers do the walking to Chapter 9.

Working with Properties

Every object on Stage has properties, and they're not the type you go to a realtor's office to see. The properties I'm talking about are an object's *x* and *y* coordinates, its visibility or lack thereof, and its scale, to name a few. When a named instance of a movie clip is on Stage, you have an object whose properties you can modify with ActionScript.

Setting an Object's Property

When you need to change a property of an object, you can do it in one of two ways. You can use the setProperty action, which is the easiest way to go about the task but involves a few more steps, or you can refer directly to the path of the target object and then follow it up with the property you want to set. Listing 7-1 shows both ways of setting an object's property. In this case, the *y* position of a movie clip named my_movieclip is being set to 200.

Listing 7-1 Saying the Same Thing in Different Ways

```
setProperty (_root.my_movieclip, _y, 200);
_root.my_movieclip._y=200;
```

You can create a script that changes the properties of an object when a keyframe is reached, a button is clicked, or a certain set of conditions is met. The choice depends on the type of movie you're creating. For example, you can create a movie and make an object disappear when a certain frame is reached by changing its visibility to 0 — or false, for those of you who have read the Boolean section in Chapter 6. And yes, for those of you who are wondering, you can refer to a Boolean value by using true or false, or you can substitute 0 for false or 1 for true — *another* case of saying the same thing with different words.

In upcoming sections, I show you both methods of setting an object's properties using some of the most popular ActionScript properties. Unfortunately, my editor says that I have to do this chapter with fewer than 9,000 words; in other words, I can't possibly show you every property. Fear not; I get you pointed in the right direction. To set an object's property using the setProperty action:

1. **Select the object or keyframe that will trigger the change in one or more of an object's properties.**

2. **Click the arrow to the left of the word Actions.**

   The Actions panel opens, same as it always does. (Talk about consistency!)

3. **Click Actions⇨Movie Clip Control.**

   The Movie Clip Control group opens.

4. **Locate the setProperty action and double-click it.**

   The action appears in the Script pane of the Actions panel, and the parameter text boxes make another heralded appearance. Highlighted in bold red is a warning from Flash telling you that the property hasn't been set. Your cursor comes to rest in the Target field, as shown in Figure 7-1.

Figure 7-1:
Before you
can set an
object's
properties,
you must
select a
target.

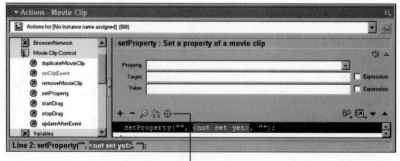

Insert Target Path button

5. **Click the Insert a Target Path button (the black button with the crosshair for a belly button).**

   Flash opens the Insert Target Path dialog box, as shown in Figure 7-2. Listed inside this dialog box you find one button for each named instance in your movie and another button for Root, the main timeline. This dialog box may look a tad frightening, but not to worry. I go to great lengths to explain target paths in Chapter 9.

Figure 7-2: You use this dialog box to select the target for the property change.

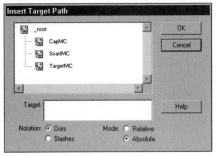

6. **Click the button for the object you want to modify.**

   The target path for the movie clip appears in the Target field.

7. **Click OK to add the target path for the object you're modifying with the action.**

   The target path appears in the Target field.

8. **Click the triangle to the right of the Property field.**

   A drop-down menu with lots of properties appears.

9. **Click the desired property to select it, as shown in Figure 7-3.**

   If, for example, you want to resize an object along its x axis, you select _xscale. This drop-down menu is quite friendly. To the right of each property is a description of the property in common English. For example, the listing for _x property reads _x(X Position). Who's afraid of ActionScript, Virginia Woolf?

10. **In the Value field, enter the new value for the property you're setting.**

    If, for example, you want to change the x position of an object and the Stage for your movie is 500 pixels wide, choose a value between 0 (the left side of the Stage) and 500 (the right side of the Stage). Of course, you can choose a value greater than or less than these values if you want the object to disappear from view.

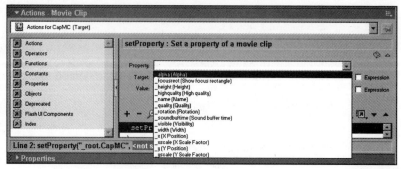

Figure 7-3:
Change the
property to
change the
object of
your desire.

An object's position is measured from its registration point, which —
unless you've changed it — is its center. If you want an object's motion
to be restrained to the *x* boundary of the Stage, you need to deduct half
the object's width from the value you select for the object's *x* position
property and half the object's height for the value you specify for the
object's *y* position property.

11. Close the Actions panel.

When the movie is published, the object's property changes when the
keyframe or object triggers the lines of code you created.

Remember that you can change more than one object property at a time.
To do this, simply add one `setProperty` action to the script for each
property you want to change. For example, you can change an object's *x*
position, *y* position, *x* scale, *y* scale, and alpha properties in one fell swoop
by applying the `setProperty` action five times, first changing the object's
`_x` property, and then changing the object's `_y` property, and so on.

As I mention earlier in this chapter, there are way too many properties in the
Actions panel for me to stuff into the itsy-bitsy amount of room I'm allowed in
this chapter. However, I give you a nudge in the right direction. Table 7-1 lists
the properties you can set for a named instance, with a description of each
property and, where applicable, the parameters you can set.

Table 7-1	So Many Properties, So Little Time	
Property	*What It Sets*	*Parameters*
_alpha	An object's opacity	0 (transparent) to 100 (opaque)
_height	An object's height in pixels	Any numeric value
_highquality	Render quality	0 (low), 1 (high), 3 (best)
_name	An object's name	Any acceptable movie clip name

Property	What It Sets	Parameters
_quality	Render quality	LOW, MEDIUM, HIGH, BEST
_rotation	Degree of rotation	A value between 0 and 360
_soundbuftime	Time before movie streams	An integer
_visible	An object's visibility	True or 1 (visible); false or 0 (invisible)
_width	An object's width in pixels	Any numeric value
_x	An object's x position	Any numeric value
_xscale	An object's x scale	Any numeric value (100% is the original scale of the object)
_y	An object's y position	Any numeric value
_yscale	An object's y scale	Any numeric value (100% is the original scale of the object)

You may notice that the focusrect property is missing from this table. The reason is that focusrect is a global value and does not apply to individual instances of movie clips.

Wherever you see any numeric value listed in Table 7-1, keep in mind that you can enter a value that isn't applicable to the situation. For example, you can enter a value for an object's *x* or *y* position that would put it clean off the Stage.

Symbol Makeover 101: Changing the Way an Object Looks

Changing an object's properties with ActionScript is useful when you're creating games or you need to add a little razzle-dazzle to an otherwise static movie. In the following sections, I show you how to use the various properties in a movie. I show you how to program buttons to change the properties of an object in a movie I created, just to show you how this stuff works.

To follow along with the following steps, locate the file set_properties.fla in this chapter's folder on the CD that accompanies this book. Copy the file to your hard drive, and use your operating system to disable the file's read-only attributes.

Changing Herman the mouse

To get an idea of the power ActionScript gives you, you change the properties of a lovely little critter I call Herman. Herman the mouse was imported into the document and nested in a movie clip. Remember that you can't change the properties of a movie clip unless it is to a named instance. In this instance, I christened the movie clip `Herman`. To begin Herman's makeover:

1. **Choose File⇨Open.**

   The Open dialog box appears.

2. **Locate the set_properties.fla file you copied to your hard drive and open the file.**

   Flash opens the file.

Before you go rushing off to the next section, let me explain what's happening. I've already positioned the movie clip on Stage and named it `Herman`. Cute little critter, isn't he? On the left side of the movie are five buttons, appropriately named for what they do to gullible `Herman`. You program each button to make `Herman` do something different. Notice that I followed the ActionScripter Code of Good Housekeeping and set up a separate layer for the buttons.

Moving an object

When you start scripting action games, you change the position of an object by changing its `_xposition` and `_yposition` properties. To move Herman when the button is clicked:

1. **Click the Move Me button to select it.**

2. **Click the arrow to the left of the word Actions.**

   The Actions panel opens.

3. **Click Actions⇨Movie Control.**

   The Movie Control group opens.

4. **Locate the `setProperty` action and double-click it.**

   The action appears in the Script pane of the Actions panel. Your cursor has come to rest in the Target parameter text box.

5. **Click the Insert a Target Path button (the black button just above the Script pane and a smidge to the left).**

   The Insert Target Path dialog box opens. Notice that a button named Herman is already in it. Whenever you label an instance of a movie clip, a button that represents the instance's target path is added to this dialog box.

6. **Click the Herman button and then click OK to close the dialog box.**

   Herman's path is added to the script. When the action is executed, Flash knows where to find Herman.

7. **Click the triangle to the right of the Property field.**

   A drop-down menu drops down.

8. **Choose _x property.**

   The property is added to the script.

9. **In the Value field, type** 500 **and click the Expression box.**

   When the button is clicked, Herman moves to the *x* coordinate, 500. This step is all you need to do for Herman to move in one plane. To get him to move in both directions, you need to change another property. Yep, you guessed it — it's the *y* position.

10. **Double-click the** setProperty **action.**

    The action is added below the line of code you just created.

11. **Repeat Steps 5 and 6 to add** Herman's **path to the code.**

12. **Click the triangle to the right of the Property field.**

    The drop-down menu appears again.

13. **Choose the _y property.**

    The property is added to the script. Changing this property changes Herman's *y* position — as long as you don't enter the same *y* coordinate where Herman is located.

14. **In the Value field, type** 50 **and click the Expression box.**

15. **Close the Actions panel.**

    When the button is clicked, Herman moves to the following position on Stage: (500, 50). If you don't believe me, choose Control⇨Test Movie. Click the Move Me button, and Herman moves to the upper-right position of the Stage.

Rotating an object

Now that you've moved Herman, take him for a spin. To do this, you change the _rotation property. You can change an object's property in two ways. You used the first method if you moved Herman in a previous section. To rotate Herman, you use the second method. To take Herman for a spin:

1. **Click the Rotate Me button.**

2. **Open the Actions panel and click the Properties.**

   The Properties group opens.

3. **Locate the `rotation` property and double-click it.**

   The property is added to the script, and a field named Expression opens in the parameter text box area. The expression you create sets the rotation of Herman equal to a number you choose between 0 and 360. (If you remember your geometry, a circle has 360 degrees in it.)

4. **Inside the Expression field, click just before the underscore.**

   Your cursor is blinking at the beginning of the field.

5. **Click the Insert a Target Path button just above the Script pane.**

   The Insert Target Path dialog box opens. Yup, there's Herman's button again.

6. **Click the button labeled Herman.**

   Inside the Target field, _root.Herman appears.

7. **Inside the Target field, click anywhere to the right of Herman.**

   A flashing cursor appears after the n.

8. **Enter a period (.) and click OK to close the dialog box.**

   This is called *dot syntax,* which is used to refer to an object's path or an object's property. In this case, it's referring to the rotation property of the movie clip named Herman. (Remember him? This tutorial describes how to change Herman's properties.)

   To find out about dot syntax, go back to Chapter 3.

9. **In the Expression field, click anywhere to the right of _rotation.**

   A flashing cursor appears after the n.

10. **Type =180.**

    This entry completes the expression. Your completed code should look exactly like what's shown in Figure 7-4. In plain English, the expression sets the rotation property of Herman equal to 180 degrees. In other words, when the button is clicked, Herman does a headstand.

11. **Close the Actions panel.**

    If you want to see Herman do the headstand, choose Control⇨Test Movie. After Flash publishes the movie, click the Spin Me button, and Herman does the headstand.

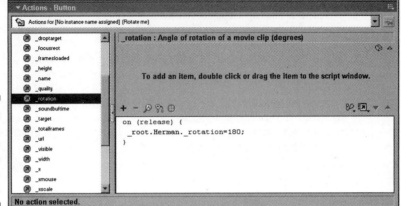

Figure 7-4:
To rotate an
object, you
change its
rotation
property.

Scaling an object

Another useful property you can change is an object's *x* scale or *y* scale or
both. Scaling an object has many uses. One that immediately comes to mind
is an e-commerce site where the size of an object increases when its button
is clicked. This feature gives the patron a better look at the item, of course,
and — if the patron has available credit — a good excuse to purchase the
bauble. The scale property works on percentages. An object's original scale
is 100, or 100 percent of its size. Enter a number larger than 100, and the
object grows; smaller than 100, and it shrinks. I don't know about you, but
the thought of a large mouse simply terrifies me, so in the following steps,
I show you how to program the button to shrink Herman down to size:

1. **Click the Scale Me button and then open the Actions panel.**

2. **Click Actions➪Movie Clip Control.**

   The Movie Clip Control group opens.

3. **Locate the** setProperty **action and double-click it.**

   The action is added to the script, and your cursor is flashing in the
   Target field just above the Script pane.

4. **Click the black Insert a Target Path button.**

   The Insert Target Path dialog box opens.

5. **Click the button labeled Herman and then click OK.**

   The dialog box closes, and the target path to Herman is added to the
   code.

6. Click the triangle to the right of the Property field and choose _xscale from the drop-down menu.

The property is added to the script.

7. In the Value field, type 50 and click the Expression box.

This step shrinks `Herman` to 50 percent of his *x* dimension, or width.

If you were to leave the script as is, `Herman` would be a tall, skinny mouse. To shrink him proportionately, you need to change his *y* scale by an equal amount by following Steps 3 – 7; the only difference is that you choose the _yscale property in Step 6. Your finished script should look exactly like what is shown in Figure 7-5.

8. Close the Actions panel.

When the movie is published and the button is clicked, `Herman` is cut down to size.

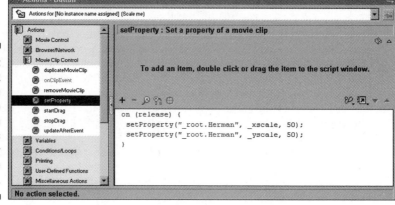

Figure 7-5: To shrink Herman down to size, you change his *x* and *y* scale properties.

```
on (release) {
    setProperty("_root.Herman", _xscale, 50);
    setProperty("_root.Herman", _yscale, 50);
}
```

Changing an object's opacity

You change the alpha property of an object to change its opacity. An object that is fully opaque has an alpha value of 100; an invisible object has an alpha value of 0. Any setting in between yields a degree of transparency. To make `Herman` fade away:

1. Click the Fade Me button and then open the Actions panel.

2. Click Actions⇨Movie Clip Control.

The Movie Clip Control group falls in for duty.

3. **Double-click the `setProperty` action.**

   The action is added to the script and your cursor is beamed up to the Target field.

4. **Click the Insert a Target Path button just above the Script pane.**

   The Insert Target dialog box opens.

5. **Click the Herman button and then click OK to close the dialog box.**

   The path to `Herman` is added to the script.

6. **Click the triangle to the right of the Property field and choose `_alpha` from the drop-down menu.**

   The `_alpha` property is added to the script.

7. **In the value field, type 25 and click the Expression box.**

8. **Close the Actions panel.**

   If you followed these steps exactly, after the movie is published `Herman` fades by 75 percent when the button is clicked.

Hiding an object

Last but not least, you can program the Hide Me button to make `Herman` pull a Houdini and disappear from view. To hide `Herman`:

1. **Click the Hide Me button and then open the Actions panel.**

2. **Click Actions⇨Movie Clip Control.**

   The Movie Clip Control group opens.

3. **Locate the `setProperty` action and double-click it.**

   The action appears in the right pane of the Actions panel, and the parameter text boxes open. Your cursor is flashing in the Target field.

4. **Click the black Insert a Target Path button.**

   The Insert Target Path dialog box opens.

5. **Click the button named Herman and then click OK to close the dialog box.**

   `Herman`'s target path is added to the script.

6. **Click the triangle to the right of the Property field and choose `visible`.**

   The property is added to the code.

7. **Click inside the Value field, type** false, **and then click the Expression box.**

Visible is a Boolean property. You either see an object or you don't.

When you're working with properties that have Boolean values, you can substitute 0 for false or 1 for true.

8. **Close the Actions panel.**

The Hide Me button is programmed to hide Herman when it's clicked.

Now it's time to check out your handiwork and make sure that everything is programmed properly. To test the movie, choose Control⇨Test Movie. After the movie is published, click each button to put Herman through his paces. Notice that after you change the property, you can't get Herman back to his original state. Or can you? Of course you can, by creating more ActionScript. For now, you can click the convenient little button labeled Reset, at the bottom of the movie. To see what makes the button tick, close the Test Movie window. When you're back in movie-editing mode, click the button and open the Actions panel to see how I programmed the button. After examining the script, you see that the actions set Herman's properties back to their original values when the button is clicked.

If Herman didn't do the ditty-bop when you clicked the buttons, locate the setpropertiesfinal.fla file, which you find in this chapter's folder on the CD that comes with this book. Copy the file to your hard drive, disable its read-only attribute, and open it in Flash. Compare the code on each button to the code you created, to see where you've gone awry.

Getting an Object's Properties

What you can set, you can get. And what is already set can be got, too. If you think that I just went on a literary tirade, I didn't. The two sentences make perfect sense. The ActionScript getProperty function enables you to create a variable and set it equal to a property of an object. Why is this concept important to a fledgling ActionScript programmer? Well, properties change. If you create a variable that's equal to an object's property, when the property changes, the variable changes. Suppose that an object is 10 pixels wide and it is positioned over a bar 100 pixels long, and its motion is constrained between x position 0 and x position 100. If you create a variable and set it equal to the object's x position, the value of the variable changes from 0 to 100 as the object moves, which means that you can use the variable to vary an object's property (the volume of a soundtrack, for example) by a percentage between 0 and 100. These are the rudimentary steps for creating a slider. In Chapter 16, I show you how to use an object's *x* position property to control the volume of a movie's sound and to pan the sound from the left speaker to the right speaker with a ready made slider I carefully crafted for your viewing enjoyment.

You can get a particular property of an object in two ways: by using the getProperty function and by addressing the movie clip by its target path and then adding the property you want to retrieve. As you gain more experience in ActionScript, you may find the second method more to your liking. It's quicker, especially if you enter the code directly in Expert mode. Whichever method you find suits your preference, remember that you first have to create a *variable,* something in which to store the object's property. In most cases, you use this function on a keyframe.

To get an object's property using the getProperty function:

1. **Select the keyframe where you want to create the variable.**

   If the frame you've selected isn't a keyframe, press F6 to create a keyframe.

2. **Click the arrow to the left of the word Actions.**

   The Actions panel opens.

3. **Click Actions⇨Variables.**

   The Variables group snaps to attention.

4. **Locate the set variable action and double-click it.**

   The action appears in the Script pane of the Actions panel, and the parameter text boxes pop up.

5. **In the Variable field, enter a name for the variable.**

   You can't just pick a name out of the air for a variable. For a refresher course on what you can and can't call your variables, refer to Chapter 6.

6. **Click anywhere inside the Value field.**

   Your cursor flashes at you, waiting for you to proceed to Step 7.

7. **Click Functions.**

   The Functions group is at your beck and call.

8. **Locate the getProperty function and double-click it.**

   In the value field, getProperty appears, followed by two parentheses with nothing between them, your clue that Flash is waiting for you to fill in this information, please.

9. **Click between the parentheses, and then click the black Insert a Target Path button just above the Script pane.**

   The Insert Target Path dialog box opens.

10. **Locate the button for the named instance of the movie clip whose property you want to get and click OK.**

    The movie clip's target path is added to the script.

11. **After the target path, type a comma (,).**

    You might say that the comma separates the wheat from the chaff, but in this case, the comma separates the target from the property you're retrieving.

12. **Click the Properties button on the left pane of the Actions panel.**

    You've got properties, but no real estate license.

13. **Double-click the property you want to retrieve.**

    The property is added to the script. Listing 7-2 shows a script using the `getProperty` function. The results of this script would store the *x* position of a movie clip named `slider` in a variable named `value`.

14. **Click the Expression box.**

    If you forget to click the Expression box, Flash reads the value as string data.

Listing 7-2   Using the `getProperty` Function

```
value = getProperty (_root.slider, _x );
```

If you look at Listing 7-2, you see only one line of code, but you go through quite a few steps to get the result. The more direct method for getting an object's property is to create the variable and set its value equal to the property of the movie clip object. Here's how:

1. **Select the keyframe where you want to create the variable.**

   Remember that when you use ActionScript on the timeline, you can assign it only to a keyframe.

2. **Click the arrow to the left of the word Actions.**

   The Actions panel appears.

3. **Click Actions➪Variables.**

   The Variables group awaits your command.

4. **Locate the** `set variable` **action and double-click it.**

   The action appears in the right pane of the Actions panel, and the parameter text boxes open for business.

5. **In the Variable field, enter a name for the variable.**

6. **Click anywhere inside the Value field.**

7. **Click the Properties button.**

   The Properties group opens.

8. **Double-click the property you want to get.**

   The property appears in the Value field.

9. **In the Value field, position your cursor before the property you just added.**

10. **Click the black Insert a Target Path button.**

    The Insert Target Path dialog box opens.

11. **Click the button for the named instance from which you want to retrieve the data.**

    The target path appears in the Target field.

12. **Add a period (.) directly after the target path and click OK.**

    The target path is added to the script. Adding the period (or *dot*, as it is referred to in ActionScript) tells Flash that the property is separate from the named instance. If, for example, the instance from which you want to retrieve the property has a target path of `_root.pendulum` and the property you want to get is `_x` (*x* position), the value for this property equals `_root.pendulum._x`. If you leave out the dot between the object and the property, Flash thinks that you're looking for a variable, not a movie clip's property. Listing 7-3 shows the direct method of getting the value of an object's property.

13. **Click the Expression box.**

    That's how you get an object's property. Remember that when you assign an object's property to a variable, you need to click the Expression box, or else Flash thinks that the variable's value is string data.

Listing 7-3   Getting the Value of an Object's Property

```
value = _root.slider._x;
```

Notice how much simpler this code is than the code shown in Listing 7-2. Both lines of code retrieve the same value. After you gain some experience in ActionScript, you can enter code like this by switching to Expert mode and typing it. It's quick. It's easy. And, after you see the results of your labor, it's fun.

If you're retrieving the property of an object that changes repeatedly (for example when a slider is dragged to a new position), create a new movie clip and put nothing in it. Name the movie clip Script_holder or something like that. Drag an instance of the movie clip on Stage (best to put it on a separate layer called Actions because there'll be nothing but code in it). Enter the ActionScript for the properties you want to retrieve and be sure to use the Enter Clip event. The variable you assign the code to is updated continuously.

Working with Functions

A *function* is ActionScript code that you can use anywhere within your movie. Each function performs a different task. You have lots of predetermined Flash functions you can have fun with: functions you can use to perform collision detection (`testhit`) as well as functions to scroll blocks of text. I show you how to use some of the more popular functions in Chapters 14, 15, and 16. In the meantime, if you want to experiment on your own, open the Functions section in the Actions panel and move your cursor over the various functions. A tooltip appears giving you a description of what the function's used for.

Calling a Function without Running Up a Long-Distance Bill

When you need to use one of the preset Flash functions, or one you've created, you call it. The location from which you call a function depends on the function and the set of circumstances involved. For example, the `getProperty` function is attached to a named instance of a movie clip. Table 7-2 shows a few examples of how various functions are called.

Table 7-2 Call Any Function, and the Function Will Respond to You

Function	Description
`_root.beginTimer=getTimer()`	The variable `_root.beginTimer` is set equal to `getTimer` (function).
`pos = getProperty (_root.myClip, _x);`	The variable `pos` is set equal to the x property of `myClip`.

You can use the `function` action to create a custom function for lines of code you use repeatedly throughout a movie.

Generating Random Numbers

When you change the property of an object — such as its alpha, x position, y position, x scale, or y scale — you set it equal to a value. Whenever the event that triggers the property change occurs, the value remains the same because Flash is, of course, evaluating an expression. However, if you set the value of the expression that evaluates the property equal to a random value, the result is different every time the event occurs. To create this randomness, you use a method, named `random`, from the Math object group. The random method of the Math object generates a random number between 0 and 1. Follow along with the steps in this section, where I show you how to use this little gem to create random motion.

Creating a function to generate random numbers

To follow along with these steps, locate the file random.fla in this chapter's folder on the accompanying CD. Copy the file to your hard drive and use your computer's operating system to disable the file's read-only attribute.

To show you how to create random movement with the random method of the Math object, I've created a file named random.fla and all the graphics. In the upcoming steps, I show you how to program random movement by creating a random number. But you're going to generate the random number in a function that you define. To create the function that generates random movement:

1. **Launch Flash, choose File⇨Open, and then locate and open the random.fla file you copied to your hard drive.**

   Flash opens the file. The scene I've already set for you is a movie clip of a friendly mouse named Herman and a button. Herman is on every mouse's field of dreams, a large piece of cheese full of holes.

2. **Click the first frame in the Actions layer and then click the arrow to the left of the word Actions.**

   The Actions panel opens.

3. **Click Actions⇨User Defined Functions and then double-click** `function`.

   Flash adds the action to your script and two parameter text boxes appear above the Script pane.

4. **In the Name field type** moveMe, **and in the Parameters field, type** mc.

   The parameters are passed onto the function. In this case the function I've christened moveMe works with a movieclip or mc.

5. **Click Actions⇨Variables and then double-click** `set variable`.

   The action is added to your script and two parameter text boxes appear above the Script pane.

6. **In the Name field type** posX.

   This variable stores a randomly generated number that determines the x position on stage.

7. **Click the Value field. In the left pane of the Actions panel, click Objects⇨Core⇨Math⇨Methods, and then double-click** `random`.

   The random method of the Math object is added to your script. Your cursor should be flashing to the right of two parentheses.

8. **Enter *400 and click the Expressions check box.**

   Now you're probably wondering, why 400? Right now, Herman is at the center of the Stage, which is 550 pixels wide; an *x* position of 275. Herman has height, and he has girth, so those factors must be considered when determining what number the random method of the Math object is multiplied by. After some experimentation, I arrived at 400 as the ideal number so that part of Herman would not disappear off Stage when a large number is generated. Remember to click the Expression box or Herman will just sit there and do nothing when the ActionScript executes.

The lines of code to complete the random motion are similar, with just a few subtle changes. My motto has always been "Why work harder when you can work smarter?" In the remaining steps, I show you how to work smarter.

9. **Right-click (in Windows) or Ctrl+click (on the Macintosh) anywhere within the Script pane.**

   A pop-up menu appears.

10. **Choose Copy.**

    The line of code you just entered is copied to the clipboard.

11. **Right-click (in Windows) or Ctrl+click (on the Macintosh) anywhere within the Script pane.**

    The pop-up menu pops up again.

12. **Choose Paste.**

    You now have two lines of identical code.

13. **Change the variable name to: posY and change the value to: Math.random () * 300.**

    As you can see, all you have to do is change the X to a Y and change 400 to 300 instead of re-entering all the code. (Isn't cut-and-paste wonderful?)

    Before moving on to Step 14, where you create the code that bends Herman at the waist, let me explain what the code you just generated does. This line of code creates random movement on the *y* axis by changing the *y* position property of Herman. This movie has a *y* dimension of 400 pixels. The value of 300 compensates for Herman's height.

    If you find that modifying copied and pasted code in the parameter text boxes is a pain — after all, the text display in these boxes is painfully small (pun intended) — click the triangle near the upper-right corner of the Actions panel and then choose Expert mode. You can now modify the code by typing directly in the Script pane of the Actions panel. You can also copy, cut, and paste in Expert mode. When you're done modifying the code, click the triangle again and choose Normal mode.

14. **Right-click (in Windows) or Ctrl+click (on the Macintosh) and choose Paste from the pop-up menu.**

    The first line of code is pasted below the last line of code you created.

15. **Change the Name and Value so this line of code reads as follows: _posRotate=Math.random ()*45;.**

    Again, cut-and-paste saves you lots of steps by creating the foundation for the line of code. This code creates a random rotation between 0 and 45 degrees.

Now that you've generated the random numbers, it's time to create the rest of the function. The random numbers generated by the code you just created will be used to change the x, y, and rotation properties of an object. Yes, you're thinking, but this isn't an object, it's a function. There is only one parameter for this object, mc, or movie clip. The movie clip the function works with is on the root timeline, so the properties are addressed to _root.[mc].

16. **Click Actions⇨Miscellaneous Actions, and then double-click** evaluate.

    The Expression field opens.

17. **In the Expression field type: _root[mc]._x=posX.**

    When evaluated, this expression changes the ._x property of the movie clip the function is used on. The movie clip is designated by _root [mc], where _root is the main timeline and [mc] refers to the function's sole parameter.

18. **Right-click (Windows) or Ctrl+click (Macintosh) and choose Copy from the drop-down menu.**

    The code is copied to the clipboard.

19. **Right-click (Windows) or Ctrl+click (Macintosh) and choose Paste from the drop-down menu.**

    The code is pasted into the Script pane.

20. **In the Expression field, modify the line of code so that it reads:** _root[mc]._y=posY.

    This line of code uses the random number stored by the posY variable to change the ._y property of the movie clip the function addresses.

21. **Right-click (Windows) or Ctrl+click (Macintosh) and choose Paste from the drop-down menu.**

    That's right Virginia, another line of code to modify. But cut and paste sure beats creating it from scratch.

22. **Modify the code you just pasted so that it reads as follows:** _root[mc]._rotation=posRotate.

    This line of code uses the random number from the posRotate variable to change the ._rotation property of the movie clip the function is used on. The code for your finished function should look like Figure 7-6.

    And that's how you create a function. Now all you have to do is use the function to make Herman hip-hop around his field of dreams.

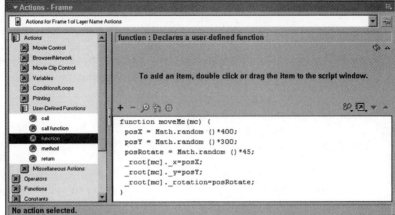

Figure 7-6:
The function
is randomly
functional.

23. **Select the button and then open the Actions panel.**

    The title of the Actions panel should read: Actions-Button. If it doesn't
    select the button until it does.

24. **Click Actions⇨Miscellaneous Actions and double-click** `evaluate`.

    The Expression field expresses itself above the Script pane.

25. **In the Expression field, enter the following code:** moveMe ("Herman").

    This line of code executes the `moveMe` function. You may be wondering
    why the Herman movie clip is listed between parentheses instead of by
    its target path. That's because you're addressing a parameter of the
    function, the (mc) parameter. In this case, the movie clip is `Herman` and
    it's a string literal value, so the name appears between quotes.

26. **To test your ActionScript wizardry, choose Control⇨Test Movie.**

    The movie is published and opens in another window. Click the button
    you've just programmed and then click it again. Every time you release
    the button, Herman flits to a new location on the slab of cheese.

This isn't the only use for the Math.random object. Use it whenever you
need to generate a random value. You can use the random method of the
Math object to generate a random number in a guessing game or randomly
select an element from an array, for example. Put your thinking cap on and
have fun with this tool.

I know what you're thinking. That's a lot of work to make Herman hip-hop to
the barber shop. But what happens if you want more than one object in your

movie to boog-a-loo down Broadway? Do you write the same code three, four, five, six — ad infinitum, ad nauseum — number of times? This would surely induce a bad case of carpal tunnel syndrome and you'd be in for a visit to an orthopedic specialist. But hey, that's why you put it all in a function instead of creating the same code umpteen zillion times. To learn how to get the most out of the function you just created, please leave the file open and read on to the next section.

Putting a function to work

When you create a function, you create code that you can use on more than one movie clip in your production. After you create the function, all you have to do is refer to it by name.

If you just randomly happened upon this section because you thought it was cool or you spotted it in the table of contents and thought it would be cool or your pet cat put its paw in this section because it looked cool, you'll first need to read the preceding section in order to understand how a function is created and then this will all make sense.

To use the function you created in the random.fla file on more than one object, do the following:

1. **Select the layer named Herman.**

2. **Open the document Library.**

   Lo and behold, there's a Mouse2 and Mouse3 movie clip.

3. **Drag an instance of the Mouse2 and Mouse3 movie clip on Stage.**

4. **Select one of the mice you just added to the document and open the Property inspector.**

5. **In the <Instance Name> field enter:** Minnie.

6. **With the Property inspector still open, select the second mouse and name it:** Millie.

   Make sure you don't select Herman by mistake. Your goal is to have three named instances: Herman, Minnie, and Millie.

7. **Select all three mice and using the Align panel, center them to Stage.**

   You now have three mice occupying the same piece of real estate.

8. **Select the button and then open the Actions panel.**

   If the Actions panel doesn't read Actions-Button, you know what to do — reselect the button.

9. **Select the second line of code, right-click (Windows) or Ctrl+click (Macintosh) and then choose Copy from the drop-down menu.**

   The code is copied to the clipboard.

10. **Right-click (Windows) or Ctrl+click (Macintosh) and then choose Paste from the context menu.**

11. **Modify the line of code so that it reads:** moveMe("Minnie").

12. **Right-click (Windows) or Ctrl+click (Macintosh) and then choose Paste from the context menu.**

13. **Modify this line of code to read:** moveMe("Millie").

    The finished code for your button should look like Figure 7-7.

14. **Choose Control⇨Test Movie.**

    Flash publishes the movie in another window. Click the Move Me button and the three mice should jump to a new position on Stage. Click the button again and your three blind mice run randomly around the Stage. Every time you click the button, the moveMe function executes three times, one for each mouse, thereby placing each mouse at a unique location.

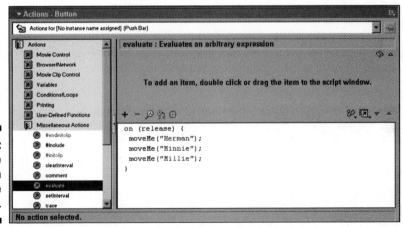

Figure 7-7:
You can use
a function
on multiple
items.

Now you have an idea of how powerful a function can be. When you create a document where the same thing happens with many movie clips, create a function instead of creating the same code over and over again and then call the function as outlined previously. Your wrists will thank you; your local orthopedic specialist won't.

Part III
Using Not-So-Elementary ActionScript, My Dear Watson

The 5th Wave   By Rich Tennant

@RICHTENNANT

SCREEEEEK

"Is this really the best use of Flash MX ActionScript animation on our e-commerce Web site? A bad wheel on the shopping cart icon that squeaks, wobbles, and pulls to the left?"

In this part . . .

*I*f you jumped straight to this part because you thought you might find a certain level of coolness for your ActionScript movies, well you're right, and at the same time you're wrong. The actions — in and of themselves — will do nothing to increase how cool or uncool your movie is; that task rests with you, the movie's author. Having said that, I will tell you that you can create more coolness than the law allows by using the actions presented in this part. Many of the chapters in this part have one or more exercises where I've given you a head start by creating the graphics. You get to do the fun part: creating the ActionScript. For example, in Chapter 8, I show you how to create the script for a clock that keeps perfect time for your movies.

If you're a wordy kind of Flash author, you'll appreciate Chapter 10, which is all about creating Dynamic and Input text. In Chapter 11, I show you how to create interactive stuff for your Flash movies; like buttons and menus. In Chapter 13, I show you how to deal with the arch nemesis of thee that dabble in ActionScript: the bug.

Chapter 8

Modifying and Creating Objects

. . . .

In This Chapter

▶ Working with ActionScript objects

▶ Keeping time with the Date objects

▶ Modifying object colors with the Color objects

▶ Modifying sounds with the Sound objects

. . . .

*I*n Flash, you've got several types of objects to work with:

  ✔ Physical objects (your garden-variety movie clips)

  ✔ Objects you use to get information, such as the current date and time

  ✔ Objects you use to modify physical objects in your movie, such as sound and color

  ✔ Other objects you use with movie clips, strings, and arrays

The last three objects on the list are in groups in the Actions panel. When you get into ActionScript object, you find there are lots of objects are at your disposal, probably more objects than you can ever use. If you've read the book from page 1, you've already used some of those objects, and I thank you for being such a diligent fan of my prose (or at least of ActionScript). In this chapter, I show you how to use what I feel are some of the more useful ActionScript objects. In Chapters 14, 15, and 16, I show you how to use these objects and a few others with ActionScript elements to create some cool things for your Flash movies.

The Actions panel's got lots of books. And some of these books have books within a book. To add some actions to your scripts, you have to click this book icon, then click that book icon, then click another book icon, and so on. Rather than bore you with a lot of words, I'm going to show the path to each action as shown in the following example: Click Actions➪Movie Control and then double-click goto.

Using ActionScript Objects

Flash has a number of preset objects that perform various functions or retrieve various data. Each object has a number of methods you use to perform an action or retrieve some data. The Date object retrieves the current date information from the host computer (the computer playing the Flash movie). Before the end of this chapter, I show you how to create a digital clock that you can add to your Flash movies. Another useful object is the Sound object. You can use it to control sounds and soundtracks in your Flash movies. Figure 8-1 shows the Object actions at your disposal.

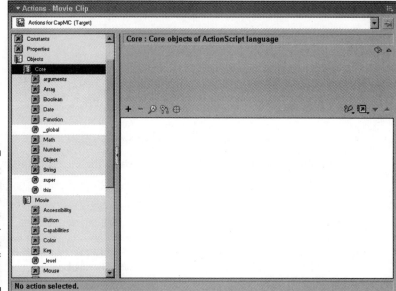

Figure 8-1: And when you click the Objects button — yikes! That's a ton of objects!

Creating Objects

When you decide to use one of the ActionScript objects in a movie, you must first create an object. You can create an object by first creating a variable and then using the object's `new` operator. The objects, such as the Date object, that return data, are the ones that use the `new` operator; for example, `myDate=new Date()`.

Many objects need to be kick-started, or, as they say in ActionScript-speak, *initialized.* When you use other objects, such as the Sound or Color objects, you need to create an instance of them. And sometimes you even need to create a new object to get the job done, such as when you use the setTransform Color object method to tint a bitmap image.

Working with Date Objects — Keeping Web Surfers Up-to-Date

One useful object that adds a bit of interactivity and information to your Flash movies is the Date object. The Date object has methods for retrieving various date and time information from the computer's clock. The information in a Date object is variable, which means that it keeps changing as the clock ticks and the calendar turns. To create a Date object, you first create a variable and then create a new Date object. In the following sections, I show you how to get the current date and time and create a working clock that you can use in your Flash movies.

Initializing a Date object

Before you can get the date or time, you have to initialize the Date object. To initialize the Date object:

1. **Select the keyframe or object in which you want to initialize the Date object.**

   If the Date object is used globally throughout the movie, initialize the object on the first keyframe.

2. **Click the arrow to the left of the word Actions.**

   The Actions panel opens.

3. **Click Actions⇨Variables.**

   The Variables group opens.

4. **Double-click the set variable action.**

   The action appears in the Script pane of the Actions panel, and the parameter text boxes beg for your attention.

5. **In the Variable field, enter a name for the variable.**

   This variable holds the information gathered by the Date object. Choose a meaningful name, such as currentDate, or, if you're working with the time, currentTime.

6. **Click inside the Value field and in the left pane of the Actions panel, click Objects⇨Core⇨Date.**

   The date group opens looking for all the lonely people.

7. **Double-click** `new Date`.

   The new Date method is added to the script. Remember to click the Expression box, otherwise Flash thinks this is string literal data.

This is all you do to initialize the date object. Before the Date object returns any data, you must create a new variable and set it equal to the variable that initialized the Date object, followed by one of the Date methods. Listing 8-1 shows the ActionScript to initialize a Date object.

Listing 8-1   Initializing a New Date Object

```
mydate = new Date();
```

Getting the current date

After you initialize a Date object, you can use the Date object's methods to get the current date from the computer. You can use quite a few methods to get the date. The most common are

- ✔ `.getDate:` Returns the current date of the month as a number.

- ✔ `.getDay:` Returns the day of the week as a number. The week begins on Sunday, which is represented as 0, and ends on Saturday, which is represented as 6.

- ✔ `.getMonth:` Returns the month of the year as a number. January is represented as 0; December, as 11.

- ✔ `.getFullYear:` Returns the current year as a 4-digit number; for example, 2001.

To retrieve the current date using any of the listed methods, you must first create a variable and set it equal to the Date object, appended by the object method that retrieves the date information you want. Here's how:

1. **Select the keyframe or object where you want to create a new Date object.**

2. **Create a new Date object.**

   If you don't know how to create a Date object, please read the section "Initializing a Date object," earlier in this chapter. Name the Date object **mydate**.

3. **Click the arrow to the left of the word Actions.**

   The Actions panel opens.

4. **Click Actions⇨Variables.**

   The Variables group opens.

5. **Double-click the `set variable` action.**

   The action is added to the script, and the parameter text boxes open.

6. **In the Variable field, enter a name.**

   If you've read other sections on setting variables, you know that my advice is to enter a variable name that makes sense. This step is no exception. For example, if you're getting the current month, `month` is a good name for the variable.

7. **In the Value field, type mydate.**

   This is the name of your Date object. If, for some reason, you choose a name other than `mydate`, enter the name you used when creating the Date object.

8. **In the left pane of the Actions panel click Objects⇨Core⇨Date⇨ Methods.**

   The Date methods are displayed.

9. **Double-click the method that retrieves the information you want.**

   For example, to get the current month, double-click the `getMonth` method.

10. **Click the Expression box.**

    If you don't click the Expression box, Flash thinks that this is string literal data and sets the variable equal to the text you've entered in the Value field rather than the date information needed for your movie.

11. **If your script calls for additional date information, repeat Steps 5 – 10.**

    When you retrieve additional date information, you need to create a new variable for each additional Date method you need. For example, if you need to get the current day, you create a new variable named `day` and set it equal to `mydate.getDay()`. Listing 8-2 shows the ActionScript needed to get the current month, date, and year.

Listing 8-2   Using ActionScript to Get the Current Date

```
mydate = new Date();
date = mydate.getDate();
month = mydate.getMonth();
year = mydate.getFullYear();
```

The ActionScript shown in Listing 8-2 would have to be modified if you were to display it in a dynamic text box. The viewer will be confused when January is displayed as 0 rather than 1. To correct this, update the month variable in the next line of code to read month=month+1, remembering to click the Expression box. If you want to display the month's actual name, you create an array with the names of the month, as shown in Listing 8-3. The same holds true if you're using the .getDay method to retrieve the current day. If you display the result returned using the value returned by the .getDay method, Sunday is 0, Monday is 1, and so on. Listing 8-3 shows the ActionScript needed to display the current month, date, day, and year. The lines of code preceded by two forward slashes are comments.

Listing 8-3   Displaying the Current Date

```
// Set day array
myday = new Array("Sunday", "Monday", "Tuesday", "Wednesday",
        "Thursday", "Friday", "Saturday");
// create date object and variables for day, month,date, and
        year
mymonth = new Array
        ("January","February","March","April","May","June"
        ,"July","August","September","October","November",
        "December");
mydate = new Date();
day = mydate.getDay();
month = mydate.getMonth();
currentdate = mydate.getDate();
year = mydate.getFullYear();
display_day = myday[day];
display_month = mymonth[month];
current_date = display_day+", "+display_month+"
        "+currentdate+", "+year;
```

The last three lines of code in Listing 8-3 modify the information retrieved by the Date object so that it is displayed in the expected format. A variable called display_day is created to display the day by its name rather than by a number. The value of the variable is plucked from the myday array. If, for example, the day of the week is Wednesday, the getDay method returns 4. The 4th element of the myday array is Wednesday. When the ActionScript gets to the line display_day = myday[day], the value of the variable day is 4, which sets the value of the variable display_date to Wednesday.

The variable display_month works in the same manner. When the getMonth method of the date object returns a value of 4, the month of May is plucked from the mymonth array because the first element of an array is always 0.

To see a completed calendar, copy to your hard drive the calendar.fla file from this chapter's folder on the CD that accompanies this book and use your computer's operating system to disable the file's read-only attributes. Open the file in Flash and then choose Control⇨Test Movie. After you're done staring at the current date, close the window to return to movie-editing mode. To see the ActionScript that makes the calendar work, click the first frame on the Actions layer and then choose the arrow to the left of the word Actions to open the Actions panel.

Getting the current time

You use the Date object when the current time is called for in a movie. Before you can get the current time, however, you have to initialize a Date object. If you have been faithfully reading this chapter from the beginning, I don't put you through the drudgery of reading the text again. If you have jumped to this section because you need to add the current time to your movie, please read the "Initializing a Date object" section earlier in this chapter. The Date object has many methods for working with time. Here are the most common:

- getHours: Returns the current hour from the computer's clock as a number. Flash retrieves time information in military time. Midnight is 0; 11:00 p.m. is 23.

- getMinutes: Returns the current minute from the computer's clock as a whole number.

- getSeconds: Returns the current second from the computer's clock as a whole number.

To see how you can use these methods to display the current time in your movie, please read the next section. The steps show you how to create a working digital clock.

Crafting a clock without a cuckoo

Before the Date object was introduced in Flash MX, you needed to know JavaScript to display the time in your movies. JavaScript, although somewhat similar to ActionScript, isn't the most user-friendly scripting language in the world. In this exercise, I show you how to use ActionScript to create a working clock you can add to your Flash movies.

To follow along with this exercise, locate the time.fla file in this chapter's folder on the CD that accompanies this book. Copy the file to your hard drive and use your computer's operating system to disable the file's read-only attributes.

To create a working clock, you initialize a Date object and use several of its methods to return the current hour, minute, and second. The information retrieved is based on a 24-hour clock. Unless your Web surfers are military (or ex-military), you need to convert the time to a 12-hour clock. In this section,

I introduce you to the conditional statement. A *conditional statement* evaluates a Boolean expression. One set of actions occurs if the Boolean expression is true; if it's false, a different set of actions occurs.

For more information on Boolean expressions, see Chapter 6. For the ultimate reference on conditional statements, check out Chapter 12.

Creating an ActionScript to get the current time

Okay, now that I've got all the disclaimers and legal information out of the way, it's safe to start building your clock. To create a working clock with ActionScript:

1. **Launch Flash, choose File➪Open, locate the time.fla file you copied to your hard drive, and open it.**

   Notice that you don't have a whole lot to work with: one dynamic text box is on Stage. Actually it's a dynamic text box in a movie clip.

2. **Click the movie clip to select it and then click the arrow to the left of the word Actions.**

   The Actions panel opens.

3. **Click Actions➪Variables.**

   The Variables group opens.

4. **Double-click the** set variable **action.**

   The action is added to the script, and the parameter text boxes open. Notice that Flash adds a line of code, onClipEvent(load). This little line of code tells Flash when the actions that follow should be executed. In this case, the variable is initialized when the movie clip loads. I know, you don't know what a clip event is because I haven't covered it yet. That happens in the next chapter. But what you can do with a clip event when crafting a clock is so cool, I just had to give you a preview.

5. **In the Variable field, type** mydate.

6. **Click inside the Value field. Then, in the left pane of the Actions panel, click Objects➪Core➪Date, and then double-click** new Date **and make sure to click the Expression box.**

   The Date object is added to the script and initialized.

   It took a bit of clicking to get to the date object. You can streamline the process of adding an action to your script when you know exactly which action you need to use. Click the Index — the Index book has all the actions listed alphabetically — and ditty-bop to the action you need without having to click open all those books.

7. **On the left side of the Actions panel, click Actions➪Variables and then double-click the** set variable **action.**

   The action is added to the script, and the parameter text boxes open.

8. **In the Variable field, type** hours.

9. **In the Value field, type** mydate. **Then, on the left side of the Actions panel, click Objects⇨Core⇨Date⇨Methods, and double-click** getHours. **Again, make sure you click the Expression box or Flash takes you literally and thinks this is string data.**

   This line of code creates a new variable whose value is derived using the getHour method of the Date object. When the line of code is executed, the variable returns the current hour from the computer's clock. You're a third of the way home! You still need to get the current minute and the current second, though.

10. **Create a new variable named** minutes **and set its value to** mydate.getMinutes().

    You create this variable exactly as you created the hours variable. Follow Steps 7 – 9, and substitute **minutes** in the Variable field and use the getMinutes method rather than getHours in Step 9. Remember to click the Expression box after you enter the value.

11. **Repeat Steps 7 – 9, except this time create a variable named** seconds **and set its value equal to the** getSeconds **method of the Date object. Remember to click the Expression box when you enter the value.**

    Now you've got all your variables set, ready to record the current time from the computer's operating system. Your ActionScript at this point should look exactly like what is shown in Figure 8-2.

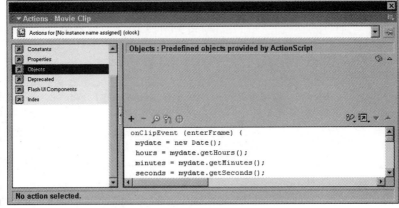

Figure 8-2: To get the time of day from Flash, you need variables.

Converting the time to a 12-hour clock

Now that you've created the ActionScript to get the current time, you need to convert it to 12-hour time. If you're creating a clock for a military site, feel free to skip this section. To convert the time to a 12-hour clock:

1. **Click Actions➪Conditions/Loops icon and then double-click the** if **action.**

   The if action is added to the script. In the parameter text box area, a field named Condition opens.

2. **In the Condition field, type** hours<12.

3. **Click Actions➪Variables and then double-click** set variable.

   Again, your friendly parameter text boxes open.

4. **In the Variable field, type** AMorPM.

5. **In the Value field, type** AM.

   Do not click the Expression box. You want AM to be displayed as text in the final working clock.

   The code you've created so far displays AM whenever the current hour is less than 12, or between midnight and noon. Of course, you want the clock to read PM between noon and midnight.

6. **Click Actions➪Conditions/Loops and then double-click** else if.

   Again, the Condition field appears above the Script pane which was previously plain Jane and not a plane in Spain.

7. **In the Condition field, type** hours>12.

8. **Click the Actions➪Variables and then double-click** set variable.

   The parameter text boxes all open wide and says "Ah."

9. **In the Variable field, type** AMorPM; **in the Value field, type** PM.

   The code you just created in Steps 6 – 9 resets the AMorPM variable to PM as soon as the hours variable is greater than 12.

   Your next task is to convert the 24-hour clock to a 12-hour clock. When a new day dawns, it's the 0 hour on a military clock, yet you know that it's really midnight. After you get past noon, it's 1 o'clock, not 1300 hours. Again, you use conditional statements to make the conversion.

   When you create a new statement, you need to click the curly brace that ends the last statement. Otherwise you end up nesting a statement within a statement and all sorts of weird and wacky things are likely to happen.

10. **Click the curly brace at the end of the conditional statement you just created, click Actions➪Conditions/Loops and then double-click** if.

    The if action is added to the script, and the Condition field opens.

11. **In the Conditions field, type** hours<1.

12. **Click Actions➪Variables and then double-click the** set variable **action.**

    The action is added to the script, and the parameter text boxes materialize.

13. **In the Variable field, type** hours; **in the Value field, type** 12 **and click the Expression box.**

14. **Click the curly brace that ends the last statement you created, click Actions⇨Conditions/Loops and then double-click** if.

    Flash adds the action to the script, and the parameter text boxes flex their muscles.

15. **In the Conditions field, type** hours>12.

16. **Click Actions⇨Variables and then double-click** set variable.

    The action is added to the script, and those pesky parameter text boxes wait for you to enter some text.

17. **In the Variable field, type** hours; **in the Value field, type** hours-12 **and then click the Expression box.**

    The lines of code created in Steps 10 – 17 reset the clock to 12-hour time. The first conditional statement sets the value of the variable hours to 12 if it was less than 1, which makes the clock read 12 during the witching hour. The second conditional statement subtracts 12 from the hours variable after it's larger than 12, converting the 24-hour clock to a 12-hour clock. Your ActionScript to this point should look exactly like what is shown in Figure 8-3.

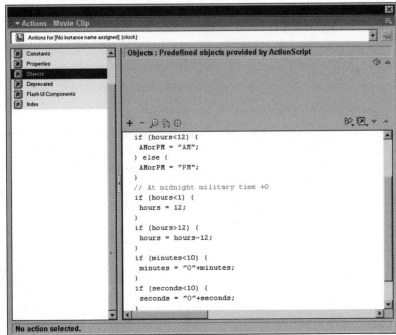

Figure 8-3: You use conditional statements to convert the clock to 12-hour time.

```
if (hours<12) {
  AMorPM = "AM";
} else {
  AMorPM = "PM";
}
// At midnight military time +0
if (hours<1) {
  hours = 12;
}
if (hours>12) {
  hours = hours-12;
}
if (minutes<10) {
  minutes = "0"+minutes;
}
if (seconds<10) {
  seconds = "0"+seconds;
}
```

Displaying the time

Now that your clock is running on 12-hour time, you must complete a few housekeeping chores before you can take the clock for a spin. The first thing you need to do is to set up the display. When the clock starts ticking from 0, the seconds and minutes that are less than 10 are displayed as a single digit and then jump to double digits. The shift is somewhat jarring to the eye, so you need to add a 0 to the display whenever the seconds or minutes are less than 10. Last but not least, you need to create the variable that displays the time:

1. **Click Actions⇨Conditions/Loops and then double-click** if.

   The action is added to the script, and the Condition field opens.

2. **In the Condition field, type** minutes<10.

3. **Click Actions⇨Variables and then double-click the** set variable **action.**

   Another action is added to the script, and the parameter text boxes appear.

4. **In the Variable field, type** minutes; **in the Value field, type** "0"+minutes **and then click the Expression box.**

   The code you created in Steps 1 – 4 adds a 0 before the minutes variable when the variable's value is less than 10. Notice that the 0 is in quotation marks, which means that Flash displays it as a string literal rather than add the value 0 to the variable. Now you've got to do the same thing for seconds.

5. **Click the curly brace at the end of the statement you just created, click Actions⇨Conditions/Loops and then double-click** if.

   The action is added to the script, and the Condition field opens.

6. **In the Condition field, type** seconds<10.

7. **Click the Actions⇨Variables and then double-click the** set variable **action.**

   Yet another action is added to the script, and the parameter text boxes open.

8. **In the Variable field, type** seconds; **in the Value field, type** "0"+seconds **and then click the Expression box.**

   Now that you've got the seconds displayed properly, you need to tie everything together by creating the current_time variable that displays all the results in the dynamic text box that's neatly housed in the movie clip that is idly resting on Stage, waiting for you to finish writing your ActionScript so it can fulfill its purpose and show viewers what time it is.

9. **Click Actions⇨Variables and then double-click** set variable.

   Okay, you should know the drill by now. The parameter text boxes open, and you've got more stuff to do.

10. **In the Variable field, type** current_time; **in the Value field, type** hours+":"+minutes+":"+seconds+" "+AMorPM **and then click the Expression box.**

    Your finished ActionScript for the clock should look exactly like what's shown in Figure 8-4.

    The line of code you just created simply compiles everything for display. The colons between the quotation marks are displayed as string literal values, serving to separate hours, minutes, and seconds. The last bit of punctuation is the space between quotation marks that separates the time from results displayed by the AMorPM variable.

11. **To test the clock, choose Control⇨Test Movie.**

    Flash publishes the movie and — wait! Time is standing still. The clock reads the time but doesn't update it. To get the clock to update in real time, you need to do one more thing. Remember at the start of this section when I introduced you to a clip event? The reason the clock didn't start ticking is the fact that the code ran only once, when the movie clip loaded. In order for the clock to keep on ticking, it has to take a licking. Just kidding — you need to specify another clip event.

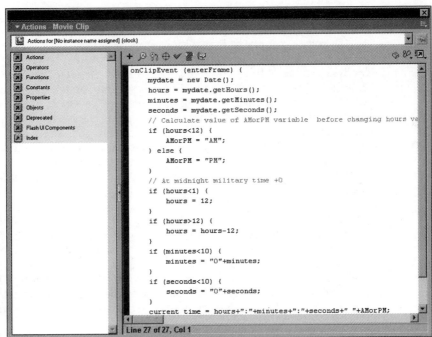

Figure 8-4: This script does everything except cuckoo on the hour.

12. **Close the window to return to movie-editing mode.**

13. **Select the movie clip and click the arrow to the right of the word Actions.**

    The Actions panel opens. It should read Actions-Movie Clip. If it doesn't, reselect the movie clip.

14. **Select the first line of code,** `onClipEvent (load) {`.

    After you select the line of code, the parameter text boxes for the `on` action open. But they're not really text boxes; all you see are a bunch of radio buttons. These are the clip events you'll come to know and love — well maybe you'll just respect them — in Chapter 9. The load clip event is added automatically every time you create ActionScript in a movie clip. And if you don't want the actions to execute when the movie clip loads, well, you choose another clip event.

15. **Click the EnterFrame radio button.**

    Holy scriptography, Batman, the first line of code now reads, `onClipEvent (enterFrame) {`. This clip event executes the code that follows every time the frame is entered. So then, it's a single frame movie clip, which means that frame is always entered. And that's what it takes to keep the clock ticking.

16. **Choose Control⇨Test Movie.**

    The clock is updated in real time.

There's a couple of things to note about this last exercise. You could have done all this by entering the code in the first frame on the main timeline. If you did it in this manner, you wouldn't have a clip event to handle the code, and the code would execute only once. Then you'd have to add another frame and write the following script for the frame: `gotoAndPlay (1)`. When the movie looped back to frame 1, the code to read the time would execute. By creating this code in a movie clip, you save the trouble of having to create another keyframe. And you do one other thing as well — you create modular ActionScript.

Whoa, Nellie! Modular ActionScript? Yup. By putting your ActionScript in a movie clip, you can take it anywhere, even to another movie. After you save a document with a ActionScript in a movie clip, you can use it in another movie by choosing File⇨Open as Library, navigating to the file and then clicking Open. After you click Open, Flash opens the file's document Library. Drag the movie clip with the modular ActionScript into the current document Library or drag it on Stage. Your modular ActionScript clock works just fine in this movie.

If, for any reason, your clock ticked when it should have tocked, copy to your hard drive the time_final.fla file from this chapter's folder on this book's CD. Disable the file's read-only attribute, open the file in Flash, and compare the ActionScript to what you've created.

Working with the Color Object

You use the Color object when you want to transform the color of a movie clip. Like other objects, the Color object has different methods that perform different functions. The Color object has the following methods:

- ✔ getRGB: Returns the numeric RGB value that was set the last time the setRGB method was called.

- ✔ getTransform: Returns the transformation data that was set the last time the setTransformation method was called.

- ✔ setRGB: Sets the RGB color of a Color object and uses the hexadecimal format.

- ✔ setTranform: Sets the color transformation for a Color object.

Creating a new Color object

Before you can change the color of an object in your movie, you must first create an instance of the Color object that references your movie clip.

To create an instance of the Color object:

1. **Select the frame or object in which you want to create an instance of the Color object.**

2. **Click the arrow to the left of the word Actions.**

   The Actions panel makes another appearance.

3. **Click Actions⇨Variables and then double-click the** set variable **action.**

   The parameter text boxes open.

4. **In the Variable field, type** mycolor.

   You can choose any variable name you want. However, choosing a name like mycolor makes it easier to remember what you're using the variable for.

5. **Click inside the Value field. Then, in the left pane of the Actions panel, click Objects⇨Movie⇨Color.**

   The Color object methods are ready for use.

6. **Double-click** new Color.

The name appears in the Value field with a pair of parentheses. Congratulations. You've just created your own color object. Now you need to tell Flash which object in your movie you want the color object to modify.

7. **First click between the parentheses; then click the Insert Target Path icon that looks like a cross-hair.**

The Insert Target Path dialog box opens.

8. **Click the button for the movie clip whose color you want to transform.**

An instance of the Color object has been created.

After you have an instance of the Color object targeted toward a movie clip, you can modify the movie clip's color using one of the Color object methods. To see how you use the Color object to transform an object's color, please read the next section.

Transforming an object's color

After you create an instance of the Color object and target it toward a movie clip, you're ready to change the object's color. An object or keyframe can be used to trigger the color change.

Using the .set RGB method

The setRGB color method uses the hexadecimal color format to specify the color transformation. The hexadecimal format uses a combination of letters from *A* through *F* and numbers from 0 through 16 to set a color. Jet black in hexadecimal format is #000000, and pure-as-the-driven-snow white is #FFFFFF. By combining the different variations of the three two-digit hexadecimal numbers, the full-color RGB palette can be achieved. To change an object's color using the setRGB method:

1. **Set up an instance of the Color object.**

You can't change an object's color until you set up an instance of the Color object. It's an ActionScript law. If you don't know how to do this task, please read the "Creating a new Color object" section, a few paragraphs back from the words you're now reading.

2. **Select the keyframe or object that will trigger the color change.**

3. **Click the arrow to the left of the word Actions.**

The Actions panel opens.

4. **In the left pane of the Actions panel, click Objects⇨Movie⇨Color⇨ Methods, and then double-click the setRGB method.**

The text setRGB() appears in the Script pane and two parameter text boxes open: Object and Parameters.

5. **In the Object field, enter the name of the color object.**

This is the name you chose when you created an instance of the color object in Step 1.

6. **In the Parameters field, enter the value of the color.**

Right below the field, notice the Flash programmers give you the correct formatting for the color 0xRRGGBB. If you wanted to change the color of the object to blood red, you'd enter 0X990000.

When the script is executed, the movie clip object targeted by the instance of the Color object changes its color. Listing 8-4 shows a few lines of ActionScript that change a movie clip named color_clip to a pale yellow when a button is clicked.

Listing 8-4   Changing an Object's Color

```
on (release) {
mycolor = new Color(color_clip);
mycolor.setRGB( 0xFFFF99);
}
```

If you're not familiar with the hexadecimal format, click the triangle to the right of the Fill color well to open the color pallet. Drag the eye dropper until you see the color you want and then click the color. The hexadecimal value for that color appears in a window to the right of the color swatch.

For your viewing pleasure, I've created a document called color.fla, which you can find in this chapter's folder on the CD that came with this book. Copy the file to your hard drive and disable the file's read-only attributes. Open the file in Flash and then choose Control⇨Test Movie. Click the buttons and watch the sphere change to the same color as the button. When you're through, close the window to enter movie-editing mode. Open the Actions panel, and examine the ActionScript on the first frame and the ActionScript attached to each button.

Using the setTransform method

You use the setTransform method of the Color object when you want to change the color characteristics of a multicolored object, like a bitmap image or a vector graphic with a gradient fill. You're not *changing* the object's color; you're *tinting* it. To tint an object with the setTransform method:

1. **Create an instance of the Color object.**

   If you don't know how to create a Color object, read the section "Creating a new Color object," conveniently located earlier in this chapter.

2. **Select the object or keyframe to be the trigger that causes the movie clip to be tinted.**

   If you're tinting an object, you can assign the `setTranform` method to a button that when clicked changes the tint of an object.

3. **Click the arrow to the left of the word Actions.**

   The Actions panel opens.

4. **Click Actions⇨Variables, and then double-click** `set variable`.

   Again, Flash adds the action to the script, and the parameter text boxes open.

5. **In the Variable field, type** myColorTransform.

   If you don't like the variable name `myColorTransform`, feel free to choose another, as long as it adheres to the rules for creating a variable name.

6. **Click inside the Value field. Then, in the left pane of the Actions panel, click Objects⇨Core⇨Objects and then double-click** `new Object`.

   This line of code tells Flash to create a new object — in this case, an object that tints the movie clip you specified when you created the Color object. The actual transformation is passed from the new object, `myColorTransform`, to the Color object using the `setTransform` method. And that's the truth.

7. **Click Actions⇨Variables and then double-click** `set variable`.

   The action is added to your script and two fields open in the parameter text box area.

8. **In the Variable field, enter the name of the new object you created in Step 5.**

   If you've been following along, enter `myColorTransform`. If you decided to use some other weird or wonderful name, enter it now.

9. **In the Value field, type** myColorTransform={ra:'75', rb:'221',ga:'45',gb:'112', ba:'35',bb:'128',aa:'45',ab:'75'}.

   This line of code alters the colors of the original object by a set percentage and then applies a tint to the object. In the preceding code, the `ra` component of the script is setting the value of the red color in the original object to 75 percent. The `rb` component of the script is applying a red tint with a value of 221 in the RGB color model, and so on. You can use the following parameters to tint an object:

- **ra:** Sets the percentage of the red in the original color. Enter a value between –100 and 100.

- **rb:** Applies a red tint to an object. You can use a value from –255 to 255.

- **ga:** Sets the percentage of the green in the original color. Acceptable values range between –100 and 100.

- **gb:** Applies a green tint to an object. You can use a value from –255 to 255.

- **ba:** Sets the percentage of blue in the original color. Enter a value between –100 and 100.

- **aa:** Adjusts the percentage of alpha (opacity) in the original color. Enter a value between –100 and 100.

- **ab:** Sets the alpha value for the tint. You can use any value between –255 and 255.

10. **In the left pane of the Actions panel, click Objects⇨Movie⇨Color⇨ Methods, and then click** setTransform.

   In the Script pane, you see the line of code <not set yet>. setTransform. In the parameters text area, two fields appear: Object and Parameters.

11. **In the Object field, enter the name of the color object you created when you assigned an instance of the color object to the movie clip you're transforming.**

   When you use the setTransform method of the Color object, you have two objects, the object you created and assigned to a movie clip and the object with the transformation information.

12. **In the parameters field enter the name of the object you created in Step 5.**

   The last line of code in the script links the color transform object with the Color object you created for the movie clip.

And that, dear reader, is how you tint an object. The whole process may seem a little daunting at first, but after you work with it for a while, it becomes second nature. You can use the setTransform color method to good effect when you're creating an e-commerce site and you want to give visitors an idea of what a product looks like in a different color.

To get a better idea of how the various settings for the setTransform color method modify an object, create a Flash movie and then import a bitmap image into it. Convert the bitmap to a symbol. Apply the Advanced Color effect to it, and drag the sliders for the effect's various settings to see how each setting changes the tint of the bitmap. You don't even have to publish the movie to do this task; you can experiment with different values for each setting and see the change in movie-editing mode. The red, green, blue, and alpha settings on the left side of the Advanced Effect dialog box have the same effect as the `setTransform` method's ra, ga, ba, and aa parameters. The settings on the right side of the Advanced Effect dialog box have the same effect on the image as the `setTransform` method's rb, gb, bb, and ab parameters.

Modifying Sounds in Your Movies

Another useful object is the Sound object. You can use the Sound object's various methods to control the sounds in your movies. Before the Sound object came along, you could change an individual sound in your movie by changing its synch settings in the Property inspector. You could also stop all sounds in a movie by using the stopAllSounds action. The Sound object gives you more flexibility. It has methods that you use to control the characteristics of a selected sound or globally, for all sounds in your movie.

Importing sounds into your movie

You can work with sounds in Flash in one of two ways. You can either create a movie clip with nothing but a soundtrack and use the loadMovie action to load it into your movie, or you can import a sound directly into a document, assign an ActionScript identifier to it, and then modify the sound.

When you choose the first method, you can create a button that your viewers can click to decide whether or not they want to hear the soundtrack you've deemed worthy of the movie. You assign the loadMovie action to a button and then load the soundtrack movie into a higher level than the base movie. I always like to use level 99 for loading soundtrack movies. It's easy to remember and makes me think of Agent 99 from the old Get Smart television series. To load a soundtrack movie using a button, you create the code shown in Listing 8-5.

Listing 8-5   Loading a Soundtrack Movie

```
on (release) {
   loadMovieNum("soundtrack.swf", 99);
}
```

This method is explored in greater detail in Chapter 16, when you create a working sound controller.

When you choose the second method of working with a sound, you import it into the movie. When you import a sound into a movie, it becomes part of the document Library. After you add a sound to the document Library, you can refer to it with ActionScript by creating linkage for the sound. Creating linkage for a sound makes it possible to start, stop or otherwise modify the sound using methods of the Sound object.

To create linkage for a sound in the document Library:

1. **Choose Window⇨Library.**

   The document Library opens.

2. **Select the sound you want to create linkage for.**

3. **Right-click (Windows) or Ctrl-click (Macintosh) and choose Linkage from the drop-down menu.**

   The Linkage Properties dialog box appears.

4. **Click the Export for ActionScript check box.**

   Flash creates an ActionScript identifier for the sound. The default identifier is the name of the sound file: for example, loop1.wav. You can create a different identifier if you like.

5. **Accept the default Identifier, or alternatively, enter a name in the Identifier field as shown in Figure 8-5.**

   If you enter your own identifier, don't use any spaces between words. Keep it short and simple, but descriptive so you can remember the name when you attach the sound to a sound object. I know. I show you how to do that in the next section.

6. **Click OK.**

   The sound file now has an ActionScript identifier.

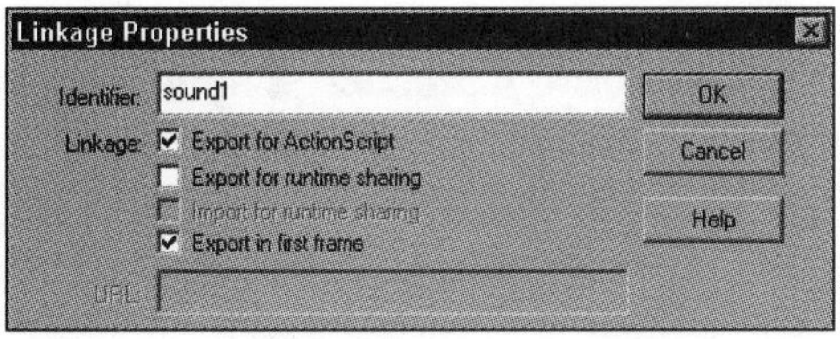

Figure 8-5:
You can create linkage to refer to a sound directly from the document Library.

Creating a new Sound object

Before you can control a sound with one of the sound methods, you have to create an instance of the Sound object and then attach the sound you want to control to it (see Figure 8-6). To create a new Sound object:

1. **Select the keyframe or object where you want to create the Sound object.**

   If the sound will be used throughout the movie, creating the Sound object in the first frame of the movie is a good idea.

2. **Choose Window⇨Actions.**

   The Actions panel opens.

3. **Click Actions⇨Variables and then double-click** `set variable`.

   The set variable action is added to the script, and the parameter text boxes appear.

4. **In the Variable field, enter a name for the Sound object.**

   If you want to control more than one sound in the movie, choose a name like `mysounda`.

5. **Click inside the Value field. In the left pane of the Actions panel, click Objects⇨Movie⇨Sound, and then double-click** `new Sound`.

   The Sound object is created.

   After you create a Sound object, you have to target the sound you're going to control with the Sound object's methods. To do this, you attach a sound to the Sound object by referencing the sound's target path.

6. **Click the Actions⇨Objects⇨Movie⇨Sound⇨Methods, and then double-click** `attachSound`.

   In the Script pane, the code `<not yet set>.attach.sound` appears. Above the Script pane, two fields appear: Object and Parameters.

7. **In the Object field, enter the name of the sound object you created in Step 4.**

8. **In the Parameters field, enter the ActionScript identifier for the sound.**

   This is the name (identifier) you specify when you set the linkage properties for the object. When you refer to an object by an identifier, the identifier must be in quotation marks, for example: "sounda."

If you want to attached a soundtrack movie you loaded with the loadMovie action, in the parameters field, enter the level you loaded the soundtrack movie into, for example: `_level99`. You don't have to put quotes around the level.

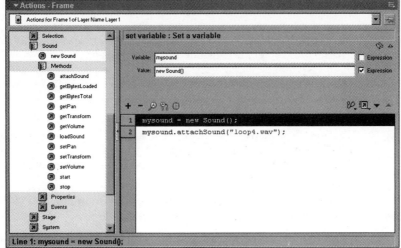

Figure 8-6:
To modify a
sound, first
you must
create a
Sound
object.

Using Sound methods to modify Sound objects

After you create a Sound object, you can use any of the Sound object's methods to modify the sound. You can start a sound, stop a sound, pan the sound toward the right speaker or the left, and control a sound's volume.

Starting a sound

You can start a Sound object wherever you want. If, for example, you've imported a sound with a little jingle in it that you want to play at a particular frame, do the following:

1. **Select the frame you want the sound to start playing on.**

   You can only apply ActionScript to a keyframe. Press F6 to convert a regular frame to a keyframe.

2. **Create a new Sound object and then use the** `attachSound` **method to target the movie clip to the Sound object.**

   If you don't know how to create a Sound object, read the earlier section "Creating a new Sound object."

3. **Click the arrow to the left of the word Actions.**

   The Actions panel opens.

4. **Click the Objects➪Movie➪Sound➪Methods, and then double-click** start.

   In the Script pane the code, <not yet set>.start appears. Above the Script pane, the Object and Parameters fields appear.

5. **In the Object field, enter the name of the sound object you want to start.**

   If all you want to do is start the sound, you're done. However, you can control how many seconds into the sound clip it starts playing and control the number of times it plays. When you accept the default and enter no parameters, the sound starts at the beginning and plays once.

6. **In the Parameters field, enter the number of seconds you want to offset the start of the sound, followed by a comma, and then enter the number of times you want the sound the loop.**

   For your convenience, below the Parameters field, the Flash programmers entered the proper syntax (seconds offset, loops) you use to offset and loop the sound. This is displayed right below the Parameters text box. If you just want to offset the start of the sound, enter the seconds offset value and nothing else. If you only want to loop the sound, enter 0 for the seconds offset, type a comma, and then enter the number of times you want the sound to go loop-de-loop. Publish the movie, crank up the volume, and enjoy. Listing 8-6 shows the code for a sound object that starts eight seconds into the sound clip and loops three times.

Listing 8-6   Starting a Sound

```
soundc.start(8,3)
```

Stopping a sound (hush!)

You can also use ActionScript to stop a sound from playing. If you've created a movie clip with a soundtrack in it, you can give viewers the option of turning the sound off. You can also have a sound stop playing when the movie advances to a certain frame. To stop a sound from playing:

1. **Select the keyframe or button that will cause the sound to stop playing.**

2. **Click the arrow to the left of the word Actions.**

   The Actions panel makes another appearance.

3. **Click Objects➪Movie➪Sound➪Methods, and then double-click** stop.

   The stop method of the Sound object is added to the script. Above the Script pane, the Object parameter text box appears.

4. In the Object field, enter the name of the sound object you want to stop playing.

Listing 8-7 shows a line of code that stops a Sound object named `soundc` from playing. Ah, the sounds of silence.

Listing 8-7   Creating Silence

```
soundc.stop()
```

Panning a sound

You can also use a Sound object to pan a sound. When you *pan* a sound, you alter the balance between the speakers. When a sound is played in Flash, by default the sound is split 50–50 between each speaker. You can alter the balance by using the Sound object's `setPan` method. You can use a keyframe or button to trigger the change. To set the pan of a sound:

1. Select the keyframe or button that will trigger the event change.

2. Click the arrow to the left of the word Actions

The Actions panel opens.

3. Click Objects⇨Movie⇨Sound⇨Methods, and then double-click `setPan`.

The method is added to the script. Above the Script pane, two parameter text boxes appear, Object and Pan.

4. In the Object field, enter the name of the sound object you want to pan.

5. In the Pan field, enter the value by which you want to pan the Sound object.

Enter a value between –100 (the sound plays only in the left speaker) and 100 (the sound plays only in the right speaker).

Listing 8-8 shows a line of ActionScript code that pans a Sound object named `soundc` toward the right speaker.

Listing 8-8   Panning for Sound, Not Gold

```
soundc.pan(75)
```

Controlling sound volume: Turn that down!

You can also use a Sound object method to soundly control the volume of a sound. You can use this method to accentuate an important part of your movie by having a sound play louder or softer. You can use a button or keyframe to trigger a change in sound volume. To control the volume of a Sound object:

1. **Select the object or keyframe that will trigger the volume change.**

2. **Click the arrow to the left of the word Actions.**

   The Actions panel opens.

3. **Click Objects⇨Movie⇨Sound⇨Methods, and then double-click** setVolume.

   The setVolume method is added to the script. Above the Script pane, two fields appear, Object and Parameters.

4. **In the Object field, enter the name of the sound object whose volume you want to control.**

5. **In the Parameters field, enter a value.**

   You can enter any reasonable value greater than 0. You can also enter a value greater than 100, which is the full volume of the original sound. Values greater than 100 increase the volume of a sound but distort it — take my word for it. I tested values up to 700 and didn't dare go higher for fear of breaking my PC's speakers. Listing 8-9 shows a line of ActionScript that reduces the volume of a Sound object named soundc to 75 percent of its original volume.

Listing 8-9   Turning the Volume Down

```
soundc.setVolume(75)
```

In Chapter 16, I show you how to create a sound controller for your movie soundtracks. The controller has sliders to set the volume and pan the sound as well as buttons to start and stop the soundtrack.

Chapter 9

Creating Interactive Elements

· ·

· ·

*T*he movie clip is the king of ActionScript. Movie clips are the objects you can fold, spindle, and mutilate with ActionScript. You can resize them, shrink them, and multiply them by applying the right action in the right place. You can use movie clips as reusable animations that you summon with ActionScript. Or you can use them to house a single graphic — for example, a laser beam for your favorite alien space invader game. You then use ActionScript to bring the laser beam to life and zap the big, bad Klingons into the next dimension.

In this chapter, I show you how to communicate with movie clips from the main timeline and how movie clips can communicate with each other. I also show you how to create movie clips and load other Flash movies into movie clips. For those of you who want to know all about the movie clip's prodigy offspring, the user-defined component, by the time the chapter is over, I show you how to create one — a movie clip with a super-high IQ that you can reprogram on the fly.

The Actions panel's got lots of books. And some of these books have books within a book. To add some actions to your scripts, you have to click this book icon, then click that book icon, then click another book icon, and so on. Rather than bore you with a lot of words, I'm going to show the path to each action as shown in the following example: Click Actions➪Movie Control and then double-click goto.

Understanding Targets and Paths: A Tale of Many Timelines

A movie clip has a timeline, even a movie clip with only one item and a single frame. You can address a movie clip's timeline from the main timeline. You can also get assets from a movie clip from the main timeline, such as data from variables or arrays. Movie clips can talk to each other too — well, not in the literal sense. (If I were to visit a Flash site and hear movie clips engrossed in conversation, plotting to overthrow — never mind.) It's probably better to say that movie clips can communicate with each other and the main timeline. For example, when one movie clip gets done strutting its stuff, it can stop itself and call another movie clip into action.

You can get this interactivity between movie clips by addressing a movie clip's target path. If you want an action on one timeline to affect a movie clip on another timeline, you need to show Flash the way by telling it which path to follow. The movie clip is the target, and the way there is the path. To give you an idea of what a path in ActionScript looks like, consider the following: `_root.mymovieclip`. This is the path to a movie clip named `mymovieclip` from the main, or root, timeline. This concept may seem a little scary, but — trust me — it isn't. You don't have to know each and every path for each and every movie clip in your movies. Flash has in the Actions panel a handy tool that is so tiny, so miniscule, that you almost miss it the first time you wander into the Actions panel. There, just above the Script pane, sitting there on a level plane, not in Spain, nestled up close and personal to other icons that can, is a tiny, black button with a crosshair for a belly button that you use to insert a target path in your script (see Figure 9-1).

When you need to insert a target path, simply click the black button, and the Insert Target Path dialog box opens, as shown in Figure 9-2. This innocuous little box has a button for every named instance of a movie clip in your movie. To insert a target path, you simply click the proper button and — voilà — the name of the target path appears in the Target field, near the bottom of the dialog box. You can now add to the target path if necessary. For example, if you're referencing the target path of a variable, you simply need to add a dot (.) and the name of the variable, and then Flash knows right where to find it. The same statement is true if you need to get the property of a movie clip, such as its x or y position. Simply add a dot (.) after the target path in the Target field and finish off the code with the property. After you've selected a target path, click OK. Then you can add whatever other bit of ActionScript you need in the Actions panel.

If you take a good look at Figure 9-2, you notice a few choices you have to make. On the left side of the dialog box is a section labeled Notation. It refers to slash notation, from Flash 4, and dot notation, which was introduced in Flash 5. Unless you're creating a movie for Flash 4, stick with the default dot notation.

Insert Target Path button

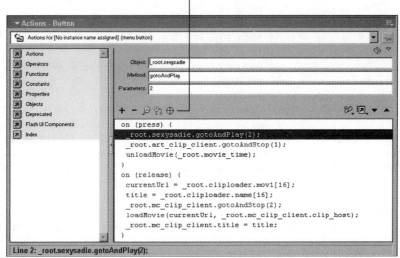

Figure 9-1: You click this little black icon to insert a target path in your Action-Script.

Figure 9-2: Inserting target paths is as easy as clicking a button.

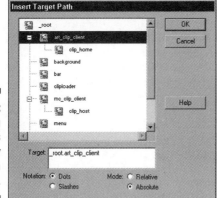

For more information on dot and slash notation, refer to Chapter 3.

On the lower-right side of the Insert Target Path dialog box is a section labeled Mode. It tells Flash whether to look for the target path on the same timeline (in Relative mode) or to use the root timeline as a starting point (in Absolute mode).

Using absolute paths

An *absolute path* always has its base (root) on the main timeline of the movie and that's the absolute truth. The base timeline of a movie is always addressed in ActionScript as _root followed by a dot (.), which is then followed by a named instance of a movie clip. If a movie clip is nested within a movie clip, the nested movie clip is a *child* to the movie clip. If an action calls a child of a movie clip, you add another target within the path. If, for example, an action is calling a movie clip named io, which is a child of a movie clip called venus, the path from the root timeline is _root.venus.io. When you achieve the honored rank of ActionScript Genius, you manually enter target paths like this one in Expert mode. In the meantime, your friend the Insert Target Path dialog box has it all mapped out for you. All you need to do is choose the Absolute mode option and then click the button for the movie clip you want to target. If a button has a plus sign (+) beside it, it means that more than one named instance (target) is in the path; in other words, one or more movie clips is nested within the main movie clip. Click the plus sign to expand the target path and display all the instances along the path. You can view a target path to a nested movie clip in Absolute or Relative mode. Figure 9-3 shows a target path in Relative mode to a movie clip that is a child of another movie clip. Relative mode? It's coming up in the next section; just wanted to give you a preview.

An instance of a movie clip always has the same absolute path, whether you're calling it from another movie clip or another level.

Using relative paths

When you use a relative path, you're addressing the timeline of the movie that calls the action. It's kind of like addressing yourself. If, for example, you have a movie clip named cerealFlake within a movie clip named cerealFlakeBox and you want the address to get the *x* property of cerealFlake from cerealFlake, the target path is _x.cerealFlake. Notice the absence of _root. from the path. Whenever you see this, it's a dead give-away that the path is relative, not absolute. Again, not to worry. If you prefer to write your ActionScript code in Normal mode while creating Flash movies in your humble (or not so humble) abode, just choose Relative mode and click the button of your choice. When you choose the Relative mode, you are able to address only targets on the same level. Figure 9-4 shows the Insert Target Path dialog box in Relative mode.

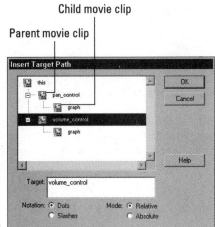

Child movie clip

Parent movie clip

Figure 9-3:
This movie clip is a child to the parent.

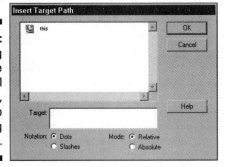

Figure 9-4:
Creating a relative path is all relative, thanks to this dialog box.

Using path aliases

You don't use a path alias to protect the identity of a movie clip in a witness protection program. You do use a path alias when you want to quickly reference a movie clip without referring to its full target path. You have three aliases to work with: _root, _parent, and _this. To understand how this concept works, consider a hypothetical movie clip family. It has a parent movie clip named jackAndjill, and nested within jackAndjill are two other movie clips, Joseph, and Gillian. Figure 9-5 shows a visual representation of the movie clip family and their relation to each other and the root timeline.

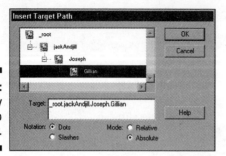

Figure 9-5:
A happy
movie clip
family.

In Figure 9-5, everything begins at the main timeline: _root. The jackAndjill movie clip is parent to the Joseph movie clip, and the Joseph movie clip is parent to the Gillian movie clip. If you're creating a line of code in the Gillian movie clip to stop the Joseph movie clip from playing, you have three ways to do it:

- **Absolute mode:** _root.Joseph.stop
- **Relative mode:** _Joseph.stop
- **Relative mode using alias:** _parent.stop

You can use the Insert Target Path dialog box when using the first two methods or enter the path manually in Normal mode by typing the path directly into a field in the appropriate parameter text box, or in Expert mode by typing the path directly into the Script pane of the Actions panel. The third and quickest solution is to manually enter the alias in either Normal mode or Expert mode.

Another useful alias is this. You use the this alias when you're referring to the movie clip calling the action. Think of this as a movie clip addressing itself. For example, to get the *x* property from within a movie clip that is calling the property, simply enter this._x.

Producing a Movie Clip

The movie clip is the heart of interactivity within a Flash movie. A movie clip can contain a stationary graphic element or elements you modify with ActionScript, or it can be a full-fledged animation with multiple layers and a timeline with many frames. Creating the movie clip is your first step. You can create ActionScript within the movie clip itself or let actions from another movie clip or the main timeline control the movie clip. After a movie clip is created, it resides in the document Library until you create an instance of it on the timeline and label it.

For more information on creating a movie clip and labeling an instance of a movie clip, refer to Chapter 7.

Programming a movie clip

When you use ActionScript within a movie clip, you can control the movie clip from within itself or have the movie clip function as a majordomo of sorts and control other movie clips. A movie clip plays as soon as it appears on the timeline. If you're using multiple movie clips in a single frame movie, you don't want the clips to play when the movie begins.

Suppose that you create a single-frame Flash movie for a commercial Web site. The main movie has a user interface composed of buttons programmed to play movie clips that are all on Stage within the movie's single frame. All the action and interaction come from the movie clips, which begin to play, of course, as soon as the movie loads, unless you use ActionScript to prevent that from happening. To do this task, you create each movie clip with a blank first frame; *no* graphics. On the first frame, you use the stop action to prevent the movie clip from advancing to the second frame when it is loaded. You create all the graphics and animation for the movie clip beginning on the second frame, using as many frames as you need to complete the effect you're after. After the movie clip has finished playing, you want it to stop and no longer be visible. On the last frame of the movie clip, you use the goto action to have the movie return to frame 1, which is blank. To put the whole thing together, you program each button to play frame 2 of the appropriate movie clip when the button is clicked. Figure 9-6 shows the timeline of a movie clip that is dormant until a button tells it to get physical and start playing.

First keyframe is blank with a Stop action

Movie clip begins playing on frame 2

Movie clip stops and goes to first keyframe

Figure 9-6:
To control a movie clip, you add actions to its timeline.

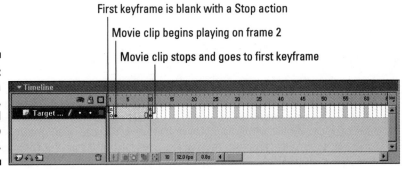

Duplicating a movie clip

Before you started using ActionScript, when you needed more than one of an object, you dragged it from the document Library and placed it on Stage. With ActionScript, you can clone movie clips with the `duplicateMovieClip` action. This little gem is really useful when you create a cool movie clip of a moving star, for example, and want to duplicate it to create a moving star field.

A duplicated movie clip begins playing on the first frame, no matter what frame of the parent movie clip is playing when the cloned clip is created. The `duplicateMovieClip` action has parameters you set that determine the name of the duplicated movie clip, as well as the number of movie clips that are spawned from the original. Listing 9-1 shows the format and parameters for the `duplicateMovieClip` method.

Listing 9-1   The duplicateMovieClip Method Parameters

```
_root.myMovieClip.duplicateMovieClip( newName, depth );
```

In this listing, I've already entered the target, and instance of a movie clip with the path: `_root.myMovieClip`. When you use this method in your ActionScript, you replace `newName` with a name for the duplicated movie clip and replace `depth` with the number of copies you want to create. If, for example, you were to create one copy of a movie clip called `myMovieClip`, the code would read `_root.myMovieClip.duplicateMovieClip(_root.myMovieClip1,1)`. If you're creating more than one copy of a movie clip, the easiest way to do it is to set up a loop that uses a counter to create the names of the duplicated movie clips as well as the number that are cloned.

To see a While loop used to duplicate a movie clip, wile away a few minutes and read Chapter 5.

Loading a Movie into a Movie Clip

When you use the `loadMovie` action, you can load the movie either into a level or into a target. When you choose a movie clip as the target, you open a new world of possibilities. You can place the target anywhere on Stage, and the movie you're loading appears right there. You can also create a movie clip that can be dragged, giving the viewer the option of moving the loaded movie to a different position in her browser.

For more information on using the `loadMovie` action, take a peek at Chapter 5. If you need to know how to create an object that can be dragged *right now,* drag yourself over to Chapter 11.

When you load a movie into a level, the movie inherits the same dimension as the main movie. When you load a movie into a target movie clip, you have more control over the process; create the target with the exact dimension of the movie(s) that you want to load into a target.

Creating a target movie clip

When you create a movie clip for the sole purpose of loading other movie clips into it, the target movie clip hangs about on Stage until you load a movie clip into it. Therefore, the movie clip should not be seen — or heard, for that matter — until it is summoned. To create a target movie clip that won't be visible when loaded:

1. **Choose Insert⇨New Symbol.**

   The Symbol Properties dialog box appears.

2. **Enter a name for the movie clip, choose the movie clip behavior, and click OK.**

   The Symbol Properties dialog box closes, and Flash enters symbol-editing mode.

3. **Create a new layer and label it** Actions.

4. **Click the first frame in the Actions layer and then click the arrow to the left of the word Actions.**

   The Actions panel opens.

5. **Click Actions⇨Movie Control and double-click** stop.

   The stop action is added to the first frame of the movie clip.

6. **Create a second keyframe on the Actions layer by pressing F6 and then add the** stop **action to this frame.**

7. **Rename the first layer** Target.

8. **Click the second frame in the Target layer and press F6 to convert it to a keyframe.**

9. **Create a rectangle with no fill the same size as the movies you want to load into the target.**

   You use the Property inspector or Info panel to size the rectangle precisely. Use the movie's background color for the rectangle's stroke color; the rectangle is never visible when the movie is loading. It merely serves as a template for the movie you're loading into the target. If you're loading a large movie into the target, you may consider adding the word Loading. This action alerts your viewers that something is happening.

10. **Position the rectangle so that its upper-left corner is at the center of the stage.**

    Flash loads the new movie from the upper-left corner of the target movie clip, which means that you must align the upper-left corner of the movie clip to center stage. You can use the Property inspector to align the rectangle perfectly. Just enter 0 in the X: and Y: fields, as shown in Figure 9-7.

11. **Click the Back button or current scene button to return to movie-editing mode.**

12. **Choose Window⇨Library.**

    The document Library opens.

13. **Drag an instance of the target movie clip on Stage and, using the Property inspector, give the movie clip instance a name.**

    Remember you give a movie clip instance a name by entering it in the Property inspector's <Instance Name> field. Without an instance name, you won't be able to refer to the target clip with ActionScript. If you have a complex movie, you should also put all your movie clips on their own layers.

Registration point coordinates

Registration point

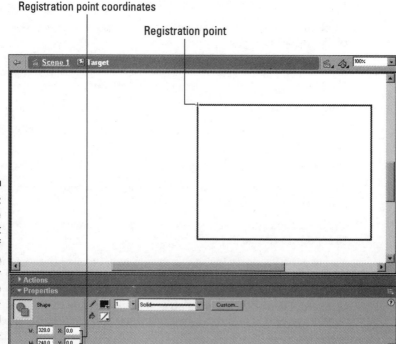

Figure 9-7:
Align the upper-left corner of the movie to the center of the symbol-editing window.

14. Position the movie clip.

You won't be able to see the actual movie clip. The only thing you have to go by is the movie clip's registration point, which shows up as a little white dot on Stage.

Now that you've got the target movie clip on Stage, all you have to do is write the ActionScript that loads movies into the target clip, a task I show you how to do in the next section.

 If you have lots of movie clips on Stage with blank first frames, all you can see is the movie clip's registration point: a white dot. To make the individual movie clips easier to identify, create a Guide layer, use unfilled circles to surround the clip's registration point, and create a line of text next to each movie clip showing the movie clip instance's name. After you create the Guide layer and label it, lock it. When the movie is published, the guide layer isn't seen, but it's a tremendous help when you're trying to identify each individual movie clip on Stage.

Creating the ActionScript to load the movie

After you have created the target movie clip, you create the ActionScript to load the movie into the target. To do this, you use the `loadMovie` action. To load a movie into a target:

1. **Select the keyframe or object that you want to trigger the loading of the movie.**

2. **Click the arrow to the left of the word actions.**

   The Actions panel opens.

3. **Click Actions⇨Miscellaneous Actions and then double-click** `evaluate`**.**

   The Expression field opens above the Script pane.

4. **Click the black Insert a Target Path button just above the Script pane.**

   The Insert Target Path dialog box opens.

5. **Click the target path button for the target movie clip.**

   The clip's target path appears in the Target field.

6. **In the Target field, type** .gotoAndStop (2) **and then click OK.**

   Make sure that you enter the action exactly as I have it in this step, including the dot (.) before `goto`. If you prefer, after you click the button to insert the clip's target path, click OK to exit the Insert Target Path dialog box. After you're back in the Actions panel, you can enter the dot followed by the action in the Expression field.

7. **Click Actions⇨Browser/Network Control and then double-click** `loadMovie`.

   The action is added to the script, and three parameter text boxes appear above the Script pane.

8. **In the URL field, enter the name of the movie you're loading.**

   This path is the one Flash uses to find the movie clip. If you enter the path incorrectly, the movie doesn't load. If the movie you're loading is in the same directory as the main movie, you need to enter only the movie's filename; for example, about.swf.

9. **Click the triangle to the right of the Location field and choose Target from the drop-down menu.**

10. **Position your cursor in the blank field to the right of location and then click the Insert a Target Path button.**

    Yep, you've been here before. This is your old friend the Insert Target Path dialog box.

11. **Click the button that represents the target path of the movie clip into which you're loading the movie.**

    The target is added to the script. Listing 9-2 shows ActionScript that loads a movie named `about.swf` into a movie clip instance named `movie_host`. The second line of code advances the target movie clip to its second frame, and the third line of code loads the movie.

Listing 9-2   Loading a Movie into a Target

```
on (release) {
  _root.movie_host.gotoAndStop(2);
  loadMovie ("about.swf", _root.movie_host);
}
```

Modular ActionScript

When you create an effect with ActionScript on the main timeline, the script is executed when the frame is reached. If you want to use the same effect several times within the same movie, or in other movies, create the effect in a movie clip. Then, you have a reusable effect that you can drag from the document Library whenever you need it. You can also use the effect in other movies by using the Open As Library command to open the .fla file where the desired movie clip is located and then drag it into the current movie's document Library or directly onto the Stage.

Using the onClipEvent Action

The ability to add actions to movie clips makes it possible for you to use a single movie clip several times in a movie and program each clip differently. If, for example, you have a movie clip with a graphic in it, you can use ActionScript to resize the graphic or change its color when the instance of the movie clip loads. The original movie clip symbol is safe and secure in the document Library. The code you attach to any instance of the clip doesn't change the symbol from which the instance was created. When you assign an action to a movie clip in Normal mode, the onClipEvent action is automatically added to the script. By default, Flash handles an action you add to a movie clip when the clip loads. This is also known as an *event handler*. In other words, the ActionScript is executed (handled) when a certain event occurs. Listing 9-3 shows ActionScript that changes the *x* position of a movie clip to 500 when the clip loads. Notice the use of the alias this instead of referring to the full target path of the movie clip.

Listing 9-3   Using the onClipEvent Action

```
onClipEvent (load) {
  _this._x=500;
}
```

When you add ActionScript to a movie clip, you can choose one of the following events:

- ✔ load: The action is handled whenever the movie clip first appears on the timeline and loads.

- ✔ enterFrame: The action is executed as each frame in the movie clip is played.

- ✔ unload: The action occurs after the first frame of the clip plays.

- ✔ mouseMove: The action occurs whenever the mouse is moved.

- ✔ mouseDown: The action is executed whenever the left mouse button is pressed.

- ✔ mouseUp: The action executes whenever the left mouse button is released.

- ✔ keyDown: The action occurs whenever a key is pressed. You use the Key.getCode to tell Flash which key is being pressed.

- ✔ keyUp: The action is executed whenever a key is released. You use the Key.getCode method to tell Flash which key is pressed.

Figure 9-8 shows the onClipEvent action's events as they appear in the parameter text box area. To specify an event, click it. You can choose only one event.

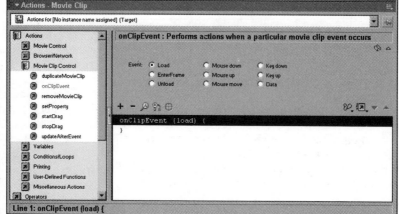

The last movie clip event, data, is one I rarely use. If you decide to use the data movie-clip event, here's what happens. The action takes place when data is received as the result of a loadVariables or loadMovie action. When you specify this event handler with a loadVariables action, the event occurs only when the data is first loaded. If you specify the event with a loadMovie action, the data event occurs every time a section of data from the movie is loaded.

Calling All Movie Clips with the with Action

If you don't like referring directly to a movie clip's target path, Flash has an action to make life easier for you; the with action. The way the action works is like this: *with* a certain object, this action occurs, or these actions occur. You can use the with action to reference an actual object, such as the math object. When you're beginning, your most common use for the with action is to assign an action to a movie clip without having to create the target path and action with dot syntax. To use the with action:

1. **Select the keyframe or object that you want to trigger the action.**

2. **Click the arrow to the left of the word Actions.**

   The Actions panel opens.

3. **Click Actions⇨Variables, and then double-click** with**.**

   The action is added to the script, and the Object parameter text box appears above the Script pane.

4. **To select the target path of a movie clip, click the black Insert a Target Path button.**

   The Insert Target Path dialog box appears.

5. **Click the button for the movie clip that becomes the object and then click OK.**

   The target path is added to the script.

6. **In the left side of the Actions panel, double-click the action that you want to occur with the object.**

   If, for example, you want to advance to a specific frame in the movie clip, you add the goto action to the script and specify to which frame you want the movie to advance.

   Listing 9-4 shows two sections of code. The first line addresses the movie clip directly by its target path, followed by the action. The remaining lines of code use the with action to accomplish the same thing. The first method is a bit harder to master, but involves fewer steps.

Listing 9-4   Using the with Action

```
_root.musicClip.gotoAndPlay (2);
with (_root.musicClip) {
    gotoAndPlay (2);
}
```

Creating a User-Defined Component — A Movie Clip That Is Wise Beyond Its Years

When you create a movie that you have to update after a time, or if other Flash authors are working on the project with you, using one or more user-defined components can greatly simplify matters. So what the heck is a user-defined component? A movie clip with a PhD from Harvard? Not quite. A *user-defined component* (the movie clip formerly known as smart clip in Flash 5) is a movie clip whose parameters you can change on the fly. User-defined components can have graphic elements whose properties you can quickly change, or they can be a storehouse for variables, a list of objects, or an array that you or another Flash programmer can quickly and easily change without having to modify the code.

Creating a clip and defining its parameters

All user-defined components begin life as a humble movie clip. To create a user-defined component:

1. **Create a movie clip with variables or properties for which you want the capability of changing quickly.**

   One excellent use for a user-defined component is in an e-commerce site where the prices of items need to be updated frequently. You can also create a user-defined component that performs a specific function, such as pausing a movie. Rather than having to rewrite the code every time you change the length of time the movie is paused, you change the user-defined component's parameters.

2. **After you create the user-defined component, choose Window⇨ Library.**

   The document Library opens.

3. **Click the movie clip you just created to select it.**

4. **Right-click (in Windows) or Ctrl+click (on the Macintosh).**

   The document Library context menu appears.

5. **Choose Component Definition.**

   The Component Definition dialog box appears, as shown in Figure 9-9.

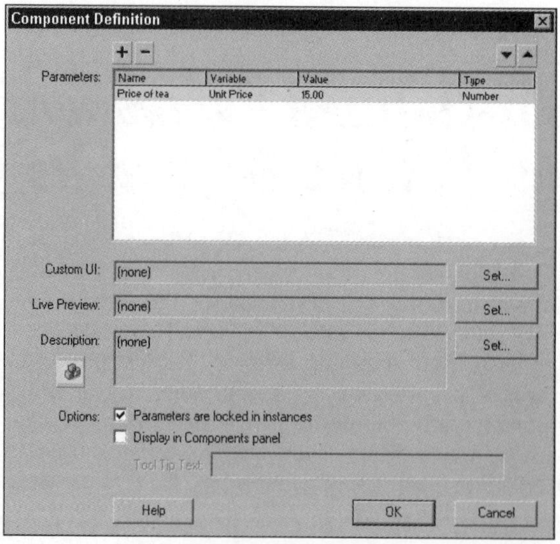

Figure 9-9:
Create a user-defined component whenever your movie has values that you need to frequently change.

6. **Click the plus sign (+) to add an object to the component.**

   The word `default` appears in the Type column.

7. **Double-click `default` in the Type column.**

   A triangle appears next to the word `default`.

8. **Click the triangle.**

   A drop-down menu appears.

9. **Choose one of the following:**

   - **Default:** Lets you enter a string or number value.

   - **Array:** Sets up a blank array that can grow or shrink according to your needs.

   - **Object:** Lets you create a group of objects. This is similar to an array and can grow or shrink according to your needs.

   - **List:** Lets you create a list of several choices, such as values or items. The list option is similar to an array, but the values cannot be changed after an instance of the user-defined component is created; you can only choose an item from the list.

   - **String:** Lets you create a string literal object. Use this object in a component when you want the capability of changing a dynamic text box housed within the component.

   - **Number:** Lets you create numeric data. You can display the contents of this object within a dynamic text box as well. As an added bonus, you can use this object in an Expression and Flash actually does the math. For example, you can add this object to a user-defined component that is used in an e-commerce Flash design where the price of a catalog object changes frequently.

   - **Boolean:** Lets you define whether or not an object is enabled or disabled. An example can be shown if you drag an instance of the Flash UI Scroll Pane component on Stage. Open the Property inspector and look at the parameters for the Scroll bars. They're both set to auto. Choose false for either scroll bar and the scroll bar is no longer visible.

   - **Font Type:** Lets you define a specific font type to be used with a textfield object.

   - **Color:** Lets you modify the color of a textfield object. You can also use this object when creating a user-defined component that uses the Color object.

10. **Double-click a value to define it.**

    The editing you can do depends on the type of item the value is associated with. If the value is for a variable, you can change the variable. If the value is for an object, list, or array, the Values dialog box appears. Click the plus button (+) to add a value to the list; click the minus button (–) to delete an item from the list. To move an item up or down the list, click the appropriate arrow.

11. **Double-click the current listing in the Name field.**

    The listing is highlighted.

12. **Enter a name that describes the information this row of the user-defined component contains.**

    You can have multiple rows of items in a user-defined component. You can have a changeable variable in one row, an array in the next, and an object list in the next. If you're dealing with a variable, enter the name of the variable as it appears in the actual frames of the user-defined component.

13. **In the Description field, add any notes to help you or other programmers working on the project.**

    The information you add in this field can range from memory joggers to instructions on how to use the user-defined component. If you're sharing the user-defined component with other designers or selling the user-defined component, this is a good place to enter copyright information.

14. **Choose Lock in Instance to prevent other users from renaming the parameters in the Clip Parameters panel.**

    Choosing this option prevents other programmers from changing the parameters of an instance of the user-defined component on Stage.

15. **Click OK.**

    The user-defined component is programmed and ready for use.

Setting user-defined component parameters

After you define a clip's parameters, you're ready to use it in your movie. To use a user-defined component, you create an instance of it on Stage. If, for example, you create a user-defined component that pauses a movie for a number of seconds, select the keyframe where you want the movie to pause, and then drag an instance of the user-defined component on Stage. You then set the clip's parameters to determine how long the movie pauses. To set a component's parameters:

1. **Create an instance of the user-defined component on Stage.**

2. **Click the triangle to the left of the word Properties and click the Parameters tab.**

    The component's parameters are displayed in the Property inspector.

3. Double-click a Value field you want to set as shown in Figure 9-10.

- If the field you double-click is a variable, the default variable value is highlighted. Enter a new value.

- If the field is an object, a drop-down menu of all the objects on the list appears. Click an object to select it.

- If the field is an array, a list of all the elements in the array appears. Double-click an element to change its value. Click the plus sign (+) to add an element to the array. Click the minus sign (–) to delete an element from the array. Click the Up arrow to move an element up the order; click the Down arrow to move an element down the order.

4. Close the Property inspector.

The new values are used the next time an item from the user-defined component is called.

Figure 9-10:
You can
change a
user-
defined
component's
parameters.

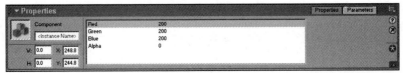

Chapter 10

Sending and Receiving the Written Word

In This Chapter

▶ Creating and working with dynamic text

▶ Loading external data

▶ Creating input text

▶ Creating rich formatted text

*B*efore you began working with ActionScript, most likely you used text to display the written word in your Flash movies. With ActionScript, you can use text boxes to display data stored within variables or to accept data from your movie's viewers. The data you send and receive can be humorous, cantankerous, or downright serious. That decision is in your hands; after all, you are the creator of your Flash movies.

In this chapter, I show you how to create dynamic text boxes that display data from other parts of your movies. I also show you how to create input text boxes. When you have the need for feedback or input from those that view, input text is the only thing that will do.

The Actions panel's got lots of books. And some of these books have books within a book. To add some actions to your scripts, you have to click this book icon, then click that book icon, then click another book icon, and so on. Rather than bore you with a lot of words, I'm going to show the path to each action as shown in the following example: Click Actions⇨Movie Control and then double-click goto.

Working with Dynamic Text

You use *dynamic* text to display string values stored within variables. *Variables* are containers for information that can change throughout the course of your movie. When you use dynamic text, you can display the changing information whenever you want — or whenever you think that viewers of your movie will want. You can use any supported font for dynamic text and size it really, really big or miniscule. In other words, you have lots of options. And remember, the alphabet may be only 26 letters, but when you work with the alphabet, you have every possible word in the English language at your fingertips. Oh, the power!

Creating dynamic text

Before you can display a variable's contents, you need to create a dynamic text box. After the text box is created, you can have the box display a variable's content when a button is clicked, a frame is reached, or a movie clip is loaded. To create a dynamic text box:

1. **Select the Text tool and then click and drag it on Stage.**

   A bounding box appears as you drag the tool. Don't be too concerned about the size of the box; you can change it to the proper size after you've set the text parameters.

2. **Click the arrow to the left of the word Properties.**

   The Property inspector opens.

3. **Click the triangle to the right of the Text Type field and choose Dynamic Text.**

   The text box is now set up to receive information from a variable in your movie, as shown in Figure 10-1.

Figure 10-1:
You use this panel to dynamically create dynamic text.

Text type   Line type

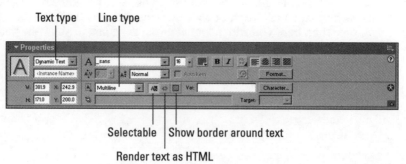

Selectable | Show border around text

Render text as HTML

4. **Click the triangle to the right of the Line Type field and choose one of the following:**

   - **Single Line:** This default option displays the contents of the text box as a single line.

   - **Multiline:** You use this option to display the contents of the text box in multiple lines. If you choose this option, Flash automatically creates a new line when the text exceeds the boundary of the text box.

   - **Multiline no wrap:** You use this option to display text as multiple lines. Flash creates a new line whenever a character is a breaking character creating by pressing Enter (Windows) or Return (Macintosh).

5. **Click the Selectable button and viewers will not be able to select the text.**

   Dynamic text is selectable by default. When the Selectable button is clicked, that means anybody can select the text in a box. Click the button to toggle this option between selectable and not selectable.

6. **Click the Render text as HTML button to use HTML text tags.**

   This option applies to text data that you load into your movie. I show you how to work with the HTML tags in the "Creating rich text" section, which is coming up soon.

7. **To display a border and background for your text box, click the Show Border Around Text button.**

   When the movie is published, Flash displays a background and border around the text.

8. **Enter a name in the Var field.**

   If you don't enter a Var (short for variable) name, guess what? Like Sergeant Schultz of *Hogan's Heroes,* the dynamic text box knows nothing, and you see nothing — except maybe a border and background if you chose that option. Remember to use the proper naming convention for the variable's name. If you're choosing a variable that has already been declared in the movie, make sure that you choose the proper variable and enter the name correctly. If you enter the variable name incorrectly, your script doesn't perform properly.

9. **To embed any fonts with the dynamic text box, click the Character button and choose an option.**

   If you don't know the answer to the age-old question about whether it is nobler to embed or not to embed, check out *Flash MX For Dummies* by Gurdy Leete and Ellen Finklestein (published by Hungry Minds, Inc.).

10. **If you're going to use the dynamic text box with any of the new Flash UI components, enter a name in the <Instance Name> field.**

    Before the end of this chapter, I show you how to create a dynamic text box with scroll handlers. It's cool. It's fun. It's easy.

11. **Resize and align the text box as needed.**

    You can manually resize the text box by clicking it with the Text tool and then dragging the handle, which is a small rectangle in the lower-right corner of the text box. Position the text box by selecting the Arrow tool and then clicking and dragging the box to the position you want; or use the Align panel to align the text box to the Stage or another object.

    After sizing and aligning the text box, it's ready to display the named variable's data.

Even though it's awfully tempting, do not attempt to resize a text box with the Property inspector. The text will be resized proportionately to the text box and your font sizing goes right out the window. Talk about your skewed text.

Loading text data from external sources

The more you work with ActionScript, the more uses you find for dynamic text. If you have large amounts of text data to display, entering the data in the Actions panel can become a tad bothersome; you've got so much text and only a small panel in which to create it. Plus, you have no spell checker. The solution is to create the text in your favorite word processing program and then load the text into a dynamic text box.

Creating the text data

When you create text data in your word processing program, you have to declare the variable within the document and then create the data. To create text data and declare a variable:

1. **Launch your favorite word processing program.**

    While your word processing program is loading, think of a name for the variable. If you've already created the dynamic text box in which the data is displayed, make sure to use the same variable name.

2. **In the first line of the document, enter the name of the variable.**

    For example, if the name of the variable is `company_mission`, the first line in your document reads `company_mission=`.

3. **Complete the document by entering the text you want to display in a dynamic text box.**

   After you create the text, make sure to run it through your word processor's spell checker. Typos on Web sites show a lack of professionalism.

4. **Save the document as a .txt file.**

   Your text file is ready for use in Flash. If your word processing program throws up a red flag warning you that all formatting will be lost, disregard it. All the text formatting attributes are handled by the dynamic text box in which the data is displayed after the data is loaded into the movie, a feat I show you how to accomplish in the next section.

Loading the text data

When you create a text file with for the sole purpose of loading it into a Flash movie, save the file in the same directory as the Flash movie you're creating. You can load the data into the movie at any point on the timeline before the variable is called. To load the text data into your movie:

1. **On your Actions layer, select the keyframe where you want to load the data.**

   If you've been reading each section of this book, you know that I recommend creating a separate layer for any actions in your Flash movie. If you passed Go, forgot to collect your $200, and dove right into this section of this chapter, create an Actions layer before proceeding to Step 2.

2. **Click the arrow to the left of the word Actions.**

   The Actions panel opens. Remember the Actions panel? This is a book about actions.

3. **Click Actions ⇨Browser/Network , and then double-click the** loadVariables **action.**

   The action is added to the script as loadVariablesNum and several fields appear above the Script pane.

4. **In the URL field, enter the name of the text document you created with your word processor.**

   Enter the file's full name, including the .txt extension.

5. **Close the Actions panel.**

   When the movie is published, the loaded file is displayed in the dynamic text box with the same variable name as the loaded data.

Creating rich text

When you create a text file in a word processing program, you can add HTML tags to the text. When you display the data in a dynamic text box, with the HTML option enabled, the text is displayed with the HTML attributes you assigned when you created the original document. You must use both a beginning and ending tag, as you do when you're creating an HTML document. If you apply multiple font tags to a block of string data, you cannot combine the tags; a separate beginning and ending tag are required for each tag. You can use the following HTML tags with string data that is displayed in a dynamic text box: `<A>`, `<B>`, `<I>`, `<P>`, `<U>`, `<FONT SIZE>`, `<FONT FACE>`, and `<FONT COLOR>`.

- `<A HREF="http://www.mysite.com">` string data `</A>`: The string data between the tags is hyperlinked to the specified URL.

- `<B>` string data `</B>`: The string data between these tags is boldfaced.

- `<I>` string data `</I>`: The string data you enter between the tags is italicized.

- `<P>` string data `>` `</P>`: These tags begin and end a paragraph that neatly sandwiches your string data.

- `<U>` string data `</U>`: You use this tag to underline the string data between the tags.

- `<FONT SIZE="x">` string data `</FONT>`: You use this tag to set the font size of the text where *x* is the font size in points.

- `<FONT FACE="XXXX">` string data `</FONT>`: You use this tag to format the font style where XXXX is the name of the font. For the font to be displayed properly, it must be loaded on the viewer's computer; otherwise, it reverts back to the viewer's system font.

- `<FONT COLOR="#xxxxxx">` string data `</FONT>`: You use this tag to specify the color of the string data between the tags where #xxxxxx is the color specified in hexadecimal format.

Figure 10-2 shows a document created in a word processing program that uses HTML tags to format the text. To create string data with rich text formatting:

1. **Launch your favorite word processing program and create the text data you want to display in your Flash movie using the methods outlined in the section "Creating the text data," a little earlier in this section.**

2. **Add the HTML tags to the string data you want to format.**

   Remember to use an ending HTML tag where you want the formatting to end.

3. **Save the document as a .txt file.**

Remember to save the file in the same directory as the Flash movie in which it is used.

4. **Launch Flash and open the movie in which you want to use the word processing file.**

5. **Use the** `loadVariables` **action to load the file into the movie.**

If you jumped right to this section because you like rich text formatting, you may not know how to load the file into the Flash movie. If this is the case, check out the "Loading the text data" section, earlier in this chapter.

6. **Using the Text tool and the Property inspector, create a dynamic text box.**

7. **Choose the Multiline option for text type and click the HTML button.**

If you want to display a border and background around the text, click the Show Border Around Text button as well. If you're not familiar with dynamic text, read the "Creating dynamic text" section, earlier in this chapter.

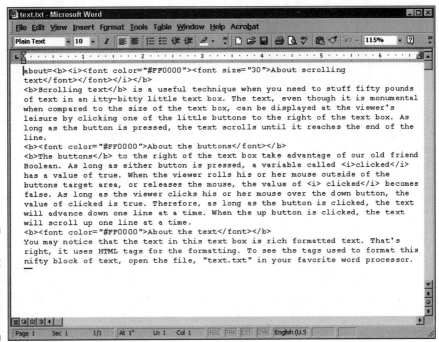

Figure 10-2:
You format
your rich
text in a
word
processor.

8. In Property inspector, select a font size, font style, and font color.

Remember that all your formatting has been done in the file you created in your word processing program. The options you choose in the Character panel are applied to any unformatted string data in the file.

That's all there is to it. After you close the Character panel and publish the movie, the rich text is richly displayed in the dynamic text box with the same variable name. Figure 10-3 shows the string data from the document shown in Figure 10-2 displayed in a dynamic text box. Pretty, isn't it?

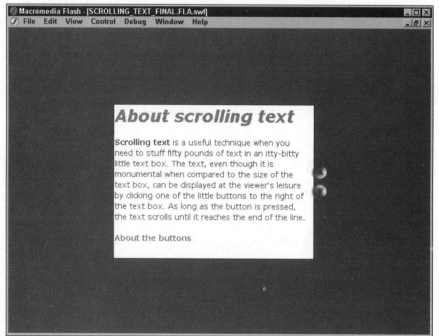

Figure 10-3: Here's some rich-looking text.

Working with Input Text

You use input text when you want to get some information from your movie's viewers. The information can be string literal data, numeric literal data, or numeric data. This data is assigned to a variable that you use to display the submitted data in a dynamic text box, add the data to an array, or transfer the data to a variable, where it's evaluated with a conditional statement. The result of the evaluation determines what happens next in the Flash movie.

For more information on working with variables, plant a bookmark on this page and check out Chapter 6. For more information on conditional statements, place a well-conditioned bookmark on this page and review Chapter 12. The color of the bookmark is at your discretion.

Creating input text

Before you can accept any data from your movie's viewers, you've got to set up an input text box. It's a law. You generally use a button to transfer the data to a dynamic text box or other variable. To create an input text box:

1. **Select the Text tool and then click and drag the tool on Stage.**

   A bounding box appears as you drag the tool. In most cases, you accept a limited amount of data, so a single line is plenty. Release the mouse button when the box is about the right length.

2. **Click the triangle to the left of the word Properties.**

   The Property inspector pops up.

3. **Click the triangle to the right of the Text Type field and choose Input Text.**

   The text box is now set up to receive information from the viewers of your movie, as shown in Figure 10-4.

Text type   Variable

Figure 10-4:
After this
box is set
up, viewers
can enter
data into it.

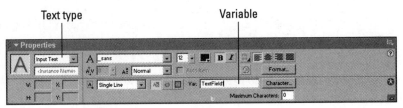

4. **Click the triangle to the right of the Line Type field and choose one of these options:**

   - **Single Line:** This default option accepts the data as a single line.

   - **Multiline:** You use this option to accept multiple lines of data, which Flash wraps to another line if the text exceeds the boundary of your text box.

   - **Multiline no wrap:** When you use this option, Flash only wraps the text to another line when the user presses Enter or Return.

• **Password:** If you choose this option, each character the user enters is shown as an asterisk, enabling the viewer to keep his or her password hidden from onlookers.

5. **Decide whether you want a border and background for your text box.**

   Click the Show Border Around Text button and Flash displays a background and border around the input text box. You should use this option whenever you create an input text box; otherwise, it can't be seen unless the viewer happens to click it. After clicking an input text box, a flashing cursor appears in it, which signifies to viewers that they can enter data.

6. **Enter a name in the Var field.**

   Use the same variable name as the dynamic text box in which the data is displayed or as the variable name in the conditional statement in which the data is evaluated.

7. **In the Max Chars field, enter a value.**

   The value you enter limits how many characters the input text box accepts. When you enter a value in the Max Chars field, your movie's viewers can type until they induce carpal tunnel syndrome; still, the input text box never displays more characters than the value you enter.

8. **Click the Character button, and then click one or more of the buttons to embed the font character set.**

   If you don't choose any option in this section, the viewer can enter any character and it is transferred to the input text box's variable. If, however, you want to limit the type of character the variable accepts, choose one of the Character options. For example, if you want only numeric data transferred to the variable, click the Only radio button, and then click the Numerals (0–9) check box.

9. **Resize and align the text box as needed.**

   You can manually resize the text box by clicking it with the Text tool and then dragging the rectangular handle in the lower-right corner of the text box. Select the box with the Arrow tool and drag the box to the desired position; or use the Align panel to align the text box to the Stage or another object.

   After you size and align the input text box, it's ready to receive data.

Creating hyperlinked text

You know those Web pages where you see those nasty little lines of text that are blue in color with an ugleeeeeeeeeeeeeeeeeeeeeee line underneath? You may know these are hyperlinks to other Web pages. In Flash MX, you can now create text hyperlinks of any size or color you want. You can have them open up in another browser window and all sorts of cool stuff. Yeah, big time Web designers can do that stuff, too, but they've got to create something called a Cascading Style Sheet to do it. You don't — you can create hyperlinked text with a little help from the Property inspector. Here's how:

1. **Select the Text tool, click a spot on Stage where you want the text to appear, and type something.**

   Your words of wisdom appear on Stage.

2. **Click the arrow to the left of the word Properties.**

   The Property inspector opens.

3. **Select the text and then specify the font size, font color, and alignment of the text.**

4. **In the URL field, enter the URL of the site you want the text to link to, as shown in Figure 10-5.**

   If the HTML document the text links to is in the same Web site, you can enter the relative path to the document; for example, `myPage.html`. If the linked document exists in another Web site, enter the entire URL; for example, `http://www.dasdesigns.net`.

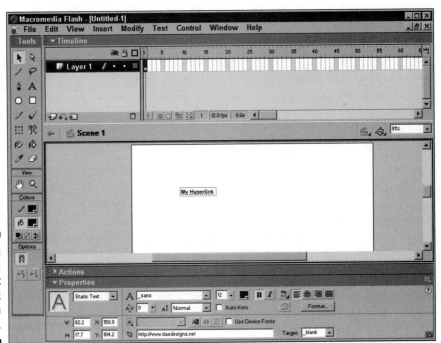

Figure 10-5:
Creating a text hyperlink in Flash is easy.

5. **Click the triangle to the right of the Target field and choose one of the following options:**

- **_blank** opens the linked document in a brand-new, unnamed browser window.

- **_parent** loads the linked document in the window of the frame that contains the link. If the frame isn't nested, the linked document loads in the full browser window.

- **_self** loads the linked document in the same frame or window as the link.

- **_top** loads the document in the full browser window, removing all frames.

And that's all there is to it. When the movie is published and users roll a mouse over the text, the familiar hand pops up. When the text link is clicked, the HTML page opens up in the target you specified in Step 5. HTML links in Flash couldn't be any simpler.

Scrolling Text — The Fast and Easy Way

In Chapter 14, I show you how to create a scrolling text box worthy of the greatest literature ever written. But sometimes a client — or you, for that matter — want it done yesterday. When you fall pressure to time constraints and don't have time to create a literary masterpiece scrolling text box, you can use one of the new Flash UI components to get one up and running quicker than you can say Ticonderoga, if you can say Ticonderoga. To create a scrolling text box without breaking a sweat:

1. **Select the Text tool and click the arrow to the left of the word Properties.**

   The Property inspector opens.

2. **Click the triangle to the right of the Text type field and choose Dynamic Text from the drop-down menu.**

   The Text tool is in dynamic text mode.

3. **Drag on Stage to define the area of your text box.**

   Drag across and down to define the size of your text box. Remember you can always resize the box with the Text tool if it's not perfectly sized for your design.

4. **In the Property inspector, specify the font size, font color, and alignment.**

5. **Click the triangle to the right of the Line Type field and choose Multiline.**

6. **In the <Instance Name> field, enter a name for the dynamic text box.**

   When you name the text object, you give the scroll bar a target.

7. **Select the text box with the Arrow tool, right-click (Windows) or Ctrl-click (Macintosh) and then choose scrollable from the drop-down menu.**

   Now you can dump all kinds of text in the field and it won't resize the text box.

8. **Double-click the text field.**

   When you double-click an input text field with the Arrow tool, it reverts to text-editing mode and your cursor becomes an I-beam.

9. **Place your cursor inside the dynamic text field and type away.**

If you've got copious amounts of text to enter, consider creating the text in your favorite word processing program. Spell-check the text and then copy it to the clipboard. Place your cursor inside the dynamic text box and then right-click (Windows) or Ctrl+click (Macintosh) and choose Paste from the drop-down menu. If the text box expands to accept the text, you forgot to do Step 7 from the preceding section.

Now that you've got your text in place, it's time to make it scroll. To do so, you use one of the new Flash UI components known as the Scroll Bar. This little jewel snaps to the dynamic text box like white on rice. To add the scroll bar to the text box:

1. **If you display the default panel window in the right side of the workspace, click the triangle to the left of the word Components; otherwise, choose Window⇨Components.**

   The component panel opens.

2. **Select the Scroll Bar component, drag it into the dynamic text box, and release the mouse button.**

   The scroll bar develops a magnetic attraction for the dynamic text box and snaps to right size.

3. **Open the Property inspector.**

   The parameters for the component are displayed as shown in Figure 10-6. When you release the component inside the text box, Flash associates the instance name with the Scroll Bar component.

   4. **For a horizontal scroll bar, click the word** `false` **and an arrow appears to the right of the field.**

   By default you have a vertical scroll bar to work with; otherwise, what's the use of a scrolling text field. If you want the ability to shrink the text box to less than the width of the text and use a horizontal scroll bar too, you can by following the next step.

   5. **Click the arrow and choose** `true` **to create a horizontal scroll bar.**

   That's pretty much it. When you publish the movie, the scroll bar becomes active and viewers of your published movie can crank up the juke box and scroll the day away to "Twistin' the Night Away."

   4. **For a horizontal scroll bar, click the word** `false` **and an arrow appears to the right of the field.**

   By default you have a vertical scroll bar to work with, otherwise what's the use of a scrolling text field. If you want the ability to shrink the text box to less than the width of the text and use a horizontal scroll bar too, you can by following the next step.

   5. **Click the arrow and choose** `true` **to create a horizontal scroll bar.**

   That's pretty much it. When you publish the movie, the scroll bar becomes active and viewers of your published movie can crank up the juke box and scroll the day away to "Twistin' the Night Away."

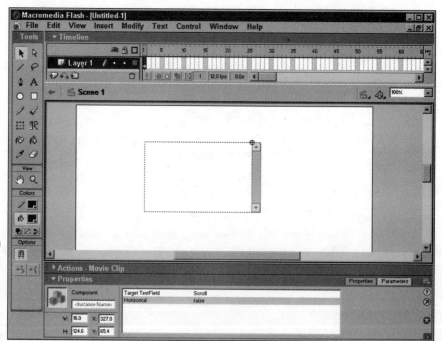

Figure 10-6:
Even
a scroll
bar has
parameters.

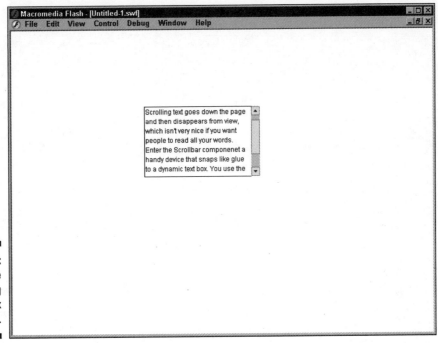

Figure 10-7:
The little
scrolling
text box
that could.

Chapter 11

Creating Interactive Buttons and Menus

*I*f you build it, they will come, but the trick is to get them to stay. To do that, you give your visitors a way to navigate around your Flash movie and give them a few toys to play with, such as drag-and-drop menus and other cool stuff. After all, what's a Flash site without a few bells and whistles?

In this chapter, I show you how to create interactive buttons that do different things depending on where the user's mouse is in relation to the button. I also show you how to create drag-and-drop items. Last, but not least, I show you how to create a fully customizable menu. Let the fun begin.

 The Actions panel's got lots of books. And some of these books have books within a book. To add some actions to your scripts, you have to click this book icon, then click that book icon, then click another book icon, and so on. Rather than bore you with a lot of words, I'm going to show the path to each action as shown in the following example: Click Actions⇨Movie Control and then double-click `goto`.

Building a Button

A basic Flash button has four states: New York, New Jersey, Rhode Island, and California. Just kidding. If you already know how to create a Flash button, by all means move on to the next section. If you could stand a brief refresher course, read the rest of this section. You have four button states to work with.

The simplest button uses one state, the Over state. When you use more than one of a button's states, you change the graphic in each state. When a user rolls his mouse over the button, he sees a different image, and the oohs and ahhs begin — at least you hope they do, if your intention was to razzle and dazzle your viewer. After you've got your viewer hooked, your Flash movie's level of coolness has just jumped up a notch or two.

When you create a button symbol, you have a timeline with four frames. When you first create a new button symbol, only the Over state has a keyframe. To add any of the other states to your button, you convert the state's frame to a keyframe. The four button states are

- **Up:** This is the default state of the button when the button is visible in the movie.

- **Over:** The graphic in this state's keyframe is displayed when the user's mouse rolls over the button.

- **Down:** The graphic in this state's keyframe is displayed when the button is clicked.

- **Hit:** The graphic in this state's keyframe isn't seen when the movie is published. It merely serves as a target area for the button. If you have a large graphic in the other three states, you definitely don't need to use the Hit state. However, if you have a dainty (read miniscule, which is just a notch or two above infinitesimal) little button, or a button made up of a graphic object and some text, use the Hit state and create a graphic large enough to blanket all the objects that make up the button.

Remember that you can also add layers to a button. For example, if you want to add sounds to a button, you add an additional layer and then add the appropriate sounds. As a rule, you add sound to the Down state or the Hit state. To create a button:

1. **Choose Insert⇨New Symbol.**

   The Create New Symbol dialog box appears.

2. **Enter a name for the button, assign the Button behavior, and then click OK.**

   Flash enters symbol-editing mode. Before you go any further, ask yourself whether you're going to have a different graphic in each state or a variation of the same graphic in each state. If you're choosing the former, go to Step 3; otherwise, go to Step 5.

3. **Convert the frame for each state you're going to use into a blank keyframe by selecting it and then pressing F7.**

4. **Create a different graphic for each button's frame.**

   Remember that you can create a new graphic for each button state or use an existing one from the document Library. Using an existing symbol reduces the file size of the published movie.

5. **Create a graphic for the Over state.**

6. **Create a keyframe for any other states you're using.**

   The graphic in the first frame is carried over to the new frames.

7. **Modify the graphic in each frame so that the viewer sees something different when the button is rolled over and clicked.**

   If you created a graphic object from scratch, you can change the object's fill and transform it with menu commands or tools. If the graphic in the first frame is a symbol from the document Library, you can change the way it looks by applying an effect to it using one of the Effects available in the Color section of the Property inspector. You can also change its scale or rotate it by using either the Free Transform tool, the Property inspector, or the Info and Transform panels. Figure 11-1 shows a button being created. This button uses all four states. Onion skins have been enabled so that you can see the graphic used in each state. Please note that the button in this screenshot has been magnified for better visibility. You may also notice that the graphic in the Hit frame looks particularly hideous. Not to worry: Any graphic you put in the Hit frame is invisible when the movie is published.

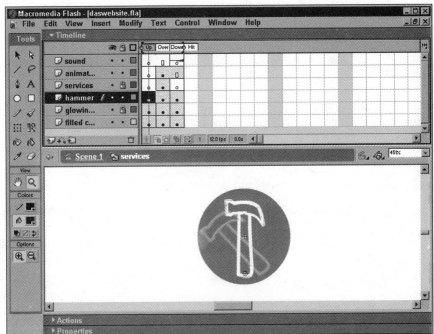

Figure 11-1:
A button
has four
neighboring
states.

8. **When you're done creating the button, click the Back button or current scene button to return to movie-editing mode.**

   The button is added to the document Library.

Even though a button has four frames, you cannot assign actions to them. The frames are simply placeholders for graphics, text, or sounds.

Programming a button

After you create a button, you program it to make it do something other than just stand there looking very button-like. You can use a button to link to another frame in your movie, load another movie, or reveal a game clue when it's clicked. You can also program a button to perform a single action when it's clicked or to perform multiple actions depending on where the user's mouse is in relation to the button. To assign code to a button:

1. **Select the button you want to program.**

2. **Click the arrow to the left of the word Actions.**

   The Actions panel opens.

3. **Choose the action you want executed as a result of the user's interaction with the button.**

   Flash adds the action to the script. The action is preceded by the default mouse event handler, on (release), as shown in Figure 11-2.

   The Release mouse event handler executes the action on the up stroke (release) of the button. You can choose from a total of nine mouse events. If you want more interactivity in your Flash buttons, read the next section, where I show you how to use the different mouse event handlers.

Event handlers

Figure 11-2:
When you
use the
Release
mouse
event
handler, the
actions are
executed
when the
mouse
button is
released.

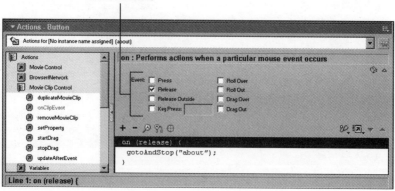

Using the mouse event handlers

When you program a button, many things can happen at the same time, or different things can happen, depending on where the movie viewer's mouse is in relation to the button. For example, you can program a button to play a movie clip when a user's mouse rolls over a button, stop the movie clip when the user rolls her mouse out of the button's field of influence, and load a movie when the user clicks the button. When you're programming a button that uses multiple mouse events, you can begin by assigning the first action to the button and then selecting an event from the parameters area, or you can use the on action. To use the on action:

1. **Select the button you want to program.**

2. **Click the arrow to the left of the word Actions.**

   The Actions panel opens.

3. **Click Actions⇨Movie Control , and then double-click the on action.**

   The default on (release) event handler is added to the script.

4. **Add the action you want to occur when the mouse button is released, or select a different mouse event handler by selecting it in the parameters area, which is conveniently located due north of the Script pane.**

   You can use more than one mouse event handler for a single action. To see what each event handler does, check out the following section.

Selecting a mouse event handler

If you decide to use one or more event handlers or use a different mouse event handler to trigger an action, you select it in the parameters area. Choose one or more of the following events:

- **Press:** The action is executed when the button is pressed (the down stroke of a button click).

- **Release:** The action is executed when the button is released (the up stroke of a click).

- **Release Outside:** The action is executed after the button has been clicked and the user releases the mouse button outside the target area of the button.

- **Key Press:** The action that follows is executed when a key is pressed.

✔ **Roll Over:** The action is executed when the user's mouse rolls over the button.

✔ **Roll Out:** The action is executed after the user's mouse rolls over and then rolls out of the button's area of influence.

✔ **Drag Over:** The action is executed when the user clicks the mouse button and drags over the button.

✔ **Drag Out:** The action is executed when a user clicks the mouse button, drags over the button, and drags beyond the button's target area.

You can use more than one mouse event handler per action. When you use multiple mouse event handlers, any event handler you assign to the action triggers it. You can also accept keyboard input to trigger an action, a feat I show you how to accomplish in the next section.

Accepting keyboard input

You can also use keyboard input to trigger an action. This mouse event handler is known as the Key Press, which is a misnomer because a computer mouse can't press a key — unless, of course, viewers have trained mice as pets that press a key on demand. In defense of the programmers, putting keyboard input with the mouse event handlers is logical, though. To use the Key Press mouse event:

1. **Select the button you want to program and then assign an action to it.**

   Flash adds the action to the script preceded by the mouse event handler you specified.

2. **Directly above the Script pane, click the Key Press event.**

   The event is selected and added to the script, and a field opens to the right of the Key Press event in the parameter text box area. If you want the Key Press mouse event only to trigger the action, deselect any other mouse events.

3. **Perform the keyboard event that you want to trigger the action.**

   For example, if you want the action executed when the Enter or Return button is pressed, press the Enter or Return key on your computer's keyboard, and Flash adds the key press to the script. Figure 11-3 shows a line of code that is executed when either the mouse button is released or Enter is pressed.

Certain keys are reserved for the system, for example: Ctrl (Windows) or ⌘ (Macintosh), Alt (Windows) or Option (Macintosh). If you choose a reserved key, the field remains blank. Click another key.

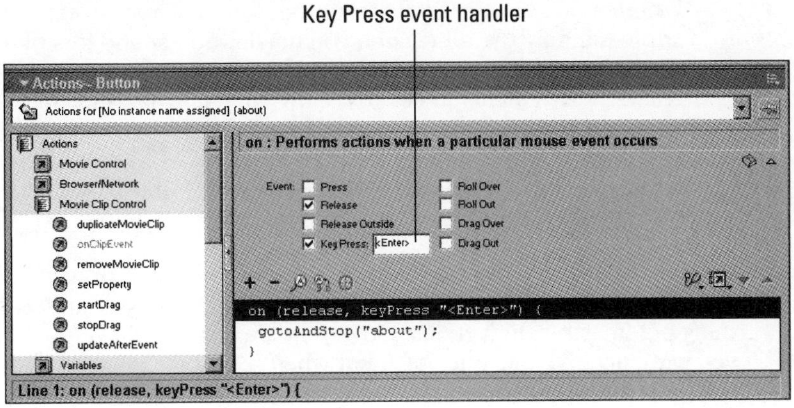

Key Press event handler

Figure 11-3:
Choose the
key press
event
handler to
trigger an
action with
a key press.

Creating an Invisible Button

Invisible buttons cannot be seen. Wow! — now there's one of my more profound statements. Even though invisible buttons can't be seen, they're useful for your ActionScripts. You can use an invisible button to create a "hot spot" on Stage that functions as a clue in a game. For example, when a user rolls his mouse over the invisible button, a clue appears, or another scene opens, advancing the player to the next level. Invisible buttons are also useful when you're displaying large blocks of text. You add a stop action to halt the movie while the viewer reads your words of wisdom. Lurking behind the text — on the button layer, of course — is an invisible button that is programmed to play the movie when clicked. Be sure to add the instruction to click the text; otherwise, the viewer may think that the movie ends with the text. Remember that the viewer has no idea you've been clever enough to use an invisible button. You also use invisible buttons when you're creating drag-and-drop objects. To create an invisible button:

1. **Choose Insert⇨New Symbol.**

   The Create New Symbol dialog box appears.

2. **Choose the Button behavior and click OK.**

   Flash enters symbol-editing mode.

3. **Click the Hit frame and then choose Insert⇨Keyframe.**

   A keyframe is born.

4. **Create a shape with one of the tools.**

   I like to use the Rectangle tool when I create an invisible button. It works with just about everything. But if you've got your mind set on a spiffy oval invisible button, knock yourself out.

Whether you use the Oval tool or the Rectangle tool, create a shape that's approximately the dimension you need. Don't spend lots of time sizing the button. Remember that the finished button is a symbol. You can resize individual instances of the invisible button as needed.

5. Click the Back button or current scene button.

Flash exits symbol-editing mode, and the invisible button is added to the document Library.

When you need to use an invisible button for an object, drag an instance of it out of the Library. When you see the button on Stage, you notice that it's anything but invisible. In fact, it's a lovely shade of aqua blue ("the better to see you with, my invisible button!"). But when the movie is published, the button is indeed invisible. The only clue that your viewers get is when their cursor changes to the time-honored pointing hand when the mouse rolls over the button.

Creating Drag-and-Drop Objects

Drag-and-drop objects are useful critters. I know that my cat drags her favorite toy and drops it wherever she pleases. In Flash, you use drag-and-drop objects in games, in e-commerce sites, or as the basis for a drag-and-drop menu — something I show you how to create before the end of this chapter.

To create a drag-and-drop object, you use ActionScript. When you create a drag-and-drop object, it begins life as a movie clip. There are two types of drag-and-drop objects you can create: one that displays the hand cursor when a user rolls her mouse over it, and one that can be dragged and dropped but doesn't change the user's cursor. Both types can be dragged and dropped in the same manner. I prefer the type that changes the user's cursor; that way, she knows that she has something she can interact with. To make this little jewel, you nest an invisible button in the movie clip.

Creating an Element That Can Be Dragged

To create an element that can be dragged, simply create a movie clip. The movie clip can have one frame, or as many frames as you want. If you want to show an animation in a movie clip that can be dragged, use as many frames as you need. After the movie clip is created, you use the startDrag action to enable dragging and use the stopDrag action to disable dragging. The event handler you use depends on whether you use a movie clip by itself or nest an invisible button in the movie clip.

My favorite method of creating a drag-and-drop object is to nest a button within the movie clip. To nest an invisible button in a movie clip:

1. **Drag from the document Library to the Stage an instance of the movie clip you want to convert to a drag-and-drop object.**

   The movie clip can be a multiframe animation or a single-frame movie clip with just a graphic.

2. **Double-click the movie clip instance to enter symbol-editing mode.**

   Flash opens the movie clip in another window.

3. **Create a new layer and label it *Invisible Button.***

   You can call the layer anything you want. Naming it Invisible Button makes it easier for you to understand what's on the layer if you have to revise the movie in a month or two. It also makes it easier for any other designer working on the project to know what the layer is for.

4. **Select the first frame on the Invisible Button layer.**

5. **Drag an instance of an invisible button from the document Library.**

   If you have no invisible button in your Library, create one using the steps outlined in the "Creating an Invisible Button" section, earlier in this chapter.

6. **Resize and align the button as needed.**

   The size and positioning of the button depend on the type of drag-and-drop object you're creating. For example, if you're creating a drag-and-drop menu with a tab in its upper-left corner, you resize the button so that it's slightly bigger than the tab and positioned directly over the tab.

7. **Click the Back button to return to movie-editing mode.**

   The invisible button is safely nestled within the object. To make it a drag-and-drop object, you use the `startDrag` action.

Using the startDrag action

You use the `startDrag` action to convert an instance of a movie clip into an object that can be dragged. The action has parameters that you can use to limit the range in which the object can be dragged. To use the `startDrag` action:

1. **Select an instance of the movie clip to which you want to assign the action.**

   If you don't have an instance of the movie clip on Stage, select it from the document Library, drag it on Stage, and then position it.

2. **Click the arrow to the left of the word Properties.**

   The Property inspector opens.

3. **Enter a name for the instance in the <Instance Name> field.**

   The name you choose appears in the Insert Target Path dialog box.

4. **Double-click the movie clip.**

   Flash enters symbol-editing mode. If your movie clip doesn't have an invisible button nested in it, follow the steps in the preceding section to add an invisible button on its own layer.

5. **Select the invisible button.**

   If you've been an efficient ActionScripter, the button is on its own layer. Follow Steps 6 – 12 to finish programming the invisible button. When you're finished, click the Back button to return to movie-editing mode.

6. **Click the arrow to the left of the word Actions.**

   The Actions panel opens.

7. **Click Actions⇨Movie Clip Control and then double-click startDrag.**

   The action is added to the script and the parameter text boxes appear, as shown in Figure 11-4. Notice that the stopDrag action is also added to this ActionScript. To figure out what that's all about, Alfie, you have to read the next section.

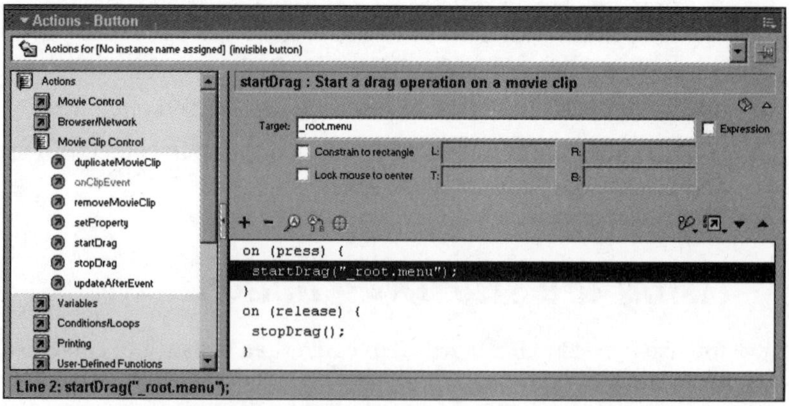

Figure 11-4:
This action
makes an
object kind
of a drag.

8. **Click inside the Target field and then click the Insert a Target Path button (the tiny black button just above the Script pane).**

   The Insert Target Path dialog box opens.

9. **Click the button for the movie clip's target path and then click OK.**

   The Insert Target Path Dialog box closes.

10. **To constrain the area in which the object can be dragged, click the Constrain to Rectangle box.**

    Four fields become active above the Script pan: L, R, T, and B.

11. **In the L (left), R (right), T (top), and B (bottom) fields, enter values to define the area in which the object can be dragged.**

    These values are in pixels. If your movie is 550 pixels x 400 pixels, the values for unrestrained motion are L=0, R=550, T=0, and B=400. Enter any values greater than L or T values, and less than R and B values to constrain the motion to a specific area of the Stage, for example, if you want to constrain dragging horizontally along a 200 pixel range, type **L=0, R=200, T=0, B=0**.

    This option constrains motion relative to the document, in other words the 0,0 coordinates are the upper-left hand corner of the Stage. To constrain motion relative to the object's position on Stage, you must nest the movie clip that will be dragged within a movie clip and name it. The constraints you apply are then based on the object's reference point when you created the symbol. In other words, the 0,0 reference point is the center of the Stage and not the upper-left corner of the Stage.

12. **Click the Lock Mouse to Center box, and the object's center will be locked to the mouse's coordinates as it's dragged.**

The actual event handler you use to begin dragging the object depends on whether you assigned the `startDrag` action to the movie clip itself or to an invisible button nested within the movie clip. If you assigned the action directly to the movie clip, use the `Mouse down` event handler. If you assigned the action to an invisible button, use the `Press` event handler.

Using the stopDrag action

After you assign the `startDrag` action to an object, it sticks like glue to the mouse, faithfully following it like a puppy on a leash (and never once stopping to lift its leg on a virtual tree). However, as with your puppy, you've got to unleash the object at some point. If you don't, the object becomes — ahem — well, kind of a drag. To cease and desist dragging, you use the `stopDrag` action. As a rule, you assign this action at the same time you assign the `startDrag` action; you just use a different event handler to tell Flash to give up the object's fatal attraction to the mouse. To assign the `stopDrag` action to an object:

1. **Open the Actions panel, click Actions⇨Movie Clip Control and then double-click the `stopDrag` action.**

   The action is added to the script using the default event handler for the object to which the action is assigned to.

2. **If you've assigned the action to a movie clip, use the** `Mouse up` **event handler; if the action is assigned to an invisible button nested within a movie clip, use the** `Release` **event handler.**

   After you publish the movie, when the movie clip or mouse event handler occurs, the `stopDrag` action executes and the object stops. Refer to Figure 11-4 to see the `stopDrag` action in action.

Assembling a Customizable Menu

Creating Flash objects with ActionScript is time consuming. After you create a Flash object you're especially proud of, you can use it in other Flash movies by using the Copy Frames command to copy all the frames used to create the effect and then use the Paste Frames command to paste them into a movie clip. Then, whenever you need to use the Flash object in another movie, you simply use the Open as Library command to open the document Library in which your little gem is stored. Drag the object into the current document's Library, and you're off to the races. If you've created everything using symbols, you can easily modify the size and colors of the objects to suit the new movie. In this section, I show you how to create a customizable menu. The finished menu has rollover buttons and can be dragged.

To follow along with this exercise, locate the modular_menu_begin.fla file, which is in this chapter's folder on the CD that accompanies this book. Copy the file to your hard drive and use your computer's operating system to disable the file's read-only attributes.

Laying out the menu

The first step involved in creating the menu is to assemble the various components and align them. To lay out the customizable menu:

1. **Launch Flash, choose File⇨Open, and then locate and open the modular_menu_begin.fla file.**

2. **Choose Window⇨Library.**

   The document Library opens. Notice that I've already created a few items for you to work with.

3. **Choose Insert⇨New Symbol.**

   The Create New Symbol dialog box opens.

4. **Type menu for the name, choose the Movie Clip behavior, and then click OK.**

   Flash enters symbol-editing mode.

5. **Create the following layers: Background, Buttons, Text, and Invisible Button.**

   Creating individual layers makes it easier for you to select and manipulate each object.

6. **Click the Background layer to select it, and then drag an instance of the Menu background graphic on Stage and center it.**

   You can center the object using the Align panel, the Info panel, or the ever-present Property inspector.

7. **Click the Buttons layer, drag an instance of the button symbol from the Library on Stage, and then center the instance just below the red line on the background graphic.**

   You've now got one button for your menu. The menu you construct in this set of steps will have four buttons.

8. **To create another instance of the first button, select the button, hold down the Alt key (in Windows) or Option key (on the Macintosh), and drag.**

   Flash creates a new instance of the button.

9. **Repeat Step 8 until you have a total of four buttons.**

10. **Position the last button just above the bottom of the menu.**

11. **Select all the buttons and then, using the Align panel, center them horizontally to the Stage.**

    The buttons align to the center of the Stage.

12. **In the Align panel, deselect the Stage button and then click the Distribute Vertical Center button.**

    The buttons are aligned and spaced. At this stage, your menu should resemble the one shown in Figure 11-5.

13. **Choose Window⇨Library.**

    The document Library opens.

14. **Drag an instance of the invisible button onto the Stage and position it over the tab.**

    The button is larger than the tab. Use the Free Transform tool to cut it down to size.

15. **Click the Text layer to select it.**

16. **Select the Text tool.**

17. **Click the arrow to the left of the word Properties.**

    The Property inspector opens.

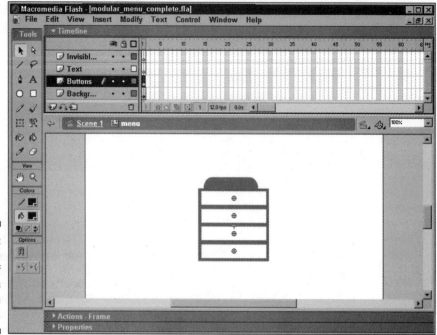

Figure 11-5:
Create
instances of
the buttons
and align
them.

18. **Choose a font style, font size, and font color.**

    For the purpose of this exercise, choose the Impact font (or a bold font, if you don't have that one on your computer), choose 14 for the font size, and choose white for the color.

19. **Type** menu **and then position the text over the tab.**

20. **In the Property inspector, change the font color to the same blue as the menu background.**

    You can quickly do this step by clicking the color swatch in the Property inspector and then clicking the menu background graphic to sample the graphic's color.

21. **Type** home **and then align the text to the left and center of the first button.**

22. **Repeat Step 21 for the rest of the buttons, but change the text to** about us, contact us, **and** links. **Your completed menu should resemble the one shown in Figure 11-6.**

23. **Click the Back button to return to movie-editing mode.**

    The menu movie clip is added to the document Library.

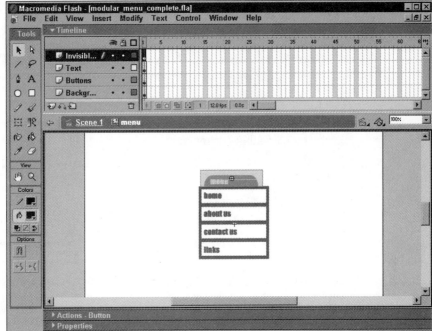

Figure 11-6:
Buttons and
text — what
more could
a menu
ask for?

Finishing the menu

The menu movie clip is now ready to use, with the exception of programming the invisible button and the menu buttons. The first step is to create an instance of the movie clip:

1. **Choose Window⇨Library.**

   The document Library opens.

2. **Click the Menu movie clip to select it and then drag it on Stage.**

   You now have an instance of the menu in your movie. Use the Arrow tool or Align panel to position the menu.

3. **Click the arrow to the left of the word Properties.**

   The Property inspector opens.

4. **In the <Instance Name> field, enter a name for the movie clip.**

   The name you choose will be part of the target path to the movie clip. Choose a name that reflects what the movie clip does. In this case, menu is an excellent choice.

Programming the invisible button

You program the invisible button to turn the movie clip into a drag-and-drop object. The invisible button — as well as the other buttons — are nested within the movie clip. Therefore, you must program them in symbol-editing mode. Here's how:

1. **Choose Edit⇨Edit Selected.**

   Flash enters symbol-editing mode.

2. **Click the invisible button and then click the arrow to the left of the word Actions.**

   The Actions panel opens.

3. **Click Actions⇨Movie Clip Control and then double-click** startDrag.

   The action is added to the script, and you've got a few parameter text boxes to deal with.

4. **Click inside the Target field and then click the black Insert a Target Path button.**

   The Insert Target Path dialog box opens.

5. **Click the movie clip's button and then click OK.**

   The target path is added to the script.

6. **Click the last line of code (the curly brace) and in the left pane of the Actions panel, double-click** stopDrag.

   The action is added to the script.

7. **Click the first line of the script, which should read** on(release).

8. **In the parameter text box area, change the event to Press.**

   The default on(release) action executes the startDrag action when the mouse is released; you need the action to start when a user presses the mouse button. Accept the default event handler — on (release) — for the stopDrag action.

9. **Click the Current Scene button or Back button to exit symbol-editing mode.**

10. **Choose Control⇨Test Movie.**

    Flash publishes the movie and opens another window. To make sure that your code is correct, click the menu and drag it. If the menu doesn't follow the mouse and stop when you release the mouse button, compare your code to the code shown in Figure 11-7.

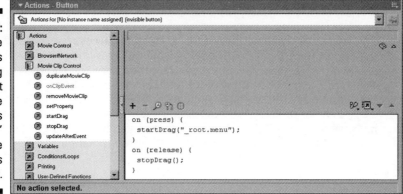

Figure 11-7:
This code
does
everything
except
paste a note
that says
"Drag me"
on the
movie clip's
back.

Programming the buttons

To make your menu fully functional, you have to program the buttons. I
know: More work! But, hey — this book is about ActionScript, a word that
you couldn't spell yesterday, and now you're creating one. Unfortunately, no
two movies are alike, so I can't instruct you on exactly how to program each
button. If you've been following this chapter from the beginning, you know
that each button is nested within the menu movie. To program the buttons,
you have to enter symbol-editing mode and then apply the necessary code to
each button. Listing 11-1 shows an example of code you may use on a button.

Listing 11-1   Assigning Code to a Button

```
on (rollOver) {
  _root.about_MC.gotoAndPlay (begin_movie);
}
on (release) {
  _root.about_MC.gotoAndStop (stop_movie);
}
on (release) {
  unloadMovieNum (1);
  loadMovieNum ("about_us.swf", 1);
}
```

If, for some reason, your menu didn't work correctly, locate the file named
modular_menu_complete.fla that is located in this chapter's folder on the CD
that accompanies this book. Use your computer operating system to disable
the file's read-only attributes. Open the file in Flash and compare the code to
what you just created.

Using the menu in other movies

The menu you create in this section is modular. To use the menu in another movie, use the Open as Library command and then drag an instance of the menu movie clip into the movie you're working on. You can then edit the movie clip in symbol-editing mode and change the text for each button. You can also modify the original symbols used to create the menu, changing their size and color to suit your movie. After that, all you have to do is program the invisible button and the menu buttons, and you're good to go. It's much quicker than creating a new menu from scratch. Trust me.

Chapter 12

Keeping Score with ActionScript and Other Delights

*W*hen you want to take a vacation, first you evaluate a set of conditions before deciding whether you can go. First and foremost, you make sure that you have the luxury of available vacation time. Second, you evaluate the state of your bank account to see whether you have enough discretionary income (also known as mad money) to afford the trip. If both those conditions are true, you take the vacation. This is a perfect example of a conditional statement. In Flash, you use conditional statements to determine what set of actions occurs next. In this chapter, I show you how to create conditional statements with string data and numeric data. I also show you how to use the mathematical operators so that your Flash movies add up. Just kidding. But the mathematical operators are quite useful when you're creating e-commerce sites and keeping score in games.

The Actions panel's got lots of books. And some of these books have books within a book. To add some actions to your scripts, you have to click this book icon, then click that book icon, then click another book icon, and so on. Rather than bore you with a lot of words, I'm going to show the path to each action as shown in the following example: Click Actions⇨Movie Control and then double-click goto.

Working with Conditional Statements

You use a conditional statement when you want Flash to evaluate a certain parameter or set of parameters. If the conditional statement is true, one set of actions occurs; if the statement is false, another set of actions occurs. Conditional statements begin with the if action, which really is quite logical, you know. It wouldn't be logical to start a conditional statement with a done deal, would it?

Consider the decision process you make when you decide whether to put the top down on your spiffy new convertible. If the sun is shining, you put the top down; otherwise, you leave the top up. In ActionScript, you would start this statement with an if, but otherwise it would be replaced by the else action. If you were to create ActionScript for this decision-making process of whether to go top-down or top-up, it would look like Listing 12-1.

Listing 12-1　Conditional Statements 101

```
If (sun is shining){
I put the top down
{ else {
I leave the top up
  }
If (sun is shining}{
I put the top down
} else {
I leave the top up
}
```

Suppose that this statement had been an actual ActionScript rather than your mind planning a Sunday drive. If the first statement had been true, the second line of the ActionScript would have been executed; if not, the line of code after the else action would be executed. In this listing, the condition is in parentheses. This is exactly as you would see it within Flash ActionScript.

Creating conditional statements

You create a conditional statement when you want to put a fork in your Flash movie's road. Which fork the movie takes depends on the outcome of the statement. The operators you use to evaluate the statement differ depending on whether you're evaluating string data or numeric data. You can assign a conditional statement to an object or a keyframe. To create a conditional statement:

1. **Select the object or keyframe where you want to create the conditional statement.**

2. **Click the arrow to the left of the word Actions.**

   The Actions panel opens.

3. **Click Actions⇨Conditions/Loops and then double-click** `if`.

   The `if` action is added to the script, and the Condition parameter text box appears.

4. **Enter the condition that must be true for the next line of the script to execute.**

   The actual condition varies from script to script. For example, if you're creating a conditional statement to evaluate the answer to a quiz, the condition may look something like this: `(answer 1=="Puff the Magic Dragon")`. Notice that a conditional statement is a Boolean expression. It can have one of two outcomes: true or false. The next step is to determine what happens if Flash evaluates the statement as true and what happens if the statement is not true.

5. **Add the action to the script that occurs if the statement evaluates as true.**

   You can have Flash execute more than one action if the statement is true. The action that you use varies, depending on the script you're creating. If the hypothetical statement in Step 4 evaluated as true, the next set of actions may congratulate the viewer on the correct answer and add 1 to his or her score. The next step is to create the action that occurs if the statement evaluates as false.

6. **In the left pane of the Actions panel, click Actions⇨Conditions/Loops and then double-click the** `else` **action.**

   The `else` action tells Flash what to do if the conditional statement is false.

7. **Add the action to the script that occurs if the statement evaluates as false.**

   In the scenario presented in Step 4, if the statement evaluated as false (the viewer entered the wrong answer), the next set of actions may be to tell the viewer that the answer was incorrect and deduct 1 from his or her score. Listing 12-2 shows the ActionScript for this scenario.

Listing 12-2   Creating and Evaluating a Conditional Statement

```
if (answer=="Puff The Magic Dragon") {
  score = ++score;
  message = "Congratulations.";
} else {
  score = --score;
  message = "Sorry, wrong answer. ";
}
```

When you create a conditional statement where Flash is evaluating string data, be sure to use the string equality operator (==) rather than the equal operator (=). If you use the equal (=) operator to test for equality with string data, the statement evaluates as false, even if it's true (equal).

Working with conditional statements that have multiple outcomes

At times, you want more than one possible outcome after a conditional statement is evaluated. To create more than one outcome based on the evaluation of a conditional statement, you use the else if action. For example, if you create a statement that displays a different message depending on how well or how poorly a player scored, you use the else if action. To create more than one outcome for a conditional statement:

1. **Select the object or keyframe where you want to create the conditional statement.**

2. **Click the arrow to the left of the word Actions.**

   Flash has this drill down pat; the Actions panel opens.

3. **Click Actions⇨Conditions/Loops and then double-click if.**

   The if action is added to the script, and the Condition parameter text box appears from out of nowhere.

4. **Enter the condition that must be true for the next line of the script to execute.**

5. **Add the action to the script that occurs if the statement evaluates as true.**

6. **In the left side of the Actions panel, click Actions⇨Conditions/Loops and then double-click the else if action.**

   The action is added to the script, and the Condition parameter text box makes yet another appearance.

7. **Enter the condition that must evaluate as true for the next line of the script to be executed.**

8. **To create another possible outcome, repeat Steps 5 and 6.**

   You can add the else if action to your script several times to create different outcomes.

9. **In the left side of the Actions panel, click Actions⇨Conditions/Loops and then double-click the else action.**

The action is added to the script. There is no condition for this action. The next line of the script is executed when all the other conditions evaluate as false.

10. **Enter the action that will occur if all the conditional statements evaluate as false.**

This action executes if all the other conditions evaluate as false. Listing 12-3 shows an ActionScript that uses the else if action to create several different outcomes depending on the score achieved in a game.

Listing 12-3   Scripting for Multiple Outcomes

```
if (score<10) {
  message = "Dumbkof";
} else if ((score>10&&score<=50)) {
  message = "Dim wit";
} else if (score>50&&score<=70) {
  message = "You can do better";
} else if (score>70&&score<=85) {
  message = "Excellent";
} else {
  message = "Brilliant";
}
```

Working with logical operators

You use logical operators when you want to evaluate a statement with two or more conditions — except for the NOT operator, which negates an individual condition. Take a look at Listing 12-3. Notice the double ampersand (&&) in the third, fifth, and seventh lines of the script. This character tells Flash that both conditions must be true for the entire statement to be true. For example, in the seventh line of the preceding script, the score must be greater than 70 and less than or equal to 85 for the statement in this line of code to evaluate as true. You have three logical operators to work with, as shown in Table 12-1.

Table 12-1	Logical Operators
Operator	*Description*
!	Logical NOT operator
&&	Logical AND operator
||	Logical OR operator

To use a logical operator in one of your scripts:

1. **Select the keyframe or object where you want to create a statement with a logical operator.**

2. **Click the arrow to the left of the word Actions.**

   Guess what? The Actions panel opens.

3. **Click Actions⇨Conditions/Loops and then double-click if.**

   The if action is added to the script, and the Condition parameter text box rears its head again. If you're using the AND or OR logical operator, proceed to Step 6; otherwise go to Step 4.

4. **Click the Operators⇨Logical Operators and then double-click the NOT (!) operator.**

   The operator is added to the script.

5. **Enter the action that the NOT operator negates.**

6. **Enter the first condition to be evaluated.**

   The condition can be string literal or numeric.

7. **In the left pane of the Actions panel, click Operators⇨Logical Operators.**

   The Logical Operators group opens.

8. **Select the Logical AND (&&) operator or Logical OR (| |) operator.**

9. **Enter the second condition to be evaluated.**

   Your conditional statement is complete.

10. **Finish up the script by adding the action that occurs if the statement is true and the action that occurs if the statement is false.**

    If you're not sure how to finish the script, see the "Creating conditional statements" section, earlier in this chapter.

Using the Logical AND operator

When you use the Logical AND (&&) operator to evaluate two conditions, both conditions must be true in order for the statement to be true. Consider the following: If my bank account has more than $800 AND my mortgage is less than $800, I pay the mortgage. In this case, two conditions have to be true in order to execute the action of paying the mortgage. If either condition is false, it is not possible to pay the mortgage — unless, of course, you write a bad check, a practice your mortgage company frowns upon. Listing 12-4 shows a statement using the Logical AND operator that is evaluated after a button is clicked.

Listing 12-4   Using the Logical AND Operator

```
on (release) {
if (guesses<10&&score>10) {
gotoAndPlay ("playGame");
   } else {
gotoAndStop ("gameOver");
   }
}
```

The second line of code in Listing 12-4 evaluates two conditions. Each condition is a Boolean statement; it evaluates as either true or false. Table 12-2 shows the possible outcomes depending on how each condition evaluates.

Table 12-2   Evaluating a Statement with the AND Operator

Condition #1	Condition #2	Statement Evaluates As
True	True	True
True	False	False
False	True	False
False	False	False

The first outcome (Condition #1 and Condition #2 being true) evaluates the entire statement as true and causes the next line in the script to play; in the example shown in Listing 12-4, the movie goes to and plays a frame called `playGame`. The other outcomes evaluate the statement as false and cause the game to end.

Using the Logical OR operator

When you use the Logical OR (||) operator to evaluate two conditions in a statement, if either condition is true, the entire statement is true. Consider this real-world example: If the sun is shining or it's partly cloudy but not raining, I leave my umbrella at home. In this case, only one of the conditions has to be true for the entire statement to be true. Listing 12-5 shows a few lines of ActionScript where a statement using the Logical OR operator is evaluated after a button is clicked.

Listing 12-5   Evaluating with the Logical OR Operator

```
on (release) {
if (user=="Bob"||password=="Open sesame") {
gotoAndPlay ("enterSite");
} else {
gotoAndStop ("notAuthorized");
}
}
```

The second line of code evaluates the two conditions. If either condition is true, the statement is true, and the next action is executed. Table 12-3 shows the possible combinations of the two conditions and how the evaluation affects the statement.

Table 12-3	Evaluating a Statement with the Logical OR Operator	
Condition #1	*Condition #2*	*Statement Evaluates As*
True	True	True
True	False	True
False	True	True
False	False	False

The first three outcomes evaluate the condition as true. In the example in Listing 12-5, a true statement causes the movie to go to and play a frame labeled enterSite; if the statement is false, the movie goes to a frame labeled notAuthorized and stops.

I rarely use the Logical NOT operator. I tried it once, and it gave me a headache, so I quit. If you're so inclined to experiment with this rascal, use the NOT operator with a statement containing a single condition. You use the NOT operator before a statement to return the negation of the statement (or the anti-Boolean, if you will).

Working with String Expressions — without Becoming Entwined

When you evaluate a string expression, a different set of protocols comes into play than when you create a variable with numeric data. If you don't follow the ActionScript protocol for evaluating a string expression, guess what? Your script falls flatter than a loaf of bread baked without enough yeast.

Creating string expressions

String data is always designated by the presence of quotation marks. When you're creating a string expression, you can combine one string with another using the + operator — a task programmers call "concatenate." For example, if you have a variable with string data in it, such as a person's name, and you want to add some text (string data, in programmer-speak) to it, you concatenate the variable with the text as follows: `"Good morning, " + name+"."` where `name` is the variable. If the data stored in the variable `name` is Jill, the expression reads: "Good morning, Jill." Notice that the variable `name` is not in quotation marks. Even though the data within the variable is string data, the variable itself needs to be evaluated as an expression in order for its contents to be displayed.

Comparing expressions with string operators

When you create a variable with string data, Flash uses the equal sign (=) to set the variable name equal to the string data you enter in the Value field. When you use the `if` action to evaluate a statement with string data, you would logically think that you could use the equal (=) sign to test for equality. Not so. You use special operators to test for equality and inequality with string data, as shown in Table 12-4.

Table 12-4	**Comparing String Expressions**	
Operator	*Function*	*Syntax*
==	Tests for equality	`name=="Jill"`
!=	Tests for inequality	name !="Jill"

Working with Mathematical Expressions: It All Adds Up

The invention of the calculator made math a no-brainer for many people: Just punch in the numbers, use the right operand, and then mash one of your fingers (I prefer the forefinger) on the equal key, and — voilà — you have an answer. With ActionScript, when you create a mathematical expression, you have to put your thinking cap on. Think back to your grade-school days, when you had to create equations, and you get an inkling of what I'm talking about. In the upcoming sections, I get you pointed in the right direction for creating your own mathematical ActionScript expressions.

Creating Mathematical Expressions

In ActionScript, you can use mathematical expressions for a number of things, such as keeping score in a game, plotting the coordinates of an object on Stage, or changing the size of an object.

You create mathematical expressions in Flash using the same operators you used in grade school. You find them by clicking the Arithmetic Operators in the Actions panel. You have lots of operators to choose from. Table 12-5 lists the most popular ones. If you're a math whiz and want to explore some of the other operators, run your mouse over the operator's name in the Actions panel, and a tooltip tells you what it does, or better yet, click the Reference icon and look it up in the online Reference panel.

Table 12-5	Mathematical Operators	
Operator	*Operation Performed*	*Syntax*
+	Adds two numbers	x+a
++	Increments a variable	++y and y++
−	Subtracts the second number from the first	x−y
−−	Decrements a variable	−−x and x−−
×	Multiplies two numbers	x × y
/	Divides the first number in the expression by the second	x/y
%	Returns a remainder of a division	c=x%y

Comparing expressions with mathematical operators

Some operators compare one side of an expression to the other. For example, y<=10 creates a Boolean expression. The expression is true if the value of y is less than or equal to 10; false if it's greater than 10. You find these operators by clicking the Comparison Operators in the Actions panel, which really is quite profound seeing as you're comparing two sides of an expression. Table 12-6 shows the operators you can use to compare expressions.

Table 12-6	Comparison Operators	
Operator	*Comparison Performed*	*Syntax*
<	Less than	7<10
>	Greater than	10>7
<=	Less than or equal to	7<=10
>=	Greater than or equal to	10>=7

About operator precedence

ActionScript operators are just like everything else on this planet: A pecking order always exists. When you have more than one operator in an expression, one operator has precedence (read: it's top dog) over the other. Consider these two equations:

y=4+3×5

y=(4+3)×5

They both have the same numbers, but return different values. In the first equation, y is equal to 19. In the second equation, y is equal to 35. The reason is that multiplication has precedence over addition and is executed first. It may help to remember a weird word, BODMAS, which is short for Brackets Open, Division, Multiplication, Addition, Subtraction. In other words, all operations within brackets are performed (have precedence) first, and then division, and then multiplication, and then addition, and then (low man again) subtraction. (I'm glad that my accountant uses a computer to do my taxes. I would be in deep sneakers if he had to remember all this stuff and the tax laws at the same time.)

Creating an expression that increments or decrements a value

Another way you can use expressions is to increment or decrement a value. If you work with an object's property — such as its width, height, scale, or position on Stage — you can get the object to move by changing the value of the object's property. If you read Chapter 7 and got Herman the Mouse to jump through the hoop, you remember that an exact value was used to move Herman and change his size. But what if you want Herman to move with every mouse click? If you've got the same value, he's only going to move once, no matter how many times the mouse button is clicked. You can create an expression that increases a value by a set amount whenever the mouse button is clicked. For example, if you want an object to move five pixels on the x axis, you create an expression that increases the x property of the object by a value of 5 whenever the expression is evaluated. Of if you want an object to move backward, you decrease the x value by a set amount. To create an expression that increases (increments) or decreases (decrements) a value by a given amount, do the following:

1. **Select the keyframe or object where you want the expression to be evaluated.**

2. **Click the arrow to the left of the word Actions.**

   The Actions panel opens.

3. **Click Actions⇨Miscellaneous Actions and then double-click** evaluate.

   The Expression parameter text box appears.

4. **Click the Insert Target Path button.**

   The Insert Target Path dialog box appears.

5. **Click the button that corresponds to the movie clip whose property you want to increment or decrement and then close the Insert Target Path dialog box.**

   The target path appears in the Expression parameter text box.

6. **Type a dot (.) and then in the left pane of the Actions panel, click Properties and double-click the object property you want to increase or decrease.**

7. **Type a plus sign (+) to increment a property or a minus sign (–) to decrement a property.**

8. **Type an equal sign (=) and then type the value you want the object property to increment or decrement by.**

   Listing 12-6 shows an expression that increases the _x property of a movie clip named Charlie by five pixels every time a button is clicked. Notice that the Press mouse event is used. If you evaluate an expression with a movie clip, you use the enterFrame clip event so that Flash continually evaluates the expression.

Listing 12-6　Creating an Expression to Increment the Value of an
　　　　　　　Object Property

```
on (press) {
  _root.Charie._x+=5;
}
```

Using the Key Object

You can program a button to accept keyboard input, and you can program a movie clip to execute an action when a key is pressed, but that limits you to only one key press, which is kind of depressing — key-wise, that is. When you use the Key object, you can program a movie clip to execute one action when one key is pressed and execute a different action when another key is pressed. Im**Press**ive, if you catch my drift. The most common way to use the Key object is with a conditional statement. Now I'll tell you something — if you don't know about conditional statements you must have fast-forwarded to this part of the chapter. Before you go too much further with the Key object, I'd like you to rewind and read the "Working With Conditional Statements" section at the start of this chapter because this section won't make much sense if you don't know how to create a conditional statement.

Okay, if you just moseyed back from reading the section on conditional statements, welcome back my friend because the show's about to begin. If you didn't mosey back from the section on conditional statements, I thank you for reading this chapter from the beginning.

So then, you use conditional statements to determine if a key is pressed and then you add the actions that occur when the key is pressed. By using a whole bunch of conditional statements, you can program a movie clip to do different things when different keys are pressed; for example, if the Up key is pressed an object moves towards the top of the screen or the object moves towards the bottom of the movie when the Down key is pressed.

When you use the key object to animate, you create an expression that increments or decrements an object property by a given value. If the words *increment* or *decrement* make you want to scurry for a dictionary, you can just scurry instead to the last section where I show you what increment and decrement are all about, as well as how to create an expression that increments or decrements a value. In that section I show an example of code that moves an object every time a button is clicked. If viewers of your movie continually have to click a button to make an object move, they'll soon become bored or end up with a sore index finger. However, when you use the Key object with a movie clip and specify the `enterFrame` clip event, the movie clip continues to change as long as the key is down (pressed).

To animate a movie clip using the key object, you create a conditional statement that determines if a specific key is pressed. The next step is to create an expression that increments or decrements a property value. In addition to the conditional statement, you need to use the `.isdown` method of the Key object, and one of the Key Constants. The Key Constants are the actual keys. You can address all the keys by using the key codes, but this involves remembering which key code goes to what key; for example, the key code for the Up key is 38. It's much easier to select `UP` from the Constants book. Follow these steps and you'll know how to animate with the Key object.

1. **Create a new Flash document.**

2. **Choose Insert⇨New Symbol.**

   The Create New Symbol dialog box appears.

3. **Choose the Movie Clip behavior, name the symbol *sphereClip,* and click OK.**

   Flash enters symbol-editing mode.

4. **Create a sphere approximately 20 pixels in diameter.**

   After you create the sphere, you can size it by opening the Property inspector and entering a value of 20 in the W and H fields.

5. **Click the Back button to exit symbol editing mode.**

   Flash adds the symbol to the document Library.

6. **Drag an instance of the symbol on stage.**

7. **Click the arrow to the left of the word Actions.**

   The Actions panel opens.

8. **Click Actions⇨Conditions/Loops and then double-click `if`.**

   The Condition parameter text box appears above the Script pane.

9. **Click Objects⇨Movie⇨Key⇨Methods and double-click `.isDown`.**

   Flash adds `Key.isDown()` to your script. In the Condition field, your cursor is flashing between the parentheses.

10. **In the left pane of the Actions panel, click Constants and then double-click `UP`.**

    The code `Key.UP` appears between the parentheses, and your conditional statement is complete.

11. **Click the Actions book⇨Miscellaneous Actions book and double-click `evaluate`.**

The Expression text parameter box opens.

12. **Enter the following code: _y-=5.**

    This line of code decreases the value of the movie clip's _y property by five pixels. Notice that a target path is not specified. That's because the property you're incrementing is a property of the movie clip.

    Notice that Flash assigned the default load clip event when you created the expression. The load clip event evaluates the expression one time, when the movie clip loads. You want Flash to continually evaluate the action, so you need to specify a different event.

13. **Select the first line of code and in the parameters area, click** EnterFrame.

    This changes the clip event to enterFrame, and the script is executed every time the frame is entered. In other words, the code is always evaluated. That's what it takes to get the movie clip to move towards the top of the screen when the Up arrow key is pressed. Your code should look like Figure 12-1.

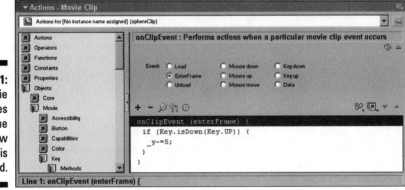

Figure 12-1: The movie clip boogies up when the Up arrow key is pressed.

Okay, I know what you're saying; big deal, the clip goes up. Well, what goes up must come down. In order to make the clip go in different directions, you create more conditional statements; in this case, one for each arrow key. The conditional statement for each arrow key evaluates an expression that increments or decrements the property for the direction you want the movie clip to move. To move the clip in different directions:

✔ To move the movie clip down, you add to the _y property.

✔ To move the movie clip to the right, you add to the _x property; subtract from the _x property to move Stage left.

✔ Repeat Steps 8-12 to create the code shown in Listing 12-7.

Listing 12-7   Animating the Movie Clip Using All the Arrow Keys

```
onClipEvent (enterFrame) {
  // Moves the movie clip up
  if (Key.isDown(Key.UP)) {
    _y-=5;
  }
  // Moves the movie clip down
  if (Key.isDown(Key.DOWN)) {
    _y+=5;
  }
  // Moves the movie clip right
  if (Key.isDown(Key.RIGHT)) {
    _x+=5;
  }
  // Moves the movie clip left
  if (Key.isDown(Key.LEFT)) {
    _x-=5;
  }
}
```

To test out your handiwork, choose Control➪Test Movie. After Flash pub-lishes the movie, press an arrow key and the sphere will start moving. Press another key to move the sphere in a different direction. If you hold any key down long enough, the sphere moves clean out of sight, never to return. To prevent against this, you need to add other conditional statements that reset the _x property or _y property of the movie clip so that it appears on the opposite side of the movie. My editor's already screaming I have too many pages in this chapter so I'll leave you on your own with that one.

To view a movie of a space ship, you can navigate over a planet's surface by copying the file alien.fla from this chapter's folder on the CD-ROM that accompanies this book to your hard drive. Use your computer operating system to disable the file's read-only attributes. Launch Flash, open the file and then choose Control➪Test Movie. When the movie publishes, press any of the arrow keys to start the ship in motion:

- ✔ Click the opposite arrow key, and the ship does a 180.
- ✔ Click the Up and Right arrow keys at the same time and the ship traverses the planet's surface diagonally.
- ✔ Hold down any of the keys and the ship pops out of the movie boundary and reappears on the other side.
- ✔ Press the Shift key to make the ship speed up.
- ✔ Press the space bar to slow the ship down.

After you're through navigating the alien craft, close the window. In movie editing mode, select the spaceship and open the Actions panel to see what makes it tick.

Scripting a Guess Number Game

The ActionScript math operators and conditional statements, combined with an input text box and a dynamic text box, are all you need to create a guess number game. In this section, I show you how to script a guess number game. I've already given you a head start by creating the graphic elements and the layers. I've also created some of the ActionScript, but am leaving the cool stuff for you to do.

Locate the file named guess_number_begin.fla, which you find in this chapter's folder on the CD that accompanies this book. Use your computer's operating system to disable the file's read-only attributes. To script a guess number game:

1. **Launch Flash and then open the guess_number_begin.fla file.**

   Flash opens the file in movie-editing mode. Before you go any further, take a look at what you have the work with. The movie's content is segregated in four layers. As always, the actions have a separate layer. The movie consists of five frames. Drag the playhead across the frames, and you see the elements I've already created. The first and second frames have two text boxes: one for displaying messages to the player and another for accepting the player's guess. frame 3 is blank; it's used for the actions that determine what happens next. Frames 4 and 5 either congratulate the player for winning the game or console him or her for losing.

2. **Click the first frame in the Actions layer and then click the arrow to the left of the word Actions.**

   The Actions panel opens for business. I've already given you a head start by creating two variables: one for the message the player sees when the game begins and the `message` variable that is set equal to the `text` variable. The content of the `message` variable changes depending on the player's guess and is displayed in the dynamic text box.

3. **Click the second line of code to select it, open the Actions panel click Actions⇨Variables, and then double-click `set variable`.**

   Look, up in the sky, it's a bird, it's a plane, it's parameter text boxes!

4. **In the Variables field, type tries; in the Value field, type 5; and then click the Expression box.**

   This line of code sets the number of tries the player has. If you're feeling generous, give your players more than five guesses.

5. **Click Actions⇨Variables and then double-click `set variable`.**

   That's right — you're going to create another variable. Variables are the lifeblood of Flash games.

6. In the Variable field, type guessNumber.

Congratulations — you've just created the variable that will keep your players guessing.

7. Click inside the Value field, click Objects⇨Core⇨Math⇨Methods, and then double-click the round **object.**

The words `Math.round ()` appear in the Value field. The `Math.round` object takes an integer that you carefully place between the parentheses and, depending on the decimal value, rounds it up or down into a whole number.

8. Place your cursor between the parentheses and in the left pane of the Actions panel, click Objects⇨Core⇨Math⇨Methods and then double-click the random **method.**

I know. You may have the Actions panel open already. The path is included for the neat freaks who close things after using them. If you're a card-carrying member of that group, please organize my file folders on your day off. The code `Math.random ()` appears between the parentheses.

9. In the Value field, type *50 **after the closing parentheses for the** Math.random **method and then click the Expression box.**

The completed line of code generates a random number between 1 and 50. To complete the line of code, you can enter the multiplication operand (*) by typing it directly from your computer keyboard or double-click the multiplication operator in the Actions panel.

10. To complete the code for this frame, create a variable named guess, **leaving the Value field blank, and add a** stop **action. Your ActionScript for the first frame of the Actions layer should resemble the one shown in Figure 12-2.**

This frame sets everything up. Before you venture forward to the next step, click the arrow to the left of the word Properties. Click each of the text boxes, and you see that the variables you created are mirrored in the text boxes. By creating the guess variable in the first frame, you declare the variable, even though it doesn't have a value yet. Click the button. If you still have the Actions panel open, you see that the movie advances to frame 3 when the button is clicked.

Please note that in Figure 12-2, the left pane of the Actions panel has been collapsed, and the panel has to be enlarged to display all the code.

11. Click the third frame in the Actions layer.

I've already converted this frame to a keyframe for you. If you still have the Actions panel open, notice that the tab is labeled Actions-Frame. If you don't have the Actions panel open, please do so now by clicking the arrow to the left of the word Actions or by clicking the arrow to the left of the word Actions, or by choosing Window⇨Actions.

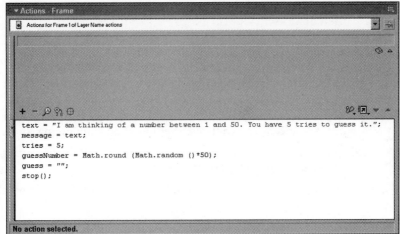

```
text = "I am thinking of a number between 1 and 50. You have 5 tries to guess it.";
message = text;
tries = 5;
guessNumber = Math.round (Math.random ()*50);
guess = "";
stop();
```

Figure 12-2:
Let the
game begin.

12. **Click Actions⇨Variables and then double-click** `set variable.`

    Parameter text boxes appear above the Script pane.

13. **In the Variable field, type** tries; **in the Value field, type** –– tries; **and click the Expression box.**

    This line of code decrements (counts down) the value of the `tries` variable. The two minus (–) signs before the variable `tries` decrement the variable by one every time the player makes a guess. You can enter the two minus (––) signs by typing them on your keyboard or by double-clicking the operator in the Actions panel.

14. **Click Actions⇨Conditions/Loops and then double-click the** `if` **action.**

    The `if` action is added to the script, and the Condition parameter text box opens.

15. **In the Conditions field, type** tries==0.

16. **In the left pane of the Actions panel, click Actions⇨Movie Control and then double-click** `goto.`

    The action is added to the script, and the parameters text boxes appear.

17. **In the Frame field, type** 5.

    This line of code advances the movie to frame 5 when the player runs out of tries.

18. **In the left pane of the Actions panel, double-click** `else if.`

    The action is added to the script, and the Condition parameter text box appears above the Script pane.

19. **In the Conditions field, type** guess==guessNumber.

20. **In the left side of the Actions panel, click Actions⇨Movie Control and then double-click** `goto`.

    The action is added to the script, and the you've got beaucoup parameter text boxes to deal with.

21. **In the Frame field, enter** 4.

    The line of code you just created instructs Flash to check the condition `guess==guessNumber`. If the condition is true, the movie advances to frame 4, and the player is congratulated on winning the game.

22. **In the left pane of the Actions panel, click Actions⇨Conditions/Loops and then double-click** `else if`.

    The action is added to the script, and the Condition parameter text box appears.

23. **In the Conditions field, type** guess<guessNumber.

24. **In the left side of the Actions panel, click Actions⇨Variables and then double-click** `set variable`.

    The action is added to the script, and again parameter text boxes keep busting out all over.

25. **In the Variable field, type** message; **in the Value field, type** "Too low. You have "+tries+" left"; **and click the Expression box.**

26. **In the left pane of the Actions panel, click Actions⇨Movie Control and then double-click** `goto`.

    The action is added to your code, and the parameter text boxes change partners.

27. **In the Frame field, type** 2 **and then click the Go To and Stop radio buttons.**

28. **The next line of code is identical to what you created in Steps 22 – 27 with the following exceptions: The condition after the** `else if` **action is:** guess>50 **and the variable** message **has a value of** "Enter a guess less than 50. You have"+tries+" left". **Be sure to click the Expression box.**

    This line of code is for game players who can't follow directions and enter a number greater than 50. They lose a try and get bumped back to frame 2 to try again.

29. **In the left pane of the Actions panel, click Actions⇨Conditions/Loops and then double-click** `else`.

    Another action is added to your script. You're getting to be quite the prolific ActionScripter! The `else` action has no parameters.

30. **In the left pane of the Actions panel, click Actions⇨Variables and then double-click** set variable.

Yep, that's right: You're going to change the variable to suit the outcome of the player's guess.

31. **In the Variable field, type** message; **in the Value field, type** "Too high. You have "+tries+" left.". **Then click the Expression box.**

32. **In the left pane of the Actions panel, click Actions⇨Movie Control and then double click** goto.

I think you know what happens now.

33. **In the Frame field, type** 2. **Your ActionScript for frame 3 should look like the one shown in Figure 12-3.**

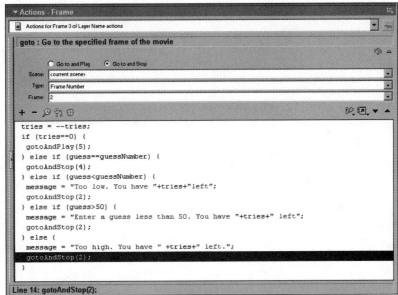

Figure 12-3:
My, that
certainly is
a ton of
ActionScript.

This is the end of the line. If all the other conditions are false, the player guessed a number greater than the number generated by Flash. The player is given the clue that the guess is too high and gets another shot at guessing the right number.

Of course, there's more to scripting the game than this. But my editor has been complaining of stress lately, so I don't want to stress her out even more by making this chapter longer than the long arm of the publisher allows. Therefore, I've created the other actions for you. It's all straightforward. In a nutshell, here's what I've done: In frame 2, the guess variable is reset to null (empty) so that the player's last guess doesn't appear in the dynamic text box. Frames 4 and 5 in the Actions layer have a simple stop action in them. The Reset buttons that appear in Frames 4 and 5 send the movie back to frame 1 when clicked, resetting the variables and effectively starting the game over again.

Please note that the Actions panel, as shown in Figure 12-2, has been modified to display all the code.

34. To test the game, choose Control⇨Test Movie.

Go ahead and play the game. You deserve a break after creating all that ActionScript.

Okay, here's the *Reader's Digest* version of what you just created. When the game begins, Flash generates a random number between 1 and 50. The player enters a guess in the input text box. After the number guesser presses the Enter button, Flash takes one turn away from the player, evaluates the guess, and displays a message telling the player the status of his or her guess. If the player guesses correctly, frame 4 plays and congratulates the player on winning. If the player runs out of tries, frame 5 plays and consoles the loser. The Reset button starts the game over.

If your game did not play correctly, locate the guess_number_final.fla file located in this chapter's folder on the CD that comes with this book. Disable the file's read-only attributes, open it in Flash, and compare the code to what you've just created.

Chapter 13

Testing Your ActionScript and Exterminating the Bugs

Creating a Flash movie with lots of bells and whistles can be a challenging endeavor. Add ActionScript, and the challenge jumps to another level, and you wonder whether the challenge will ever end. The challenge you face is not quite the fare that you see on one of those reality shows — which, in my estimation, are unreal, but I'll get off my soapbox now. When you add ActionScript to a movie, things may not happen as you had originally planned (you did plan the movie, didn't you?). When what you see isn't what you expected, or when what you see is a Flash movie frozen in its tracks, it's time to call the exterminators, and find out where the little bugs are hiding in your movie. In this chapter, I show you how to test your movies and then to debug them.

The Actions panel's got lots of books. And some of these books have books within a book. To add some actions to your scripts, you have to click this book icon, then click that book icon, then click another book icon, and so on. Rather than bore you with a lot of words, I'm going to show the path to each action as shown in the following example: Click Actions⇨Movie Control and then double-click `goto`.

Testing Your Movies

Your first line of defense against buggy ActionScript is to test your movie. When you test a movie, Flash publishes it as a .swf file, and all the effects, tweening, movie clips, buttons, and actions work — or at least you hope they do. If the movie doesn't play properly, you go back to the drawing board (actually, it's back to movie-editing mode) to figure out what went awry and where. You can test a movie in two ways: using the Test Movie command or using the Publish Preview command.

Using the Test Movie command

You can use the Test Movie command at any time to preview an entire movie or everything you've created up to that point. I recommend using the Test Movie command after you've made any major change or created new ActionScript for your movie. Catching errors is easier while the creation process is still fresh in your mind. To test your movie:

1. **Choose Control➪Test Movie.**

   Flash publishes the movie and begins playing it in another window, as shown in Figure 13-1.

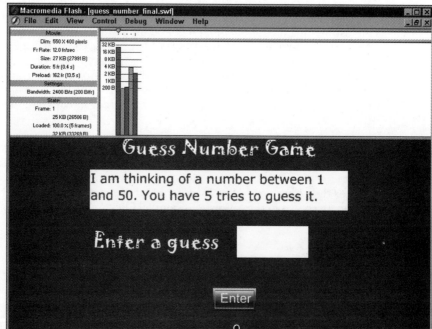

Figure 13-1:
Test your movie to find any boo-boos.

2. Choose View➪Bandwidth Profiler.

Flash opens the Bandwidth Profiler; see the graph at the top of Figure 13-1. The Bandwidth Profiler also has a pointer at the top that moves to show you which frame is playing. As you watch the movie play, pay attention to which frame the pointer is on. When an error in your movie occurs, you know right where to look. The Bandwidth Profiler also gives you lots of other information about your movie, such as its size in kilobytes, the length of the movie, and the size in kilobytes of each frame.

3. To test the movie again, choose Control➪Rewind and then choose Control➪Play.

4. To list a list of the variables in your movie, choose Debug➪List Variables.

The Output window appears, as shown in Figure 13-2. The information you get about your variables is a snapshot of each variable's value at the point you chose the List Variables command. Many variables you create change throughout the course of the movie. To see each variable updated as the movie plays, you use the Debugger, a tool I show you how to use in a later section.

Figure 13-2:
All right,
who added
that last
variable to
the movie?

```
Output                                                              X
                                                           ptions
Level #0:
Variable _level0.$version = "WIN 6,0,0,307"
Variable _level0.text = "I am thinking of a number between 1 and 50. You
Variable _level0.message = "I am thinking of a number between 1 and 50. '
Variable _level0.tries = 5
Variable _level0.guessNumber = 47
Variable _level0.guess =
Edit Text: Target="_level0.instance1"
    variable = "message",
    text = "I am thinking of a number between 1 and 50. You have 5 tries
    htmlText = "I am thinking of a number between 1 and 50. You have 5 t
    html = false, textWidth = 440, textHeight = 59, maxChars = null,
    borderColor = 0x000000, backgroundColor = 0xFFFFFF, textColor = 0x000
    background = true, wordWrap = true, password = false, multiline = tr
    selectable = true, scroll = 1, hscroll = 0, maxscroll = 1,
    maxhscroll = 0, bottomScroll = 2,
    type = "dynamic",
    embedFonts = true, restrict = null, length = 73, tabIndex = undefine
    autoSize = "none",
    condenseWhite = false
Edit Text: Target="_level0.instance2"
    variable = "guess",
    text = ,
```

If you have lots of variables in your movie, you can resize the Output window by dragging it from the lower-right corner. Figure 13-2 shows the Output window resized in this manner.

5. To display a list of the objects in your movie, choose Debug➪List Objects.

The Output window appears and displays all the objects used in your movie.

6. **When you're through testing your movie, close the window.**

   Flash returns to movie-editing mode. If your movie tested perfectly, go ahead and publish it, or if you still have more neat bells and whistles to add, create away.

 You can also add comments to your ActionScript. *Comments* are little notes to yourself — a virtual piece of string around your pinky, if you will. I show you how to add comments to your script in Chapter 3. When you've tracked down what frame your ActionScript has failed on, your comments may help you to figure out what went wrong.

Using the Publish Preview command

You use the Publish Preview command when you want to see what your Flash movie looks like in a Web browser. When you preview a finished movie — or even when you're still creating one — in a Web browser, you don't have diagnostic tools at your disposal, but you see exactly what your movie's viewers will see. To preview the movie in a browser:

1. **Choose File⇨Publish Preview or press F12.**

   Flash publishes the movie and opens your system's default Web browser.

2. **When you've finished previewing the movie, close the Web browser.**

I like to use the Test Movie command during the early stages of creation and then combine the Test Movie command with the Publish Preview command when the document is about ready to publish as a .SWF movie. When I'm using the Test Movie command, I can detect and diagnose any glitches. The Publish Preview command lets me view the overall aesthetics of the movie and the effect it will have on the viewer as well as how the effects that use ActionScript perform. (I often use these commands with my cat in my lap. If I don't end up with shredded flesh from my kitty's rapid getaway after she sees something she doesn't like, the movie passes muster.)

Testing and Debugging ActionScripts — without Toxic Chemicals

At times, you've got so many things going on in your Flash movies that you literally drive yourself batty trying to make them all work, especially when you add ActionScript to the movie. If you've been a fastidious ActionScripter, keeping all your actions in a separate layer, you're one step ahead of the game; you know where to look for potential errors. You can do a couple of other things to make your life easier when it comes time to figure out what's happening — or isn't happening — in your movie.

Using the trace Action

When you use the `trace` action, you activate the Output window. What is displayed in the Output window is up to you. You can either display a message to remind yourself what should be happening at this point in the movie. You can also display the current contents of a variable. You use the `trace` action with the object or keyframe you want to trace. For example, if you want to trace the contents of a variable at a certain keyframe, you assign the `trace` action to that keyframe. You can trace as many variables as you want. To use the `trace` action:

1. **Select the object or keyframe to which you want to assign the** `trace` **action.**

2. **Click the triangle to the left of the word Actions.**

   The Actions panel opens.

3. **Select the point in the script where you want to add the** `trace` **action.**

   If you're tracing a variable, add the action below the point in the script where you expect the variable's contents to change.

4. **Click the Actions⇨Miscellaneous Actions icon and then double-click** `trace`**.**

   The action is added to the script, and the Message parameter text box appears above the Script pane. To display a message when the movie is tested or debugged, go to Step 5; otherwise, go to Step 6.

5. **Enter the message you want displayed in the Output window.**

   When the movie is tested or debugged, the message is displayed in the Output window.

6. **To display the contents of a variable in the Output window, enter the variable's name and check the Expression box.**

   When the movie is tested or debugged, the contents of the variable are displayed in the Output window, as shown in Figure 13-3. In this figure, the `trace` action has been used twice. The first part of the text is a message; the second part displays the contents of a variable. In Figure 13-3, a loop is being traced.

To display a message and a variable at the same time, type the message in the message box with surrounding quotation marks, add the plus sign (+), and then type the variable as shown in the following example. Be sure to check the Expression box.

```
"This is loop" + i
```

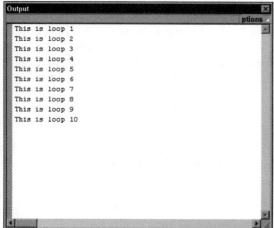

Figure 13-3:
The results of the `trace` action appear in the Output window.

Putting an End to Buggy Script with the Debugger

Your best friend when it comes to exterminating bugs in your movies is the Debug command. When you use the Debug command to test a movie, the Debugger panel opens and gives you the lowdown on what's going on in your movie. The Debugger displays the target paths of all movie clips within your movie as well as the variables within each movie clip. As a variable changes, its value updates in real time within the Debugger.

Debugging in Authoring mode

When you're creating individual parts of a movie, testing everything as you go along makes good sense. You can use the Debugger at any point while you're creating a movie. I advise using the Debugger right after you've added some complex ActionScript to the movie. Testing the code before moving on to the next part of the project is a great way to prevent a headache when you think that you've finished creating the movie but it doesn't work as planned. To use the Debugger:

1. **Choose Control⇨Debug Movie.**

   Flash publishes the movie in another window, and the Debugger opens, as shown in Figure 13-4. Notice that the panel is divided into two windows and the left window is divided in the middle. The left window displays objects and variables in your document; the right window is used to restart the movie after a breakpoint is reached. (And that's break*point*, not break dance.) The top window displays a button for each object in your movie. The bottom window has four tabs: Properties, Variables, Locals, and Watch.

   When you start the Debugger, the right window displays the message shown in Figure 13-4. The restart the movie, click the Continue button that looks like a VCR Play button.

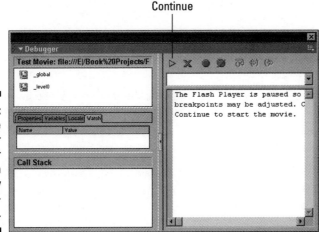

Figure 13-4: The Debugger is your prescription for buggy Action-Script.

   You can close the left window by clicking the button with the left arrow that divides the Debugger. When you close the window, the arrow turns into a right-pointing arrow. Click the arrow to close the right window and open the left. You can resize the windows by moving the cursor to toward any of the window divider bars. When the cursor changes to two parallel lines with up and down arrows, click and drag to resize the window.

2. **To display information about a particular movie clip, click its button in the top window.**

   The Debugger's bottom window displays information about the selected clip.

3. **To display a selected movie clip's properties, click the Properties tab.**

   The Debugger displays the selected movie clip's properties, as shown in Figure 13-5. If you select the level0 button, the properties of the base movie are displayed. If you've loaded additional movies with the Load Movie action, they're displayed as level1, level2, and so on.

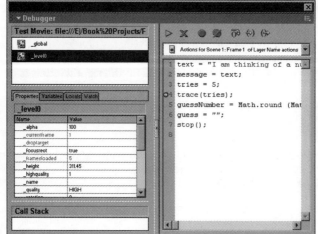

Figure 13-5:
You can
display a
movie clip's
properties
with the
Debugger.

4. To display the current contents of a movie clip's variables, click the Variables tab.

Any variables stored within the movie clip are displayed in the bottom window, as shown in Figure 13-6.

5. To display any local variables in a movie clip, click the instance's name in the top part of the left window and then click the Locals tab.

You can change the property of a movie clip, or the value of a variable from within the Debugger. Click the appropriate tab (Properties or Variable), click the field to the right of a property or variable name, enter a new value, and then press Enter or Return. The movie changes to reflect the new value you entered.

As you can see, the Debugger is a valuable tool when your Flash movie isn't performing up to snuff. Check the value of the variables in each movie clip. If the value of the variables is incorrect, you may have made an error in transferring a value from an array. If no variables are where you expect to see variables, you may have misspelled a variable's name in the heat of battle. You can easily correct this situation by selecting the object or keyframe with the dubious code, opening the Actions panel, and correcting your spelling.

If you have more information than will fit in the Debugger window, you can use the scroll bars (which automatically appear when you've got more stuff than the Debugger has space) or resize the window by dragging its lower-right corner. Most Debugger panels shown in this chapter have been resized.

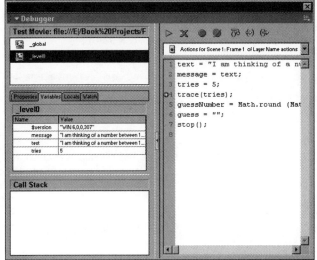

Figure 13-6:
You can track a movie clip's variables with the Debugger.

Watching a variable

The Debugger's fourth tab is labeled Watch. It has nothing to do with keeping the time. If you have several movie clips with lots of variables that you want to track as the movie plays, you can use the Watch command to track selected variables within the Watch window. To watch variables in your movie:

1. **Choose Control➪Debug Movie.**

   Flash publishes the movie and plays it in another window, and the Debugger window opens. The movie is paused, waiting for you to click the Continue button.

2. **Click the Continue button to restart the movie.**

3. **Click the button for a movie clip with variables you want to watch.**

4. **Click the Variables tab.**

   The movie clip's variables are displayed.

5. **Right-click (in Windows) or Ctrl+click (on the Macintosh) a variable you want to watch.**

   A pop-up menu with the word *Watch* on it appears.

6. **Click Watch.**

   A blue dot appears next to the variable's name, and the variable is added to the Watch list.

7. **Repeat Steps 4 and 5 to watch additional variables in the selected movie clip.**

   A blue dot appears next to the variable's name, and the variable is added to the Watch list.

8. **To watch variables from other movie clips, repeat Steps 2 – 5.**

   A blue dot appears next to any other variables you select, and they're added to the Watch list.

9. **Click the Watch tab.**

   The variables on which you used the Watch command are displayed in the lower half of the Debugger. The variables are updated in real time, as shown in Figure 13-7.

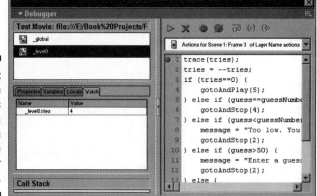

Figure 13-7:
The Watch command is like having your own private investigator on the case.

When you exit Debugging mode and return to Authoring mode, the watch still remains on the variables you selected. After you make changes to the movie, debug the movie again to see what effect your changes have on the watched variables.

10. **To remove a variable from the Watch list, right-click (in Windows) or Ctrl+click (on the Macintosh) the watched variable and then choose Remove from the pop-up menu.**

    The variable is removed from the Watch list.

You can also debug your movies remotely within a Web browser. To debug remotely, install the Flash Debug Player that was added to a directory in your computer when you installed Flash. The path to the Flash Debug Player is FlashMX⇔Players⇔Debug. To debug remotely, enable the Debugging Permitted option when you publish the movie. Then, while you're previewing the movie in a Web browser, right-click (in Windows) or Ctrl+click (on the Macintosh) anywhere within the browser window and choose Debugger from the context menu. For the Debugger to become active, you must have Flash running at the same time. To enable remote debugging, click the triangle in the upper-right corner of the Debugger and choose Enable Remote Debugging from the menu.

Doing the Breakpoint Boogie

In Flash 5 when you used the traced a variable or a property, there were times when it would scroll down the Output window so fast, you'd get dizzy watching it. The alternative was to add a stop action to the movie so the movie would stop playing and you could view the Output window without a gazillion lines flashing by at the speed of light. Which of course was a major pain if you wanted to debug other parts of your movie at the same time.

Fortunately in Flash MX there's a little jewel known as the *breakpoint.* Breakpoints are not to be confused with a Michael Jackson dance move. What breakpoints do is stop the movie at a particular line of ActionScript. You can restart the movie with controls in the debugger, which is much easier than going back to the Actions panel, removing a stop action, starting the debugger again and . . . well, you get the drift. Breakpoints speed things up.

You add breakpoints in the Actions panel by doing the following:

1. **Select the keyframe or object that contains the code you want to trace.**

2. **Open the Actions panel and click the line of code where you want to set the breakpoint.**

    You can choose any line of code in a long ActionScript. The line of code you choose is where the Debugger stops the movie so you can see what's happening.

3. **Click the Debug Options button that looks like a doctor's stethoscope.**

    The Actions panel's cold stethoscope sends a shiver down the code's virtual spine.

When you add breakpoints to a movie, in the Actions panel, click the View Options button and choose View Line numbers. When you set a new breakpoint, a red dot appears to the left of the line number. If you don't enable the View Line numbers option, guess what, you have no idea of where your breakpoints are.

4. Repeat Steps 2–4 to set additional breakpoints.

You can set as many breakpoints as you need to keep track of what's happening in your movie. For example, if you want to trace the value of a variable that appears many times in a movie, use the `trace` action each time the variable appears. This enables you to trace the value of the variable. Set a breakpoint every time you use the `trace` action. When you debug the movie, the movie stops at the breakpoints you set and you can see the value of the variable displayed in the Output panel.

After you set your breakpoints, you can debug your code by doing the following:

1. Choose Control➪Debug Movie.

Flash publishes the movie and plays it in another window. The Debugger panel is displayed (see Figure 13-8).

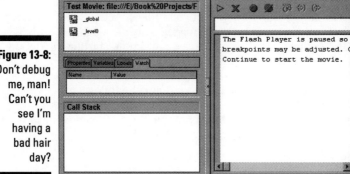

Figure 13-8:
Don't debug me, man! Can't you see I'm having a bad hair day?

2. Click the Continue button.

Flash restarts the movie and stops it at the next breakpoint, as shown in Figure 13-9. Notice the red dot to the left of the line of code where the breakpoint is set.

When you get to a breakpoint, you have several options. Choose one of the following:

✔ To continue playing the movie to the next breakpoint, click the Continue button.

✔ To stop debugging, click the Stop Debugging button and Flash continues playing the movie.

✔ To set a new breakpoint, select a line of code in the right pane of the Debugger panel and click the Toggle Breakpoint button. When you click this button, a red dot appears to the left of the selected line of code and the Debugger will pause the movie the next time this line of code occurs.

✔ To remove all breakpoints, click the Remove All Breakpoints button. This removes all breakpoints in the movie.

✔ To advance to the next action in the script, click the Step Over button.

✔ To advance to the next line of code in a user-defined function, click the Step In button. If you click this button when not in a user-defined function, the debugger advances to the next line of code that contains an action.

✔ To step out of a user-defined function, click the Step Out button.

The debugger displays a yellow arrow to the left of the currently selected line number. When you step over a line of code, the yellow arrow moves to reflect the newly selected line of code. If your movie isn't playing as planned, jot down the information from the script window at the top of the debugger and the line number of the faulty code. With this information, you can now correct the buggy line of code by modifying it in the Actions panel after closing the test movie window.

Figure 13-9:
The Debugger done put on the brakes at a breakpoint.

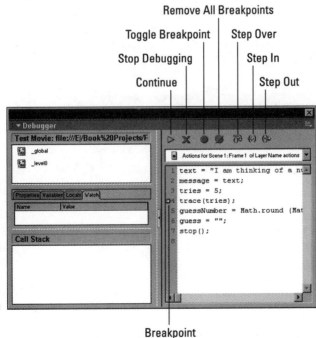

To edit breakpoints in the Actions panel, click the Debugger Options button that looks like a stethoscope and do one of the following:

- ✔ Choose Remove Breakpoint to remove a breakpoint from your script. A breakpoint is designated by a red dot to the left of the code's line number when you have the View Line Numbers option enabled.
- ✔ Choose Remove All Breakpoints to remove all breakpoints in the movie.
- ✔ Select a line of code and then choose Set Breakpoint to add a new breakpoint to your script.

When you set breakpoints in the Actions panel, they are saved with the FLA file. When you set breakpoints in the Debugger, they are valid only for the current session.

Tracing Actions with the Movie Explorer

Another excellent tool you can use to keep track of your Flash movie is the Movie Explorer, as shown in Figure 13-10. The Movie Explorer is a visual outline of all the objects in your movie. By default, the Movie Explorer shows text objects, buttons, movie clips, graphic symbols, and actions. You can add or remove items from the Movie Explorer by clicking the buttons at the top of the Movie Explorer window. You can even customize the list by clicking the last button at the top of the window and then choosing from the pop-up menu which items to display.

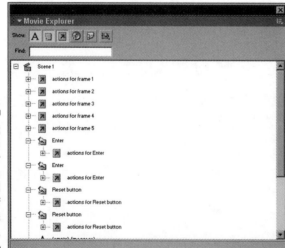

Figure 13-10: The Movie Explorer presents a visual outline of your movie's stuff.

But this book is about *ActionScript,* so I show you how to use the Movie Explorer to fine-tune your code rather than how to edit graphic objects with it. To edit ActionScript with the Movie Explorer:

1. **Choose Window⇨Movie Explorer.**

   The Movie Explorer opens.

2. **To choose the items you want displayed in the Movie Explorer, click the buttons at the top of the Movie Explorer window.**

   The chosen items are displayed. A plus sign (+) is displayed to the left of any object, such as a movie clip with actions or a nested movie clip.

3. **To expand a branch, click the plus sign (+).**

   The branch expands and lists everything used to create the object. Actions are designated by a button with an angled arrow. The label to the right of the button indicates the frame to which the actions are assigned. If the actions are assigned to a movie clip, the frame that's indicated is the frame in the main movie where the movie clip appears. To the left of the Actions button is a plus sign (+) indicating that the branch must be expanded to view the actions.

4. **To display the actions, click the plus sign (+) to expand the branch.**

   All the actions assigned to the frame are now visible.

5. **To edit the actions assigned to a frame, double-click the button with the angled arrow.**

   The Actions panel opens and the code you carefully crafted for the frame is displayed. You can now edit the ActionScript as needed.

Part IV

Integrating ActionScript Elements in Your Flash Movies

The 5th Wave · By Rich Tennant

"Well, it's not quite done. I've animated the gurgling spit-sink and the rotating Novocaine syringe, but I still have to add the high speed whining drill audio track."

In this part . . .

If it's coolness you want, it's coolness you'll get. In this part, I show you how to use several bits of ActionScript code — and other Flash delights — to create unique things for your Flash movies. Remember that coolness is relative, especially if you're from Alaska where hot is not. In this part, you'll learn to create several useful objects that you are free to distribute freely to other interested Flash ActionScripters. But do me a favor, just give them enough to whet their whistles and tell them to buy my book. Please.

Some of the things I show you how to create are sound controllers that turn the volume up and down while panning from one speaker to the next, scrolling text boxes, and a cartoon character's face with interchangeable elements, just to name a few.

Chapter 14

Creating Useful Objects

● ●

In This Chapter

▶ Animating a button

▶ Building a multi-state rollover button

▶ Crafting a custom cursor

▶ Putting together an On When Pressed button

▶ Creating scrolling text

▶ Creating a frame for a print out

● ●

*I*n ActionScript, you create expressions to evaluate things. The result of the expression depends upon the elements you're evaluating. Consider an answer for this real-life expression: *A Flash movie with motion and sound is . . .?* Most Flash movies have these elements — motion and sound — so the result depends upon the skill of the Flash author. In most cases, the result ranges from interesting to cool. When you add ActionScript to the expression and pull it off well, the result of the expression ranges from very cool to awesome.

In this chapter, I show you how to create some useful objects with ActionScript. I wouldn't go so far as to put these effects in the "awesome" category, but they rate on the high end of the cool scale. I show you how to create a couple of interesting effects with buttons and create a custom cursor. If you've got a lot to say in your Flash movies, — and you do it with text — you'll find the section on scrolling text extremely useful. And if you want to create pages that your viewers can print out, there's a section just for you toward the end of the chapter. So then, if you're ready to bring the coolness level of your Flash movies up a notch or two, turn the thermostat on your air conditioner to "chill" — or if you live in Alaska just open a window — and let the fun begin.

The Actions panel's got lots of books. And some of these books have books within a book. To add some actions to your script, you have to click this book icon and then click that book icon and then maybe even click another. Rather than bore you with a lot of words like click this, then click that, I'm going to show the path to each action as shown in the following example: Click Actions➪Movie Control and then double-click goto.

If you need to know how to create printable movie frames, I have some good news, and I have some bad news, and then I have more good news. The good news is I wrote a whole section about creating printable movie frames. The bad news is it didn't make the book. The good news (I always like to finish on a positive note) is that the entire "Creating Printable Movie Frames" section has been included as bonus content on the CD-ROM.

Creating Animated Buttons

If you're creating a full-fledged Web site with Flash, then you need some form of navigation. You can create some very cool buttons by using a different graphic in each of a button's states. To create an animated button, you create a movie clip and use it in one of the button's states, the Over state being the logical choice as motion occurs when the viewer rolls his or her mouse over the button. You've probably seen this effect before — the Flash author uses motion or shape tweening to create the motion, which becomes quite predictable after one or two passes over the button. In this section, I show you how to use ActionScript to create an animated button with random motion. To create an animated button with ActionScript:

To follow along with this exercise, locate the file named animated_button_begin.fla that you'll find in the Animated Buttons folder, which is neatly nested in this chapter's folder on the CD that accompanies this book. Copy the file to your hard drive and use your computer's operating system to disable the read-only attributes of the file.

1. **Launch Flash and open the file animated_button_begin.fla.**

   Flash opens the file and . . . look, I've already done some of the work for you! There's already a button on Stage. All you've got to do is create the movie clip and program it for random motion.

2. **Choose Insert⇨New Symbol.**

   The Create New Symbol dialog box appears.

3. **Type** Spinning Gear **for the symbol's name, choose the movie clip behavior, and click OK.**

   The Create New Symbol dialog box makes a hasty exit, and Flash enters symbol-editing mode.

4. **Name the first layer** gear; **then create a second layer and name it** actions.

   As always, make sure you segregate your actions on a different layer.

5. **Choose Window⇨Library.**

   The document Library opens.

6. **Select the first frame in the gear layer, drag an instance of the gear symbol from the Library to the Stage and center it on Stage.**

   Now you have something you can animate.

7. **Select the second frame in each layer and then choose Modify⇨ Frames⇨Convert to Key Frames.**

   The gear symbol is copied to the second frame, and you have two blank keyframes on the Actions layer.

8. **Select the first frame in the Actions layer and then click the arrow to the left of the word Actions.**

   The Actions panel opens.

9. **Click Actions⇨Variables, and then double-click** set variable.

   Two parameter text boxes appear.

10. **In the Variable field, type** this._x.

    The variable you're creating will get the x property of the gear. Using the this alias tells Flash the target path of the object is the actual object, in this case the movie clip the gear symbol is in. You can use the Insert a Target Path button to insert the target path and then double-click _x in the Actions panel, but entering the script directly into the parameter text box is just much quicker.

11. **In the Value field, type** this._x+(Math.random( )*4)-2 **and then click the Expression box.**

    The expression changes the value of the variable this._x by taking the current value of the object's _x property (or in non-programmer speak, its *x* coordinate on Stage) and changes it by adding a random number between 1 and 4 and subtracting 2 from the result. Again, you can click buttons in the Actions panel to create this line of code, but I urge you to get in the habit of typing in your own script when possible; you'll free up more time to create other cool Flash movies.

    Changing the object's _x property creates random motion along the *x* axis, but you're much better than that. You're going to create random motion on the *y* axis and then create random rotation.

12. **In the Script pane of the Actions panel, right-click (Windows) or Ctrl+click (Macintosh) and choose Copy from the drop-down menu.**

    Flash copies the line of code to the Actions panel's clipboard.

13. **In the right pane of the Actions panel, right-click (Windows) or Ctrl+click (Macintosh) and choose Paste from the drop-down menu.**

    Flash pastes the line of code into the script.

14. **In the parameter text boxes, change every instance of _x to _y.**

    You make the change by selecting the text and then typing to overwrite it, or you can use the Replace command from the Actions panel's

Options menu. Your second line of code should read: `this._y = this._y+(Math.random()*4)-2;`. This line of code generates the random motion on the y axis.

You can also find and replace items in your ActionScript by clicking the Replace button that looks like a small upright magnifying glass. You find it right next to the slightly larger, angled magnifying glass to the left and directly above the Script pane.

Now that you have the gear moving randomly about the x and y axis, it's time to add some random rotation.

15. In the Script pane of the Actions panel, right-click (Windows) or Ctrl+click (Macintosh) and choose Paste from the drop-down menu.

Flash pastes the copied line of code into the script.

16. In the Value field, change `_x` **to** `_rotation`, **change the number 4 to 360 and delete the text that reads** `-2`.

The third line of code in your ActionScript should read: `this._rotation = this._rotation+(Math.random()*360);`. This line of code changes the object's rotation property by adding a random number between 1 and 360 to its current value. You can use any number other than 360 if you please. A small number won't cause much of a change in rotation; a large number can cause large variations in rotation. I chose 360 because a circle has 360 degrees, and the motion it generated was frenetic enough to suit me. Your completed ActionScript for frame 1 should look like Figure 14-1.

Figure 14-1:
This gear will be jumping when this code is executed.

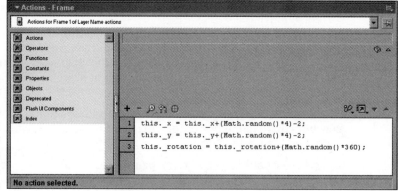

17. Click the second frame in the Actions layer.

The random motion you so carefully scripted in frame 1 will execute only once unless you tell Flash to repeat it over and over and over. In this case, you want the action to repeat over and over, so you've got to do just a wee bit more.

18. **In the left pane of the Actions panel, click Actions⇨Movie Control and then double-click** goto.

    The Actions panel should still be at the ready. If for some reason you closed the Actions panel before taking a break, wandering off into the kitchen for a cold drink, or answering the call of nature, open it now by clicking the arrow to the left of the word Actions.

    Flash adds the action to the script, and the parameter text boxes open. The default parameters tell Flash to Go to and Play frame 1, which is just what you want. Each time Flash goes back and plays between the two frames, a new random number is generated, and the gear keeps on turning and hopping about.

19. **Click the current scene button to exit symbol-editing mode.**

    The spinning gear symbol is stored in the document Library.

20. **Choose Window⇨Library and then double-click the spinner button symbol, which I've thoughtfully crafted for you.**

    Flash enters symbol-editing mode. Notice that I've already created two layers for you, MC and sound. I've already included a sound in the down frame of the button's Down frame. Notice there is no keyframe in the graphic layer's Over frame. That's because you want the spinning gear movie clip to play only in this frame. If you remember your basic buttons material, the contents of this frame show when the user's mouse rolls over the button.

21. **Click the Over frame in the MC layer and then choose Insert⇨ Keyframe.**

    Flash converts the Over frame to a keyframe, and the playhead jumps to the frame.

22. **With the Over frame still selected, drag an instance of the Spinning gear movie clip from the Library to Stage, and then center it to Stage with the Align tool.**

    The Spinning gear movie clip appears in the Over frame, as shown in Figure 14-2.

23. **Select the Down frame in the MC layer and press F7 to convert it into an empty keyframe.**

    If you don't do this, the movie clip keeps on a spinning in the Down frame, even though it's only momentarily when the button is held down. But if you're a stickler for detail, follow this step.

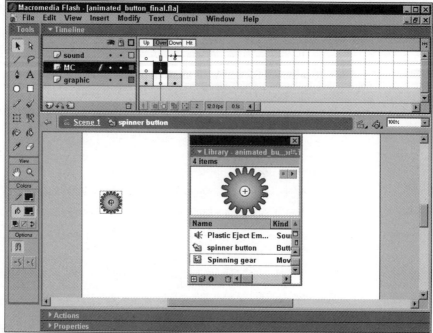

Figure 14-2:
This button will definitely spin. Very cool.

24. Click the Back button to exit symbol-editing mode.

That's it. You're done creating the button.

25. Choose Control⇨Test Movie.

Flash publishes the movie in another window. Move your mouse over the button. If you followed the steps exactly, the gear will be randomly wobbling and rotating. Click the button, the movie clip stops, the graphic in the Down frame is displayed, and the sound plays.

If your button didn't wobble or rotate, locate the file named animated_ button_final.fla. It's in the Animated Buttons folder, which is a subfolder of this chapter's folder on the CD that accompanies this book. Open the file up in Flash and compare the elements of the file to what you've just created.

Creating a Multi-State Rollover Button

You can create a standard bread-and-butter Flash button that displays different graphics, makes sounds, and does other interesting things. Even though a button has a timeline of four frames, you can't assign any actions to them. You need to do that after the button is on Stage using the On Mouse Event handler. You can use the On Mouse Event handler to make all sorts of interesting things happen. In this section, I show you how to program a button to play a movie clip when a user rolls his or her mouse over the button, stop a movie clip when the mouse rolls out of the button's target range, and load a movie clip when the button is clicked. To create a multi-state rollover button:

To follow along with this lesson, copy the rollover_buttons folder, which you'll find in this chapter's folder on the CD that comes with this book, to your hard drive. Open the folder, select all the files, and then use your computer's operating system to disable each file's read-only attributes.

1. **Launch Flash and open the file rollover_buttons_begin.fla.**

   Flash opens the file. Before you jump ahead to Step 2, choose Control⇨Test Movie. Roll your mouse over the second, third, and fourth buttons. Notice as you roll your mouse over a button, animated text appears. As soon as you roll off the button, the text stops. When you click a button, something different happens on Stage — another Flash movie is loaded.

   The animated text movie clips are always on Stage. Figure 14-3 shows the timeline for the movie. Each of the top layers houses a movie clip. The first frame of the each movie clip is blank, and there is a stop action that prevents the clip from playing when the movie loads. Each button is programmed to play the second frame of the movie clip when clicked. Your mission — should you decide to accept it — is to program the first button.

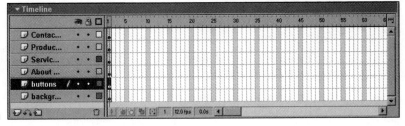

Figure 14-3:
This timeline has many movie clips.

2. **Click the first button to select it and then click the arrow to the left of the word Actions.**

   The Actions panel opens. If the title reads Actions-Frame, you haven't properly selected the button. You know the drill; click it again until the panel reads Actions-Buttons. If at first you don't succeed. . . .

3. **In the left pane of the Actions panel, click Actions⇨Browser/Network and then double-click** unloadMovie.

   The action is added to the script, and the parameter text boxes appear.

4. **Accept the default Location parameter and in the large field to the right, type** 1.

   The purpose of this action is to unload any movie that is on Stage as a result of one of the other buttons being clicked.

5. **In the left pane of the Actions panel, click Actions⇨Miscellaneous Actions and then double-click** evaluate.

   The Expression field opens above the Script pane.

6. **Click the Insert a Target Path button (the black button with a cross-hair above the Script pane).**

   The Insert Target Path dialog box opens.

7. **Click the AboutMC button and then click OK.**

   The Insert Target path dialog box closes, and the target path is added to the script.

8. **Inside the Expression field, click to the right of the target path and type** .gotoAndPlay(2).

   This line of code addresses the movie clip directly using its target path followed by the goto action. Be sure to enter the action after the target path using the exact syntax shown in Step 8; otherwise, the ActionScript will fail.

9. **Click the first line of code.**

   The mouse events are listed in the parameter text box area, but they're not text boxes, they're check boxes.

10. **Click the Release event to remove it from the script and choose the Roll Over event.**

    When the movie is published, the AboutMC movie clip plays when the user's mouse rolls over the button.

11. **Click the third line of code to select it and then right-click (Windows) or Ctrl+click (Macintosh).**

    The Actions panel context menu opens.

12. **Choose Copy.**

13. **Click the last line of code (the solitary curly brace), open the context menu as outline in Step 11, and then choose Paste.**

    Flash pastes the line of code into the script preceded by the on (release) event handler.

14. **In the parameter text box area, change the copied code so that it reads** _root.AboutMC.gotoAndStop(14).

    To change code in a parameter text box, click and drag your mouse over the code you need to modify to select it and type the revision. In this case, you select Play and replace it with Stop; select the 2 and replace it with 14. When the movie is published and this action is executed, the movie advances to frame 14 of the movie clip, which stops the movie clip from playing.

    To view all of the components I used to create each movie clip, open the document Library and then double-click the movie clip's title to see it in symbol-editing mode.

15. **Click the** (on) release **event on the line above the code you just modified.**

    The mouse events appear above the Script pane.

16. **Click the** Release **check box to remove it from the code and choose** Roll Out.

    The AboutMC movie clip stops playing when the user's mouse rolls off the button.

17. **Click the last line of code to select it and then in the left side of the Actions panel, click Actions⇨Browser/Network and then double-click** loadMovie.

    If for any reason you closed the Browser/Network book, you need to open it to select the action. The action is added to the script, and the action's parameters are displayed above the Script pane.

18. **In the URL field type** about.swf.

    This is the target path to the movie that loads when the button is released.

19. **Accept the default Location parameter and in the blank field, change the level from** 0 **to** 1.

    When the button is released, the movie loads into the first level of the movie.

20. **Click the sixth line of code you created that reads** _root.AboutMC.gotoAndStop(14);.

21. **Right-click (Windows) or Ctrl+click (Macintosh) and then choose Copy from the drop-down menu.**

    Flash copies the code to the Actions panel's clipboard.

22. Click the eighth line of code that reads on (release) { **and then right-click (Windows) or Ctrl+click (Macintosh) and choose Paste from the drop-down menu.**

The copied code is pasted into the script. This line of code stops the movie clip from playing when the button is clicked. Figure 14-4 shows the complete programming for the button. Before moving on, compare this with the code you've created.

I realize I'm making you jump back and forth between different lines of code. If you prefer, you can work in a linear fashion from top to bottom; however, by copying and pasting similar lines of code, you save quite a bit of time.

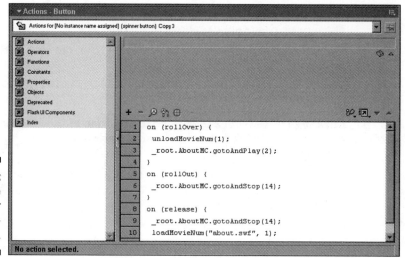

Figure 14-4:
This code makes your button multi-functional.

23. Choose Control⇨Test Movie.

Flash publishes the movie and plays it in another window. Roll your mouse over the button you just programmed, and you should see animated text; as soon as you roll off the button, the text disappears. Click the button and a movie loads, displaying information about the hypothetical company the Flash movie was created for.

As you can see, the On Mouse Event handlers give you a lot of programming flexibility when it comes to navigation buttons. For example, instead of playing a movie clip with animated text or images when a button is rolled over, you can program it to play a movie clip with a sound in it; perhaps a short fanfare to get the viewer's attention. Put on your thinking cap and come up with new and innovate ways you can use multi-state rollover buttons in your Flash movies.

Creating a Custom Cursor

Another useful object you can add to your Flash movies is a *custom cursor*. The custom cursor can be any graphic that you convert to a symbol; for example a customer's logo or a specialized cursor to suit a game you've created. In this section, I show you how to create a custom cursor that replaces the standard — ahem . . . I will be polite and say "boring" — cursor. To create a custom cursor:

To follow along with this exercise, locate the file custom_cursor_begin.fla, which you'll find in this chapter's folder of this book's CD, and copy it to your hard drive. Use your computer's operating system to disable the Read Only attributes of the file.

1. **Launch file and open the custom_cursor_begin.fla file.**

   Flash opens the file, and you see some buttons. The buttons are already programmed. You'll be creating a clever cursor that is completely clickable.

2. **Choose Insert⇨New Symbol.**

   The Create New Symbol dialog box opens.

3. **Assign the Movie Clip behavior to the symbol, type** cursor **in the Name field, and click OK.**

   You are now in symbol-editing mode.

4. **Choose Window⇨Library.**

   The document Library opens.

5. **Double click the Symbols folder, locate the symbol called** gear, **and then click and drag it on Stage.**

   An instance of the gear symbol appears in the movie clip.

6. **Using the Align panel, center the gear to Stage.**

7. **Click the Back button to return to movie-editing mode.**

   The cursor movie clip is added to the document Library.

8. **In the Timeline window, click the first frame of the cursor layer.**

   The frame is selected. Notice that the cursor layer is on top of the other layers. This is so the cursor is visible no matter what object you drag it over.

9. **In the document Library, locate the cursor symbol you just created and drag an instance of it on Stage.**

Put it anywhere. As soon as the movie is published, the custom cursor symbol develops a magnetic attraction for the user's mouse.

10. **Click the arrow to the left of the word Properties.**

The Property inspector opens. If you've been following the steps, the Property inspector shows the symbol's name (cursor) and the behavior (Movie Clip). If the Behavior field doesn't show Movie Clip, click the triangle and choose Movie Clip from the drop-down menu.

11. **In the <Instance Name> field, type cursor.**

Actually, you can type any name and it will appear on the Insert Target Path dialog box; *cursor* is just a perfectly logical name that will make sense to any other designers on the project.

12. **Click the first frame in the Actions layer.**

13. **Click the arrow to the left of the word Actions.**

The Actions panel opens.

14. **In the left pane of the panel, click Objects⇨Movie⇨Mouse⇨Methods, and then double-click hide.**

The Mouse.hide object does exactly that, hides the mouse.

15. **In the left pane of the Actions panel, click the Actions⇨Movie Clip Control, and then double-click startDrag.**

As if you didn't already know, Flash adds the action to your script, and look, the parameter text boxes are up to their old tricks.

16. **Click inside the Target field and then click the black Insert a Target Path button.**

The Insert Target Path dialog box opens.

17. **Click the button labeled cursor and then click OK.**

The dialog box closes.

18. **In the parameter text box area, click Lock Mouse to Center, shown in Figure 14-5.**

When the movie is published, the cursor movie clip sticks like glue and functions just like your normal, ho-hum, boring cursor.

19. **Choose Control⇨Test Movie.**

Flash publishes the movie and plays it in another window. Start moving your mouse, and the cursor movie clip follows. Click any of the buttons, and you'll see that the custom cursor works just like the one you've hidden. Neato.

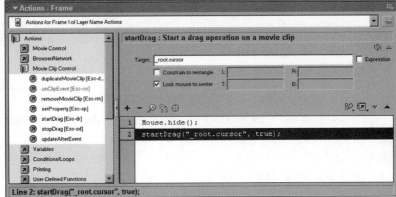

Figure 14-5: Don't know what I'm gonna do, 'cause this code's gonna make my custom cursor stick like glue.

If you create a custom cursor for a movie with multiple levels, create a separate movie with just the custom cursor in it and publish it as a Flash movie (.swf format). In the first frame of the movie you created the cursor for, use the `loadMovie` action and load the cursor movie in level 99, the highest level you can load into the base movie. Then the cursor appears on top of every object in every movie that you load into the base movie.

Building an On When Pressed Button

Have you ever visited a Flash Web site with a game, and there was this little button that made the game piece move when you clicked it, but it only moved once and you had to click the button again and again and again? And pretty soon you got a bad case of clickitis, the disease that made Microsoft famous? Discretion being the better part of valor, you made a quick exit stage left by clicking the browser Back button and getting out of Dodge. To avoid subjecting viewers of your Flash movies to the same fate, create a button that's active when the mouse button is pressed, also known as an On When Pressed button. Here's how you do it:

1. **Create a button.**

   This should be a no-brainer. Create any button with any level of coolness you desire.

2. **Choose Insert⇨New Symbol.**

   The Create New Symbol dialog box appears.

3. **Enter a name for the symbol and choose the Movie Clip behavior.**

   I know what you're thinking. I'm creating a button. Why am I creating a movie clip? Hang on, intrepid reader. Your inquiring mind will soon know the reason why.

4. **Open the document Library.**

   You've been here and done this before.

5. **Drag an instance of the button you just created into the movie clip.**

   You are nesting a symbol within a symbol. The movie clip will soon be playing at a theater near you. One button flew over the movie clip nest.

6. **Click the arrow to the left of the word Actions.**

   The Actions panel opens.

7. **Click Actions⇨Variable and then double-click** setVariable.

   Two parameter text boxes snap to attention above the Script pane.

8. **In the Variable field, type** clicked.

   A variable in a button? Hang in there.

9. **In the Value field, type true and click the Expression box.**

   That's right, this is an expression. And it's a Boolean expression to boot.

10. **In the Script pane, click the curly brace, which is coincidentally the last line of the script.**

11. **Click Actions⇨Variable and then double-click** set variable.

    Been there, done that. Please read on.

12. **In the Variable field, type** clicked.

    Hmmm, this seems familiar.

13. **In the Value field, type false and click the Expression box.**

    Now take a deep breath and look at what you've got in the Script pane. You've got the same variable, and the value is true and false when the button is released. Ah ha, the game is afoot, Watson. In order to make this button work, you've got to specify different mouse events. When the button is pressed, it's clicked, so clicked is true. When the button is released, it isn't clicked, so clicked is false.

14. **Select the first line in your script.**

    Mouse events in the Script pane. Call in the exterminators.

15. **Choose the Press event.**

16. **Click the Back button to return to movie-editing mode.**

    And that's pretty much it for the button. The movie clip is added to the document Library. Your job is to program the movie clip.

So far you've got a button that sets a variable to true or false depending on what the user's mouse is doing. To make the thing work, you've got to tell the movie clip to determine whether the button is clicked or not clicked. Remember when you nest a button in a movie clip, the button is fully functional and the cool little finger will point at the button when users roll their mouse over the button. To evaluate whether the button is clicked or not clicked, you have to create two conditional statements.

To program the movie clip:

1. **Choose Window⇨Library to open the document Library and then drag an instance of the movie clip symbol you just nested the button in onto the Stage.**

2. **Click the arrow to the left of the word Actions.**

    The Actions panel opens.

3. **Click Actions⇨Conditions/Loops and double-click if.**

    Iffy as it may sound, the if action is what makes the whole thing work.

4. **In the Condition field, type clicked.**

    The statement you've just created evaluates to see whether or not the Boolean value of the variable clicked is true. If the button nested in the movie clip is pressed, the variable is equal to the Boolean value true, so the button is well and truly clicked.

5. **Create the ActionScript that occurs if the button is clicked.**

    You can use an On While Pressed button to increment an object property, for example increase the _x and _y property of a movie clip by 1 as long as the button is pressed. That means the movie clip moves by the value specified when the button is pressed and held down.

6. **Select the first line of script.**

    The parameter text area is filled with clip events. The default clip event executes the ActionScript you just created when the movie clip loads. But wait, that's no good. You need the Flash Player to evaluate the movie clip continuously to see whether the button is clicked or not.

7. **Click the EnterFrame radio button.**

    When you choose this clip event, the actions are executed every time the frame is entered, which seeing as this is a single frame movie clip is always — at least while the Flash movie is playing, that is.

And that's it. Your button in a movie clip is good to go. For an example of a On While Pressed button in action, read the next section about scrolling text.

Building a Scrolling Text Block, or Stuffing Lots of Text in a Teeny Space

If you've got a lot to say and just a little bit of room to say it in, you've got a problem. And if you've got that problem in a Flash movie, I have the solution: scrolling text. Did you ever see those outer-space movies where somewhere in a land far, far away, the evil alien bad guy is getting ready to do hideous things to the lovely princess, and the movie producer — as clever producers are wont to do — brings you up to date with scrolling text across the screen? Well you can do almost the same thing in Flash by loading a text file into a movie and then programming a button to scroll the text up or down. To create a scrolling text block:

To follow along with this exercise, copy the folder scrolling_text (conveniently located in this chapter's folder on this book's CD) to your hard drive and use your computer's operating system to disable each file's read-only attributes.

1. **Launch Flash and open the file scrolling_text_begin.fla.**

    Flash opens the file. Now you've got the whole enchilada in front of you. Please pass the salsa. Nice author that I am, I've already created a few goodies for you to work with. On the first frame of the Actions layer, I've used the `loadVariables` action to load a file named text.txt you'll be programming the buttons to scroll. The actual text in the text.txt file is equal to a variable named `about`, which I've declared in the text document. I've already created the dynamic Text and assigned the variable `about` to it. The buttons you see on Stage are actually an individual symbol comprised of two named instances of movie clips with a button nested in them. I've already programmed the individual movie clips (Up and Down) with a bit of code that is just like the code you created when you created the On When Pressed button in the last section. (You did create the button, didn't you?)

    For more information on working with dynamic text and loading text from external sources, check Chapter 10.

2. **Double-click the buttons.**

    Flash enters symbol-editing mode. The buttons have been conveniently grouped to make your life easier. Double-clicking the button group makes it possible for you to program both buttons in one fell swoop.

3. **Click the bottom button and then click the arrow to the left of the word Actions.**

    The button is selected, and the Actions panel opens.

4. Click Actions⇨Conditions/Loops and then double-click `if`.

The action is added to your script, and the Condition parameter text box appears. Flash adds the default clip event handler, `onClipEvent (load)`.

5. In the Conditions field, type clicked.

This is the variable that was declared in the ActionScript for each button. When you type the variable's name in the Condition field, you're telling Flash to execute the action if the Boolean value of the variable is true. In this case, as long as the button is clicked, the next action will execute. This is the same code you learned how to create when you read the last section on how to create an On While Pressed button from the last section. (And you did read the last section, didn't you?)

6. In the left pane of the Actions panel, click Actions⇨Variables and then double-click `set variable`.

That's right, you've added another action to the script.

7. In the Variable field type _root.about.scroll.

You can enter the entire line of code directly into the Variable field, or you can type the target path (**_root.about**) and double-click `scroll`, which you find in the Properties book, which is neatly nestled in the Text Field book in the left pane of the Actions panel. Or if you don't like opening a zillion books, take the shortcut by opening the Index book and then scrolling to `scroll`.

An individual variable does not show up in the Insert Target Path dialog box. You have to manually enter the path for the variable.

8. In the Value field type _root.about.scroll+1 **and click the Expression box.**

This line of code takes the current value of `_root.about.scroll` and adds 1 to it, effectively scrolling the text down one line. If you don't click the Expression box, Flash thinks this is string data, and the text won't scroll.

You can also get the text to scroll by creating an expression that increments the value of `_root.about.scroll` by 1 as long as the button is pressed. To do this, you use the Evaluate action and enter the following code in the Expression field `_root.about.scroll+=1`.

9. Click the first line of code.

The first line of code determines the event handler that causes the action to execute. The default movie clip handler `load` doesn't work in this case because it evaluates the ActionScript only when the movie clip loads. You want the movie clip to be evaluated continually and when the user clicks the button, bam, the text starts scrolling. To do this you need the action to execute when the movie enters the frame the action is assigned to.

10. Click EnterFrame.

Your code for the Movie clip button should look like Figure 14-6. The code for the button that scrolls the text up is almost identical so instead of working hard, I'm going to show you how to work smarter.

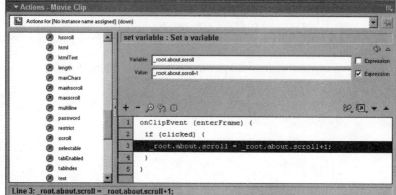

Figure 14-6:
For a text scroll, this script is the answer.

11. Click the top line of code to select it and then Shift+click the last line of code.

The entire Actionscript for the button is selected.

12. Right-click (Windows) or Ctrl+click (Macintosh) and then choose Copy from the drop-down menu.

The code is copied to the Actions panel's clipboard. Don't close the Actions panel just yet; you need it in the next step.

13. Click the top button and then click inside the right pane of the Actions panel.

14. Right-click (Windows) or Ctrl+click (Macintosh) and then choose Paste from the drop-down menu.

The code is pasted into the Actions panel.

15. Click the third line of code.

The code is selected and above the Script pane, the Variable and Value fields open.

16. In the Value field, change the plus (+) sign to a minus (–) sign.

To make the change, select the plus (+) sign and then type a minus (–) sign on your computer's keyboard. Now wasn't that a lot easier than entering all that code manually? Your finished code for the up button should look like Figure 14-7.

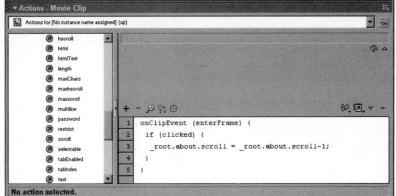

Figure 14-7:
Going up!

17. Choose Control➪Test Movie.

Flash publishes the movie and plays it in another window. Click the down button, and the text scrolls down as long as you hold the button. Click the up button, and the text reverses field and scrolls up.

If the text in your movie didn't scroll, open the file scrolling_text_final.fla in Flash and compare the code to what you've just created. The file is located in the scrolling_text folder in this chapter's folder on the CD, which — if you've been following this exercise — should be parked in your CD drive.

Chapter 15

Creating Interactive Elements

● ●

In This Chapter

▶ Creating a shopping cart

▶ Scripting a Visitor Response form

▶ Creating a Flash cartoon character

▶ Detecting collisions in Flash

▶ Building an animated mask

● ●

*T*here's so much you can do with ActionScript that it boggles the mind. I'm waiting for the day I can use it to watch my cat while I write. Nothing drastic, mind you — just a stern warning as she races right past the kitty toys I plunked down hard-earned money to purchase to tip over a wastebasket in search of a scrap of paper to play with. But that day is probably in the distant future, so I'll get back to the topic on hand: creating interactive elements with ActionScript.

In this chapter, I show you how to create some useful interactive items for a Web site. These items range from the terribly useful to the inane and impractical but terribly fun. Throughout this chapter are a number of exercises that you'll be building from source files included with the book's CD. In most cases, I've done the great majority of the work by creating the graphic elements and some of the ActionScript. But you don't get off scot-free; I leave the really cool stuff for you to do.

The Actions panel's got lots of books. And some of these books have books within a book. To add some actions to your script, you have to click this book icon and then click that book icon and then maybe even click another. Rather than bore you with a lot of words, I'm going to show the path to each action as shown in the following example: Click Actions⇨Movie Control and then double-click goto. Instead of eye strain, you can let your fingers do the clicking.

So then, you've got a Flash movie on the Web and you want some way for your visitors to get back to you. Creating a Visitor Response Form tells you what you need to know in order to create an online form and transmit the results. However, you won't find it in the book — it's incognito (wherever that is) on the CD-ROM that accompanies this book.

Building an E-Commerce Shopping Cart

With ActionScript, you can build an interactive shopping cart. By interactive, I don't mean just clicking an item that you want to purchase; I mean dragging an item off a virtual store shelf and dropping it in a shopping cart. As you add items to the shopping cart, the cash register rings up the tally. To create an online shopping cart:

To follow along with this exercise, locate the file on_line_catalog_begin.fla on the CD that came with this book, copy it to your hard drive, and use your computer's operating system to disable the file's Read Only attributes.

1. **Launch Flash and open the file on_line_catalog_begin.fla.**

   Flash opens the file. Before you go waltzing off to Step 2, Matilda, I'd like you to take a look at what I've already created. This is a four-frame movie. In the first frame's Actions layer, I've created an array for each item in the store. Each item's array is a storehouse of information about the item: title, description, and price.

   Advance to the second frame, and you see that the storefront is already set up for you. Each store item is a movie clip that the viewer drags off the shelf and into the cart. As soon as the user releases the mouse, the item is added to the shopping cart, and another one appears on the shelf to replenish inventory.

   The third frame is the same as the second. The reason for the two frames is to update the variables whenever a purchase is made. The cash register has a dynamic text block that displays the price of the items purchased.

   The fourth frame is where the purchase is confirmed. If the shopper purchases more than one of an item, it is noted here.

2. **Click the arrow to the left of the word Actions.**

   The Actions panel opens.

3. **Click the second frame on the timeline (or drag the Playhead to the second frame) and then double-click the *Carrara For Dummies* book on the top shelf.**

   This step gets you the invisible button that is nested within the movie clip. In the Actions panel, you see a couple of lines of code that I've already created for you. These lines of code start and stop the drag action.

4. **Click the line of code that reads** stopDrag ();**, click Actions⇨Movie Clip Control and then double-click** set Property.

   Flash adds the action to the script, and three parameter text boxes appear above the Script pane.

5. **Click inside the Target window and then click the black Insert a Target Path button.**

   The Insert Target Path dialog box appears.

6. **Click the button that reads** book1 **and then click OK.**

   The target path is added to the script.

7. **Click the triangle to the right of the Property field and then click** _x(position).

   The property is added to the script.

8. **In the Value field, type** 81.7 **and click the Expression box.**

   When this line of code is executed, the book returns to its original x position on the shelf. To properly align the book, you also need to adjust its y position.

9. **Right-click (Windows) or Ctrl+click (Macintosh) and then choose copy from the drop-down menu.**

   The last line of code you created is copied to the clipboard.

10. **Repeat Step 9, but this time, choose Paste from the drop-down menu.**

    The copied code is pasted into the script.

11. **Change the _x in the pasted code to _y and change the value to** 130.2.

    This line of code changes the book's y position. It should read as follows: setProperty ("_root.book1", _y, 130.2);. These two lines of code place the book back on the shelf once the purchase has been made. In other words, the store never runs out of a particular item. Talk about your perpetual inventory.

12. **In the left pane of the Actions panel, click Actions⇨Variables and then double-click** set variable.

    The action is added to the script, and two fields open above the Script pane.

13. **In the Variable field, type** bookPrice, **in the Value field type** _root.book1[2] **and then click the Expression box.**

    This line of code creates the variable that retrieves the book's price from the array. If you study the array in frame one, you'll see that the price is the third item in the book1 array. Remember that the first element in an array is always 0.

14. **In the left pane of the Actions panel, click Actions⇨Variables and then double-click** set variable.

    Yup, that's right. You're going to create a new variable. This line of code keeps track of how many times the shopper drags an item into the shopping cart. This variable is used when the order is confirmed.

15. **In the Variable field, type** _root.totalPrice.

16. **In the Value field, type** Number(_root.totalPrice)+Number(bookPrice), **and then click the Expression box .**

    This line of code creates a new variable that keeps the tally of total purchases. Notice the Math method Number precedes both sides of the equation. This method converts the string literal data from the array to numeric data that can be manipulated with mathematical operands; otherwise, you'd never get the cash register to add it all up.

17. **In the left pane of the Actions panel, click Actions⇨Variables and then double-click** set variable.

18. **In the Variable field, type** _root.CFDbought.

19. **In the Value field, type** _root.CFDbought+1 **and then click the Expression box.**

20. **In the left side of the Actions panel, click Actions⇨Miscellaneous Actions and then double-click** evaluate.

    Above the Script pane, the Expression field opens.

21. **In the Expression field type** _root.gotoAndStop(2);.

    This line of code toggles the movie back to frame 2. Remember, you're dealing with a movie clip and want the movie to toggle back to the main timeline, hence the addition of _root. Your code for the invisible button should look exactly like Figure 15-1. But don't close the Actions panel just yet. You've still got some code to create.

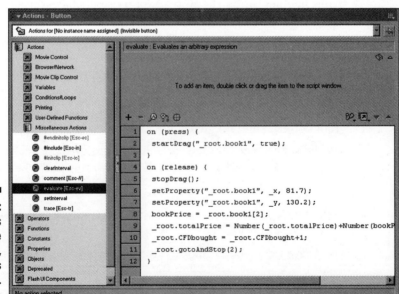

Figure 15-1: When this line of code executes, a sale is made.

Continuing with this exercise, follow these steps to create the code:

1. **Click the Back button to exit symbol-editing mode.**

   Once again you are in movie-editing mode.

2. **Click the second frame in the Actions layer.**

   The frame is selected.

3. **In the left pane of the Actions panel, click Actions⇨Variables and then double-click** set variable.

   Now comes the time to pass the price information to the variable in the dynamic text box in the cash register.

4. **Click inside the Variable field, click the black Insert a Target Path button, click the Checkout button , and then click OK.**

   Flash adds the target path to the script.

5. **In the Variable field, click to the right of** Checkout **and type** .price.

   Congratulations, you've just set the path to the price variable in the dynamic text box.

6. **In the Value field, type "$" + totalPrice, and then click the Expression box.**

   Flash now has all the information to display the price on the cash register.

7. **In the left pane of the Actions panel, click Actions⇨Movie Control, and then double-click** goto.

   Flash adds the action to the script.

8. **In the Frame field, type** 3 **and click the Go To and Stop radio button.**

   This line of code tells Flash to go to and stop at frame 3. When another item is dragged into the shopping cart, the movie reverts back to frame 2 where the price is updated and then goes to frame 3 where the viewer can add another item to the cart. Your finished code for frame 2 in the Actions layer should look just like Figure 15-2.

9. **Drag the playhead to frame 4.**

   Here's where the order is confirmed. I've already created the ActionScript in the movie's Actions layer. If you select the frame and open the Actions panel, you'll see the code shown in Figure 15-3. This code creates variables for the Dynamic text boxes, which in effect tallies the customer's purchase. Take a good look at the code and notice the value for each book's text box is set to null if the book isn't purchased. Note that in this figure, the Actions panel is displayed in Expert mode to show all the code.

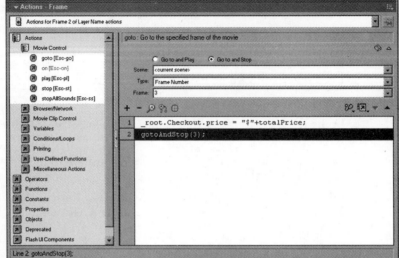

Figure 15-2: Can you say "cha-ching?"

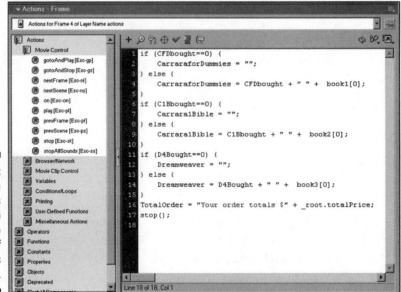

Figure 15-3: This code creates variables to confirm the number of items purchased.

10. Choose Control⇨Test Movie.

Flash publishes the movie and plays it in another window. Drag any item off the shelf, and then drop it in the shopping cart. If you've followed the steps exactly, you'll see a price in the cash register window. Drag another item into the cart, and the price will change. When you're ready to check out, click the red button and your purchases are tallied.

This movie can be further modified for use on an e-commerce site. All it needs is a Submit and Reset button. The code for the Reset button clears out the shopping cart. The code for the Submit button sends the contents of the variables to the site's administrators. The actual code behind the button varies depending upon the Web hosting service. To learn more about sending variables via the Internet, read the next section, "Creating a Visitor Response Form."

If your movie didn't add up — after you made some purchases that is — open the on_line_catalog_final.fla file in Flash and compare the ActionScript to what you've just created. Be sure to disable the file's Read Only attribute if you want to test or modify the file.

Constructing a Cartoon Character's Face

Did you ever play with a game like Mr. Potato Head or one of those games where you have to choose a nose, lips, and hair to create a goofy looking character? In this section you're going to create the Flash equivalent. I've already created the movie clips and done a great deal of the ActionScript for you.

So before I show you how to program the movie clip, let me tell you what I've already done. The noses, hairpieces, eyes, and other character parts were imported or created in a vector-based drawing application such as Macromedia's Freehand. The files were imported into Flash and converted into symbols, which of course must be movie clips because you're going to want to drag them and drop them on a shapeless face in the center of Stage. You may notice the character traits are smaller than the head. This was to fit them all into the movie. Notice that each movie clip has a blue overlay. This is an invisible button that was created by duplicating the character trait and copying it into the Hit frame of a button symbol. Each button symbol is embedded in the movie clip. You'll be programming the movie clips so that your movie viewers can drag them onto the featureless face and turn it into Fearless Frank or Sensuous Sam. The invisible button embedded in the clip changes the cursor when a user's mouse passes over it, showing the user the exact target area that can be dragged. After the user begins dragging the movie clip, it increases to its normal size. I also created some goofy animation for the eyes using motion tweening. After all, this is supposed to be a fun thing, right?

Now comes the really fun part — writing the ActionScript that enables your viewers to turn the faceless blob into Handsome Harry or, if you prefer, Gorgeous George. To create a cartoon character's face:

Copy the file cartoon_begin.fla to your hard drive from this chapter's folder on this book's CD. Use your computer's operating system to disable the Read Only attributes of this file.

1. **Launch Flash and open the cartoon_begin.fla file.**

   Flash opens the file.

2. **Click the hairpiece near the upper right-hand corner of the movie that looks like a reject from a mop factory.**

3. **Click the arrow to the left of the word Actions.**

   The Actions panel opens.

4. **Click the Actions⇨Conditions/Loops and then double-click** if.

   The action appears in the right pane of the Actions panel, and the parameter text boxes make another appearance. Flash automatically adds the onClipEvent (load) event handler to the script.

5. **In the Conditions field, type the following code:**
   this.hitTest(_root._xmouse, _root._ymouse, true).

   I know. That's a lot of code. What this line of code does is tests to see if a target (in this case, the target area of the movie clip) has been hit with the mouse. The actual name of the movie clip could have been entered, but it's much easier to use the target alias this, which refers to the movie clip's relative path.

6. **In the left pane of the Actions panel, click Actions⇨Movie Clip Control and then double-click** startDrag.

   The action is added to the script, and the parameter text boxes open.

7. **In the Target field, type** this **and then click the Expression box.**

   Again you could have referred to the movie clip instance's name, but in the case of this movie, the actions for each movie clip are the same. By using the this alias, you can copy the code and paste it into the other movie clips, which of course saves you a whole lot of typing.

8. **In the left pane of the Actions panel, click Actions⇨Variables and then double-click** set variable.

   A line of code is added to the script, and Flash adds a shocking red highlight over the text *not set yet*. This is simply Flash's way of telling you to declare the variable.

9. **In the Variable field, type** this._xscale; **in the Value field type** 100; **then click the Expression box.**

There's the `this` alias again. This line of code transforms the movie clip back to its original scale along the *x* axis. In order to transform the mop top to its proper proportions, you have to do the same for the *y* axis. Why? Because if you didn't, the wig wouldn't fit right. Right.

10. In the right pane of the Actions panel, right-click (Windows) or Ctrl+click (Macintosh) and choose Copy from the drop-down menu.

Flash copies the line of code to the Actions panel's clipboard.

11. In the right pane of the Actions panel, right-click (Windows) or Ctrl+click (Macintosh) and choose Paste from the drop-down menu.

Flash pastes the copied ActionScript, and your fingers feel much better for not having had to type it.

12. In the Variable field above the Script pane, change x **to** y.

Your finished code for this line should read: `this._yscale = 100;`.

13. Click the first line of code.

The On Clip Event handlers are listed above the Script pane.

14. Choose Mouse down.

When the movie is published, the user will be able to drag the hairpiece when his or her mouse button is pressed.

15. In the right pane of the Actions panel, click the last curly brace and in the left pane of the Actions panel, click Actions⇨Movie Clip Control and then double-click stopDrag.

The action is added to the script. The default `load` Clip event is added to the script.

16. Click the line of code that reads onClipEvent (load) {.

The clip events are listed above the Script pane.

17. Choose Mouse up.

Without this line of code, you'd never be able to drop the wig on the face without a name. Your finished code should look like Figure 15-4.

The ActionScript for the other wigs, beards, noses, eyes, and all the other features lingering on the sideline are identical. Using the `this` alias made it possible for me to copy the code from one movie clip to another. Whenever you have a lot of movie clips that use identical code, use the this alias instead of referring to the movie clip by its instance name.

18. Select the Reset button.

If you've still got the Actions panel open, you'll see the lines of code shown in Figure 15-5. In fact, you'll see more than this if you use the scroll bar. These lines of code repositioned the movie clips to their original positions and resized them so a new face could be constructed without having to restart the movie.

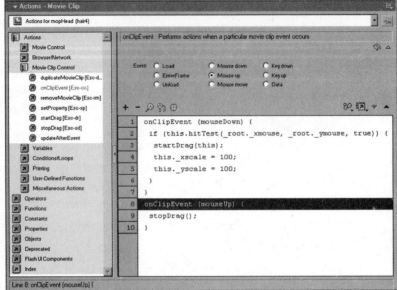

Figure 15-4:
It's so easy
when you
drop and
drag.

19. **Choose Control⇨Test Movie.**

Flash publishes the movie and plays it in another window. Go ahead, let your inner child run amuck and put together a face.

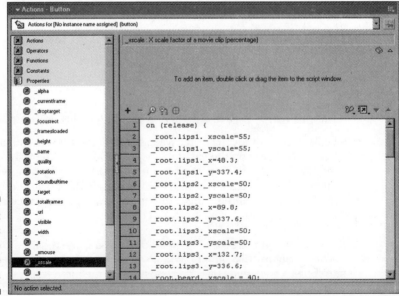

Figure 15-5:
These lines
of code
reset the
movie.

Collision Detection in Flash

The more you play with ActionScript, the more addicted you become. And when you start creating games and similar neat stuff with ActionScript, sometimes you've got to know when an object has moved into another object's area; you know, like when one object gets to know another object, real up close and personal like. Like every other object in ActionScript, movie clips must have names, or as Flash calls them, *instance labels*. You test for collision using the `hitTest` method of the movie clip object. For example, when you add `hitTest` to an ActionScript to an object that can be dragged, when you drop it on the target object, Flash detects the collision. In other words, when movie clip A encroaches on movie clip B's turf, the `hitTest` method sees all, tells all.

To see how the `hitTest` method works, copy to your hard drive the hitTestBegin.fla file that you find in this chapter's folder on the CD that accompanies this book. Use your operating system to disable the file's read only attributes.

To follow along with this tutorial, do the following:

1. **Launch Flash and open the hitTestBegin.fla file.**

   When the file opens, all you see is a bullseye and a ball. If you notice the little blue halo around the ball, that's the invisible button nested inside the ball. The button has already been programmed to execute a drag action when the button is pressed. The bullseye has been given the label of "target." For the `hitTest` method, this is the equivalent of having a kick-me sign pasted on the movie clip's back.

2. **Select the ball and then click the arrow to the left of the word Actions.**

   The Actions panel opens.

3. **Click Actions⇨Conditions/Loops and then double-click `if`.**

   The Condition parameter text box appears above the Script pane. The condition you're going to have the Flash Player test for is to see if the target movie clip has been hit when the ball is dropped. This information is useful, for example, if you've created a game where the user has to drag a game piece that looks like a state or country onto the state or country's name. You program the ActionScript so that when the user drops the game piece on the right title, Flash detects the collision. You reward the player by upping his score.

4. **In the Condition field, enter this.**

   You can use the `this` alias because the method is testing to see whether the object in question is hitting something.

5. **In the left pane of the Actions panel, click Objects⇨Movie⇨Movie Clip⇨Methods and then double-click** hitTest.

   The method is added to your script and your cursor is flashing between parentheses. This is where you need to enter either the target path for the object, or x and y coordinate that specifies the start of an area, followed by a shape; for example, **hitTest(250,200,circle)**. For the purpose of this demonstration, you're going to use a target.

6. **Click the Insert a Target Path button.**

   You know, the little black button with the crosshair that opens the Insert Target Path dialog box.

7. **In the Insert Target path dialog box, click the button labeled *target* and then click OK.**

   This little button has the same name as the movie clip with the bull's-eye. Now Flash can find the bull's-eye. The target path is added to your script and the dialog box closes. Now that you've got the target added to the script, you need to tell Flash what happens next.

8. **In the left pane of the Actions panel, click Actions⇨Miscellaneous Actions and then double-click** evaluate.

   The Expression parameter text box opens above the Script pane.

9. **In the Expression field, enter the following:**
   _root.target.gotoAndPlay(2).

   This tells the Flash Player to play frame 2 of the target movie clip when the hitTest method determines that the target has indeed been hit. I'm not going to tell you what's on frame 2; that's your little surprise for successfully completing this tutorial.

   But there's something else that you have to do when the target is hit: You have to cancel out the drag action. There's already a stopDrag action associated with the button. That's to stop the drag action if the user releases the mouse button without hitting the target. If you don't add a stopDrag action to the ActionScript that detects the collision, the other stopDrag action will not take over because after the target is hit, the Flash player looks for additional ActionScript within the movie clip, not the button.

10. **In the left pane of the Actions panel, click Actions⇨Movie Clip Control and then double-click** stopDrag.

    The action is added to the script, and the drag action invoked by pressing the button will stop when the target is hit. To take the script a bit further, you want to move the ball out of the way once the target has been hit. You do this by changing the ball's x and y properties.

11. **In the left pane of the Actions panel, click Actions⇨Miscellaneous Actions and double-click** evaluate.

12. **In the Expression field, enter the following:** this._x=500.

   This line of code causes to ball to move to the specified coordinate when the target is hit. Repeat Step 12 to change the movie clip's y property to 300. Now all you have to do is change the clip event, and the script will work like a charm.

13. **Click the first line of code and in the parameter area, click the Mouse Up radio button.**

   This tells the Flash Player to execute the script when the user releases the mouse button. Your finished script should look like Listing 15-1.

Listing 15-1   Programming the Ball Using the hitTest Method

```
onClipEvent (mouseUp) {
  if (this.hitTest(_root.target)) {
    _root.target.gotoAndPlay(2);
    stopDrag();
    this._x=500;
    this._y=300;
  }
}
```

Now that you've got everything programmed, choose Control➪Test Movie. After the movie is published, click the ball and then drop it over the target. If you didn't get a surprise, check your code against the preceding steps to see where you ran afoul of the ActionScript law, or open the hitTest_Final.fla file you'll find in this chapter's folder on the CD-ROM and compare the code to what you've created.

Creating an Animated Mask

Another way cool effect you can create in Flash is an *animated mask*. Wait a minute, I know what you're thinking, create a layer with an animation, turn it into a mask layer, and you're good to go — so simple a two-year-old can do it. But this animated mask takes it up another notch or four. When you animate a mask layer, you can animate only one symbol on the layer. A new feature in Flash MX is the setMask method of the Movie Clip Object, which you use to turn a movie clip into a mask. When you create an animated mask using ActionScript, an entire movie clip is the mask. You can use as many or as few frames as needed to create the movie clip you use as a mask. For example, if all you want is a shape to function as a mask, create a movie clip with one frame and the shape you want to mask another object in your movie. You can then make the mask a drag-and-drop mask by nesting an invisible button in the movie clip. Or if you want the ultimate in coolness, create a movie clip where things are happening, like shapes moving or letters appearing. You can use tweening to animate the letters or shapes. Then you have a mask that really makes things happen. When you use a movie clip as a mask, it can only be used on one target — yup, you guessed it — another movie clip.

To show you how easy it is to create a mask target, copy to your hard drive the maskTargetBegin.fla file found in this chapter's folder on the CD that accompanies this book. Use your operating system to disable the file's read only attribute.

If you're ready to create a mask that rivals anything you could do before ActionScript, follow these steps:

1. **Launch Flash and open the maskTargetBegin.fla file.**

   Hmmm, not a whole lot happening is there? Just a skinny little movie with a name that is near and dear to the heart of the author. And at this point of the book, I hope is near and dear to you as well. On top of the name is a skinny little line. These are both movie clips. The skinny little line is a motion tween animation. The movie clip with the name uses ActionScript to make the name dance around.

2. **Click the thin line in the middle of the banner and then click the arrow to the left of the word Properties to open the Property inspector.**

   Notice that I've already christened the movie clip "mask" for you.

3. **Click the arrow to the left of the word Actions.**

   The Actions panel awaits your command.

4. **Click Objects⇨Movie⇨Movie Clip⇨Methods and then double-click** setMask.

   The action is added to your script, and two parameter text boxes appear above the Script pane. Your cursor is blinking in the Object field. This is the object that will be the mask, which I've already named "mask" for you.

5. **Click the Insert a Target Path button.**

   The Insert a Target Path dialog box opens.

6. **Click the button that says mask and then click OK to close the panel.**

   The mask object is now set.

7. **Click inside the Parameters field, and then click the Insert a Target Path button.**

   Hey, this Insert a Target Path dialog box sure does get around.

8. **Click the bannerText button and then click OK to close the panel.**

   The target for the mask clip is now set. Your finished code should look like Listing 15-2.

Listing 15-2   Creating a Mask Target

```
onClipEvent (load) {
  _root.mask.setMask(_root.bannerText);
}
```

9. **Choose Control➪Test Movie.**

The movie is published and opens up in another window. You should see a text animation revealed from the middle out. The animated text is revealed for a short while and then the animated mask hides the animated text and then reveals it a short while later. If for any reason the animated text wasn't masked, compare your code to the maskTargetFinal.fla file in this chapter's folder on the CD-ROM that accompanies this book

The animated banner in the last tutorial was created using the 468x60 Ad Template. Templates are a great timesaver. To create a document from a preexisting template, choose File➪New from Template. Choose a template from one of the many categories. When the file opens, you see a bunch of text. Not to worry. These are instructions on a guide layer. Read the instructions, delete the layer, and you're ready to rock and roll — or line dance if you prefer country music.

Chapter 16

Creating Bells and Whistles

• •

In This Chapter

▶ Creating a jukebox

▶ Building a sound controller

▶ Creating script for a pop-up menu

▶ Scripting a mouse chaser

▶ Crafting an ActionScript quiz

• •

Your everyday ho-hum-look-ma-moving-symbols Flash sites are nice to look at, but they get a tad predictable after you've seen a few dozen. With ActionScript, you turn the mundane into the monumental, and the ho-hum, hum-drum becomes the "Wow, is it real or is it Flash?"

In this chapter, I show you how to create some very useful and entertaining elements for your Flash movies. You say you want a jukebox? No problem; with a couple of tunes and some ActionScript, you've got it. If your site could benefit from a pop-up menu, you can do that with ActionScript as well. And if you've ever been to one of those Flash sites where the author thinks his or her background music is a candidate for some sort of award when in reality the music is no better (and in some cases much worse) than the reprocessed electronic noise that rattles through the speakers in your local supermarket and you had to endure it while viewing the site, I show you how to create a stereo controller where the viewer can control the volume, pan the sound from one speaker to the next, and — ah, the sounds of silence — turn the music off.

Building a Flash Jukebox

If you like to entertain people and you like music, you can create your very own Flash jukebox for all the world — or at least all of the people that visit the Web site with the jukebox movie — to enjoy. The Flash jukebox you're going to create uses the loadMovie action to load individual movies that have nothing but a single soundtrack in them. Remember that when you load a movie into a level, it replaces any movie currently in that level. In this exercise, a soundtrack movie is loaded into Level 1 when a button is clicked. When another button is clicked, a different movie is loaded into Level 1 and so on.

To follow along with this exercise, copy the Jukebox folder from this chapter's folder on the CD that came with this book. Use your computer's operating system to disable the Read Only attributes of each file in the folder.

To create your virtual jukebox:

1. **Launch Flash and open the file Jukebox_begin.fla.**

   Flash loads the file, and look, there's already a jukebox with buttons there. You'll notice there's also an Off button. A virtual jukebox with looping soundtracks will run until the specified number of loops play (in the case of the movie soundtracks you'll be working with, that's 1,000 loops). Nobody listens to a song a thousand times, not even if it's the current #1 song. Therefore, a virtual jukebox needs an Off button.

2. **Choose Window⇨Actions.**

   The Actions panel opens.

3. **Click the uppermost button on the left side of the jukebox.**

   The Actions panel should read Actions-Button at this point. If it doesn't read Actions-Button, click the button again. The next set of actions you create programs the button to load a movie. Within the movie is a sound clip that loops 1,000 times.

4. **In the left pane of the Actions panel, click Actions⇨Browser/Network and then double-click** loadMovie.

   Flash adds the action to the script and precedes it with the default mouse event handler, on(release). Accept the default on(release) event handler.

5. **In the URL field, type** tune1.swf.

   This is the filename of a published movie with a soundtrack. It's in the Jukebox folder with the rest of the tunes the jukebox plays.

   When you're using the loadMovie action, you use the URL field to specify the path to the movie you're loading. If you keep all of your movies in the same folder, all you have to enter is the movie's name followed by the .swf extension.

6. **In the large field to the right of Location, replace the 0 with a 1.**

   When the movie is published and this button is clicked, the movie tune1.swf loads into Level 1 and begins to play. Your finished code for this button should look exactly like Figure 16-1.

   I've already programmed the other buttons for you. The actions are the same for each button; you're just loading a different movie when the button is clicked. And of course, you know each movie has a different soundtrack. The Off button uses the unloadMovie action to clear any movie out of level1, the level where the soundtrack movies for the jukebox are loaded.

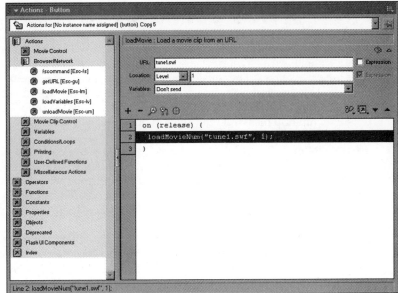

Figure 16-1:
Click the
button with
this code,
and the
jukebox will
play on.

7. Choose Control⇨Test Movie.

Flash publishes the movie and plays it in another window. Click any of
the buttons to begin playing a soundtrack. Cool, isn't it? When you get
tired of hearing the tunes, click the Off button or close the window.

If your jukebox didn't serenade you when you clicked the button you
programmed, open the Jukebox_final.fla file in Flash and compare your
ActionScript to the finished movie.

Creating a soundtrack movie

To create your own soundtrack movies, create
a new movie with a size of 1 pixel x 1 pixel. (I
know, it's a small movie. But that's okay because
you won't see anything when the movie is
loaded, but you will hear a big sound — or little
sound if you create soundtrack — with a short
song.) Import the desired soundtrack. Click the
first frame in the movie, open the Property
inspector and then click the triangle to the right
of the Sound field and select the sound you just
imported. In the Loops field, enter a high value
such as 900. Publish the movie and follow the
steps in the previous section to load the soundtrack into a movie.

Building a Stereo Sound Controller

Sound has become a staple element at many Flash Web sites. When you create a movie with an interesting soundtrack, you stimulate yet another of your viewer's senses. The music you choose should have some bearing on the actual movie, and of course you should consider the age of your viewing audience. I mean, let's face it, if your primary audience is comprised of baby boomers, hip-hop just won't get the job done. But of course no matter how carefully you choose the music, someone's not going to like it. For others it may be too loud. The solution is to give the viewer the option to turn the music off — silence is golden — or control the volume. In the following exercise, I show you how to create a Flash sound controller with ActionScript. The beauty of this controller is that after you've created it, you can use it in other Flash movies. Here's how.

Open the folder labeled Sound_controller from this chapter's folder on the CD that accompanies this book. Copy the files to your hard drive and use your computer's operating system to disable the file's Read Only attributes. Make sure the soundtrack.swf file is in the same folder.

1. **Launch Flash and open the soundController_begin.fla file.**

   Flash opens the file, and you see before you some of my best graphic work. Well not actually, but it's close. I've already created the sound controllers for you. Notice that you have two controls to work with. These are actually sliders. The slider looks like a control you might find on your home stereo system. It's nested within a movie clip. The _x property of the slider is set equal to a variable; the value of the variable is used to control the actual volume and balance between the speakers. I made the sliders movable objects with `startDrag` and `stopDrag` actions. The motion of the slider is constrained to a range of 100 pixels along the *x* axis. The slider is nested within another movie clip, which reads the _x property of the movie clip, which is set equal to the value of a variable named `level`. When the slider is all the way to the left, `level` has a value of 0; to the right, 100. So then, you've got a sliding scale from 0 to 100, perfect for cranking up the volume or turning it down. The sliders are nested within the main soundtrack control movie clip. The main movie clip is what you'll be creating the ActionScript code for.

   Before going on to Step 2, you may want to poke around each symbol to see the exact code I created for them. To do this, open the document Library and then double-click the symbol called Sound Controls. You can then poke around with all the individual elements that make up the sound controller. When you get to the individual sliders (which are nested in a movie clip called `level slider`), note the initial position or the bar slider's registration point.

For a quick refresher course on creating a symbol you can drag, turn to Chapter 11. For a refresher course on working with properties, bookmark this page and refer to Chapter 7.

2. **Double-click the sound controls movie clip.**

   Welcome to symbol-editing mode. Notice I've created three keyframes for you to work with and several layers that house the symbols used to create the movie clip. And yes, I did follow my own advice by creating an Actions layer. This is where you'll shortly be strutting your ActionScript.

3. **Click the first keyframe in the Actions layer and then click the arrow to the left of the word Actions.**

   The Actions panel opens. Your first job is to load the soundtrack — a spiffy little tune I've created for your listening enjoyment — and create the sound object. The soundtrack is a published movie with a sound that's set to loop a gazillion times or so. The first keyframe also initializes the values for the variables.

4. **Click Actions⇨Browser/Network and then double-click** loadMovie.

   The action is added to your script, and the parameter text boxes for the action appear above the Script pane.

5. **In the URL field, type** soundtrack.swf **and in the field to the right of location, type** 1.

   This line of code loads the soundtrack.swf movie into Level 1.

To use your own soundtracks with this controller, create a movie soundtrack as outlined in the "Creating a soundtrack movie" sidebar, which is located right before this very section in this very chapter. I aim to please. Name the file soundtrack and then publish it. Copy the soundtrack.swf file into the same folder, as this sound controller and your music will play instead of the soundtrack I created.

6. **In the left pane of the Actions panel, click Actions⇨Variables and then double-click** set variable.

   That's right, you're going to create a variable for the sound object.

7. **In the Variable field, type** soundtrack.

   You can use any name for this variable, but *soundtrack* is logical, wouldn't you agree?

8. **Click inside the Value field, and then in the left pane of the Actions panel, click Objects⇨Movie⇨Sound, and then double-click** new Sound. **Make sure you click the Expression box before moving to the next step.**

   Flash adds the new sound object to your script, and your cursor rests quietly between a pair of parentheses. Congratulations. You've just created a sound object.

9. **In the left pane of the Actions panel, click Actions⇨Miscellaneous Actions and then double-click** evaluate.

Above the Script pane, the Expression field opens.

10. **In the Expression field, type the following:** soundtrack.attachSound(_level1).

This expression attaches the soundtrack that will be loaded into Level 1 to the variable. The first part of the expression is the variable you created in Step 7 is followed by the obligatory dot (.) and a method of the sound object (attachSound). You can either enter the code directly as I've shown you here or double-click the attachSound method from Sound object group in the left pane of the Actions panel. For more information on the Sound object, refer to Chapter 8.

11. **In the left pane of the Actions panel, click Actions⇨Variables and then double-click** set variable.

The next two lines of code you create set the beginning positions of the pan control and volume controls. You create two variables that set the start position of each slider. The value of the variables change as your movie viewers drag the sliders to change the characteristics of the soundtrack.

12. **Place your cursor in the Variable field, click the black Insert a Target Path button and when the Insert Target Path dialog box opens, choose the Relative mode.**

This is a movie clip, and you are addressing a path within the movie clip, therefore you need to be in Relative mode. If you were addressing a path on the main timeline, you would choose Absolute mode.

For more information on Relative and Absolute modes, refer to Chapter 9.

13. **Click the plus sign (+) to the right of** pan_control **to expand the path, click** sliderBar, **and then click OK.**

The target path is added to the script, and the dialog box exits stage right.

14. **In the left pane of the Actions panel, click Properties and then double-click** _x.

15. **In the Value field, type** 50 **and click the Expression box.**

The line of code you just created sets the position of the slider bar (the movie clip instance named sliderBar) nested within the movie clip pan_control to x=50. In the next keyframe, you'll use this value to control how the sound is divided between the right and left speakers, or for you lefties in the crowd, between the left and right speakers.

16. **Repeat Steps 11 – 15 to create new variables for the movie clip volume_control and set its value equal to 75. Your finished code for the first keyframe should look like Figure 16-2.**

Creating music loops

Music has become a very important part of many Flash movies. If you've got the hankering to create your own music loops, you may want to consider investing in a program that you use to edit and mix sound samples. Two programs that work quite well for this are Acid Music (`www.soundforge.com/products/home.asp`) and Mixman (`www.mixman.com`).

This line of code sets the position of the slider bar for the sound control to 75. In other words, the sound will play at 75 percent volume when the movie begins. Now it's time to create the code for the second keyframe

When you are setting a property for a named instance of a nested movie clip, the registration point of the symbol is used. To see an illustration of this, open up the document Library and then double-click the slider bar symbol to see it in symbol-editing mode.

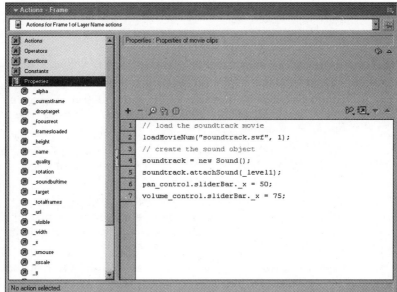

Figure 16-2:
This code sets the initial position of the sound controls.

Continuing with this exercise, to create code for the second keyframe:

1. Click the second keyframe and in the left pane of the Actions panel, click Actions➪Variables and then double-click set variable**.**

In this keyframe you'll be creating two variables that measure the current values of the volume control and pan control.

2. **In the Variable field, type** pan; **in the Value field, type** 100-(pan_control.level*2). **Be sure to click the Expression box.**

3. **In the left pane of the Actions panel, click Actions⇨Variables and then double-click** set variable.

   Yup, another variable.

4. **In the Variable field, type** vol; **in the Value field, type** volume_control.level. **Be sure to click the Expression box.**

   This variable reads the current _x property of the volume control slider, which will be a value between 1 and 100.

5. **In the left pane of the Actions panel, click Objects⇨Movie⇨Sounds⇨Methods and then double-click** setPan.

   Above the Script pane, the Object and Parameters text boxes appear.

6. **In the Object field, type the following:** soundtrack.

   Now you've done it. You've firmly attached the setPan method of the Sound object to the instance of the sound object you created at the start of this exercise.

7. **In the Parameters field type** pan.

   This is the variable that measures the current value of the slider.

8. **Repeat Steps 5 – 7 only this time attach the** setVolume **method of the sound object to the instance of the sound object. After you add the** setVolume **method to your script, in the Object field type** soundtrack **and in Parameters field type** vol.

   This line of code sets the volume by measuring the current value of the bar slider, which as you may remember is its x position. Your completed line of code for this keyframe should look like Figure 16-3.

   This keyframe's code sets the volume and pan properties of the sound based on the current position of the slider bars. But of course, the position of the slider bars is subject to change at the whim of the viewer, hence the need for the third keyframe.

9. **Click the third keyframe and type the following line of code:** gotoAndPlay (2).

   And that's all there is to setting the sound controls. By bouncing back and forth between the second and third keyframe, Flash is constantly evaluating the position of each slider control and using the _x property of each to set the volume and distribute the sound between the user's speakers.

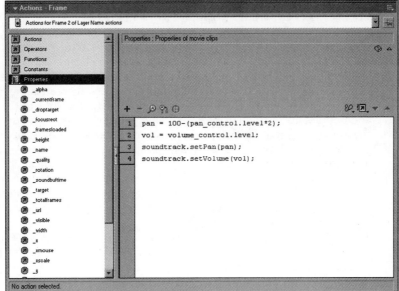

Figure 16-3:
Play it loud,
play it soft;
play it left,
play it right.

Of course there are two other controls to consider, the Stop and Reset buttons. These are invisible buttons. When the invisible button behind the word Stop is clicked, the soundtrack movie clip unloads. When the invisible button behind Restart is clicked, the soundtrack movie clip is reloaded. These are the same `loadMovie` and `unloadMovie` actions used to load a soundtrack into the jukebox you created in the previous section. If you skipped straight to this section, back up to the previous section where I show you how to load a movie soundtrack.

10. Choose Control➪Test Movie.

Flash publishes the movie and plays it in another window. As soon as the movie starts the soundtrack plays. Catchy little ditty, eh? Click the slider bars and drag them to change the volume of the sound and pan it from one speaker to another.

The beauty of this little gem is the fact that it's modular. You can use this movie clip in any Flash movie you create. Simply use the Open As Library command to open this file and drag the sound control movie clip into the current document's Library, or position it as desired on Stage. As long as you have a movie named soundtrack.swf with a looping soundtrack in the same directory, the sound will play when the movie is loaded.

Programming a Pop-Up Menu

Pop-up menus are all the rage these days. They've actually been around for quite a while. You can create them fairly easily in Flash — all you need is to create a bunch of button instances, align them, and then group them. To make the menu pop up when a button is clicked, you create a movie clip with the menu collapsed on the first frame and move the buttons to their locked and popped-up position in another frame. When the button is clicked again, the buttons revert to their original position. The biggest difficulty some people have with pop-up menus is programming the buttons after the menu is created. You're communicating across timelines and have to address the proper target path. To show you how this works, I've created a pop-up menu that you'll be exploring in the next exercise. After you see how the menu is constructed, I show you how to program the individual buttons.

To follow along with this exercise, copy the pop_up_menu.fla file from this chapter's folder on the CD to your hard drive. Use your computer's operating system to disable the file's Read Only attributes.

1. **Launch Flash and open the file, pop_up_menu.fla.**

   Flash opens the file, and you see a nice little menu tucked away in the upper left-hand corner of the Stage.

2. **Choose Control➪Test Movie.**

   Flash publishes the movie and plays it in another window.

3. **Click just above the title Web Sites R Us and drag the menu.**

   If you've been following along, you know that an invisible button is nested within the movie clip and that startDrag and stopDrag actions have been assigned to it. When you're through dragging the menu around, release the mouse button to drop it.

4. **Click the Portfolio button.**

   Pop goes the menu.

5. **Click the Portfolio button again.**

   Like a turtle retracting into its shell, the menu closes. When you're through checking out the menu, close the window to return to movie-editing mode.

6. **Choose Window➪Library.**

   The document Library opens.

7. **Double-click the Drag n Drop menu symbol.**

   Flash opens the movie clip in symbol-editing mode as shown in Figure 16-4. Notice that the movie clip is ten frames long and that there are motion tweens between the keyframes on two layers. The motion tweens are what creates the smooth motion between frames. Without the motion tweens, the menu would abruptly jump from closed to open. In this figure, frame 5 is shown, when the menu is in Pop-Up mode.

I know this is Flash 101, but when you create more than one motion tween animation, each animation must be on its own layer.

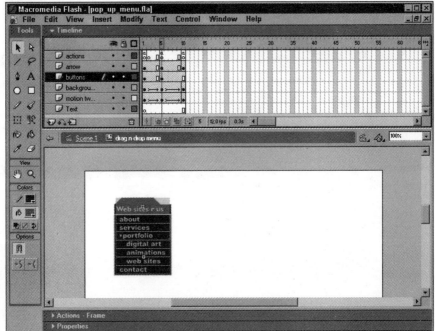

Figure 16-4
The pop-up menu is a movie clip.

8. **Drag the playhead across the frames.**

   Notice how the menu expands and contracts.

9. **Click the arrow to the left of the word Actions and then click the first keyframe on the Actions layer.**

   You see a single `stop` action in this keyframe. Thanks to the `stop` action, when the movie clip loads, nothing happens until the button is clicked. The fifth keyframe also has a `stop` action. This stops the menu when it has expanded.

10. **Click the tenth frame.**

    This is also a keyframe. It has a line of code that reads `gotoAndStop(1)`. This is what sends the movie back to its starting point.

11. **With the Actions panel still open, double-click the Portfolio button to enter symbol-editing mode and then click the Portfolio button again.**

You see the code in Figure 16-5. By now you've probably figured out exactly what is happening here. In case you haven't, let me break it down for you: When the movie clip loads, the `stop` action halts it at frame 1. When the Portfolio button is clicked, the movie plays until it reaches frame 5 where another `stop` action halts it in its tracks. This is the menu's expanded state. When the Portfolio button is clicked again, the movie plays, and the menu retracts as it travels the timeline to frame 10. At frame 10, the `gotoAndStop` action returns the movie to frame 1, where the whole cycle starts again when the Portfolio button is clicked.

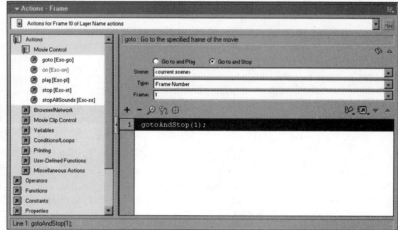

Figure 16-5: When the button is clicked, the movie will play.

Now that you know how the menu works, it's time to show you how to program the buttons. To program a button, you have to get inside the movie clip where the button is nested.

1. **If you closed the Actions panel, click the arrow to the left of the word Actions.**

2. **Double-click the About button on the Drag n Drop menu.**

   In the Actions panel, the label should read Actions-Button. If it doesn't, click the button again.

   You are now ready to program the button to play a movie clip, get another URL, or load another movie. Listing 16-1 shows a typical script you can apply to a button on a pop-up menu. Remember, each button is nested within the movie clip, which means the buttons are on a different timeline. To program each button, you merely have to address the proper timeline. If the button is addressing a movie clip instance, you use the Insert a Target Path button to add the target path to the script.

3. **After you have a button programmed, click the movie clip's title (in this case Drag n Drop menu) to return to the movie clip, and then double-click the next button you need to program.**

To program a button that is hidden within the pop-up (or drop-down if you prefer) portion of the menu, drag the playhead to expand the menu and then double-click the appropriate button. When the Actions panel reads Actions-Button, you're ready to rock and roll. If you assign an action and Flash doesn't put the default release mouse event handler before the action, you haven't properly selected the button.

Listing 16-1   Programming a Nested Button

```
on (rollOver) {
    _root.sexysadie.gotoAndPlay(2);
}
on (press) {
    unloadMovie (_root.movie_time);
}
on (release) {
    loadMovieNum (about.swf, 1);
}
```

The pop-up menu in the last exercise is a movie clip; therefore, it is modular. You can use the Open as Library command to open up this file in any other Flash movie. After you have the file's Library open, drag the menu movie clip into the current document's Library. All the objects used to create it are imported as well. Then you can modify the button text to suit the movie, as well as change the color and shape of the elements used to create the menu.

Creating a Mouse Chaser

Have you ever visited a Flash site where the author created a cool little graphic that you could drag around while the movie loaded? This is an effective effect that you can easily create. Begin by creating an interesting movie clip with some interesting effects, add a little ActionScript, and you've created a toy that will keep your viewers amused while your preloader is running. In this exercise, I've already created the movie clip with the animation. All you have to do is program the movie clip. Such a deal.

To follow along with this exercise, copy the file mouse_chaser_begin.fla from this chapter's folder on this book's CD to your hard drive. Use your computer's operating system to put a cease and desist to the file's Read Only attributes.

1. **Launch Flash and open the mouse_chaser_begin.fla file.**

   There you go; the movie clip with its cool animation is ready and waiting for you on Stage.

2. **Click the arrow next to the word Actions.**

   The Actions panel opens.

3. **In the left pane of the Actions panel, click Actions⇨Variables and then double-click** set variable.

   Two parameter text boxes appear.

4. **In the Variable field enter** diff_x **and in the Value field enter** _x-_root._ xmouse **and be sure to click the Expression box.**

   This line of code figures the distance between the movie clip and the current position mouse along the x axis of the movie. In plain English, the distance (diff_x) is equal to the current position of the movie clip (_x) minus the current position of the mouse (_root._xmouse).

5. **Repeat steps 3 and 4, only this time you'll be creating a variable named** diff_y **and set its value equal to** _y-_root._ymouse.

   Yup, you guessed it. This line of code figures how far the movie clip is from the current position of the mouse on the y axis. Now comes the fun part, creating the code that causes the movie clip to chase the mouse.

6. **Click Actions⇨Miscellaneous Actions and then double-click** evaluate.

   Oh, you say you already know what happens? Yes, that's right, the Expression text parameter box appears.

7. **In the Expression field, enter the following:** _x=_root._xmouse+ (diff_x/2).

   Whoa Nellie! That's a lot of code. In a nutshell, this sets the _x position of the movie clip equal to the current _x position of the mouse plus the value of the distance between the movie clip and the mouse (diff_x) divided by 2. All this does is create a slight lag between the chaser and the chased (which in this case is our friend the mouse). The farther away the movie clip is from the mouse, the greater the lag. When the mouse slows down or stops, the mouse chaser catches up.

8. **Repeat Steps 6 and 7, only this time the expression reads as follows:** _y=_root._ymouse+(diff_y/2).

   And this line of code dear reader, sets a slight lag between the movie clip and the mouse along the y axis.

9. **Select the first line of code that reads:** on clipEvent(load) { **and select the Mouse move event. Your code should look like Listing 16-2.**

The reason for changing the code is that if you accept the default load clip event, the code only executes once, when the movie loads. Now the code executes whenever the user's mouse finger twitches.

10. Choose Control⇨Test Movie.

Flash publishes the movie and plays it in another window. Go ahead, move your mouse and a stream of stars follows. Fun, isn't it?

Listing 16-2 Creating a Mouse Chaser

```
onClipEvent (mouseMove) {
  diff_x = _x-_root._xmouse;
  diff_y = _y-_root._ymouse;
  _x=_root._xmouse+(diff_x/2);
  _y=_root._ymouse+(diff_y/2);
}
```

If the movie clip didn't chase your mouse, open the mouse_chaser_final.fla file (which you'll find in this chapter's folder on the CD that accompanies this book) in Flash and compare the ActionScipt to what you've just created.

Creating an ActionScript Quiz

ActionScript gives you all the goodies you need to create a cool quiz game. Between arrays, variables, the program's graphic's capabilities, and the power of conditional statements, you can create a quiz that will test your viewers, entertain them, and maybe impart a bit of knowledge in the process. The quiz I created for this section tests a viewer's knowledge of the capitals of countries.

The actual movie itself (see Figure 16-6) looks fairly simple; the user is presented with a question and clicks a button to choose the answer he or she thinks is right. After a button is clicked, a new question appears, a new image appears in the window to the right, and the user is either congratulated on a correct answer or informed he or she has answered incorrectly.

It looks simple enough when you play the game — but there's a lot of ActionScript lurking underneath — so much ActionScript that you'd be bored if I laid it out step by step, action by action, blow by blow . . . okay, you get the idea. If you've been following along with this book chapter by chapter, you know how to do most of the individual steps; this section just shows you one way of combining many actions to create an interesting, entertaining, and perhaps educational movie. If you haven't read the book chapter by chapter — and you know who you are — you can still benefit from this section. I leave handy Cross References to chapters where you can get the skinny on the topic of discussion. So without further ado, I'll get the ball rolling.

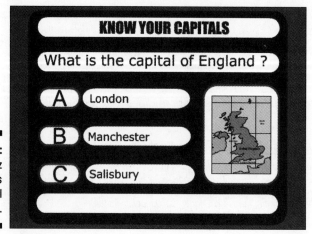

Figure 16-6:
A Flash quiz
on capitals
is a capital
idea.

To view a finished movie of this project, locate the Quiz folder which is a sub-folder of the Chapter 16 folder on this book's CD. Copy the folder to your hard drive and use your computer's operating system to disable the Read-only attributes of the files.

Initializing the arrays and variables

When you create a quiz game, you can use variables to store the questions and answers. However, this can become a tad tedious if you've got a lot of questions. And of course with a multiple choice quiz you end up with lots of answers, which may have a tendency to remind you of the quizzes you took in school.

In this capital Capital quiz, there are twelve questions, with three choices for each question. If you create variables for each question and answer, you've got — umm, where's my calculator? — 48 variables, which is a lot in my book, and more than I like to keep track of when creating ActionScript . The solution is to set up one array for the questions and one array for the answers. I recommend initializing arrays and variables in the first frame of the movie. To view the arrays and variables for this movie, you can view the listings in each section that follows or view the ActionScript in the finished movie by following these steps.

1. **Launch Flash**

2. **Open the quiz.fla file.**

   Flash opens the file, and you get your first peek under the hood of the movie.

3. **Click the arrow to the left of the word Actions.**

   The Actions panel opens.

4. **Click the first frame in the movie's Actions layer.**

   There's a whole lot of ActionScript here. In fact, both arrays are so large that they scroll right past the end of the Actions panel. Listing 16-3 shows the arrays and variables for this movie.

Listing 16-3 Initializing Arrays and Variables

```
CountryArray = new Array("England", "The USA", "Egypt",
         "Cuba", "France", "Austria", "Italy", "Sweden",
         "Venezuela", "Peru", "Morocco", "Japan");
AnswerArray = new Array("London", "Manchester", "Salisbury",
         "A", "Seattle", "Dallas", "Washington, D. C.",
         "C", "Cairo", "Giza", "Alexandria", "A", "Banes",
         "Havana", "Matanzas", "B", "Dijon", "Bordeaux",
         "Paris", "C", "Salzsburg", "Innsbruck", "Vienna",
         "C", "Salerno", "Rome", "Naples", "B", "Goteberg",
         "Stockholm", "Malmo", "B", "Caracas", "El Tigre",
         "San Carlos", "A", "Lima", "Iquitos", "Paita",
         "A", "Agadir", "Safi", "Rabat", "C", "Nagano",
         "Tokyo", "Hiroshima", "B");
SWFArray = new Array("England.swf", "USA.swf", "Egypt.swf",
         "Cuba.swf", "France.swf", "Austria.swf",
         "Italy.swf", "Sweden.swf", "Venezuela.swf",
         "Peru.swf", "Morocco.swf", "Japan.swf");
i = 0;
k = 0;
score = 0;
```

Well that certainly is a lot of code, which of course means a lot of typing. If you think I did all of that in the itty-bitty Actions panel, you don't know my motto about working smarter and not harder. The copious amounts of text were created in a word processing program and pasted into the proper spot in the newly created array.

If you create text to use in ActionScript and your word processor uses Smart Quotes, turn them off. The Script pane is dumb when it comes to Smart Quotes — it doesn't recognize them as quotes. To turn off your Smart Quotes in Microsoft Word, choose Tools➪AutoCorrect and then select the AutoFormat As You Type tab. Remove the checkmark from the Replace As You Type: "Straight Quotes" with "Smart Quotes" checkbox.

In the `AnswerArray`, notice there are three cities listed followed by a letter. The three cities are the possible answers for the identity of the first capital and the letter is the correct response. The first question asks the viewer to identify the capital of England, which is London, or Answer A.

Notice there is a third array named SWFArray. This array stores the names of published movies that are linked to each question. Compare the name of the country and its position in the CountryArray with the name of the movie and its position in the SWFArray and you see how the values in the two arrays are cross-indexed.

The final three lines of code declare some the variables used in the movie. The variables i and k are used to advance to the proper index in the three arrays when the next question is generated. And of course you have to show your viewers how many questions they've answered correctly, which falls in the hands of the variable named score whose value at the start of the movie is 0.

For more information on creating arrays and variables, browse through Chapter 6.

Creating dynamic text and other delights

Now that you've got all your arrays and variables in a row, you've got to have someplace to put them. If you have the quiz.fla file open in Flash, advance to frame 2. For those of you that are reading this in the comfort of your living room easy chair, refer to Figure 16-7. Each dynamic text box is the lucky recipient for a deserving variable. Hmm . . . if only it were that easy to win the lottery.

Here you see the whole kit-and-caboodle including several dynamic text boxes placed on Stage. These show the contents of the variables that are used to form the questions and answers for the quiz. The message text block at the bottom of the Stage informs the viewer whether he or she answered correctly or not. And that pretty little rectangle with the red border is a movie clip that serves as a target for the movie (a SWF file with a map of the country the viewer is asked to identify the capital of) that is loaded when the question is generated.

Listing 16-4 shows the ActionScript in frame 2 that fills the dynamic text boxes with a question and corresponding answers. The first line of code creates a new variable named question that combines a text string with an index from the CountryArray. Notice the variable i is used to note the proper element in the array. The second line of code creates a variable called currentURL that is equal in value to the corresponding movie you want to load with the question. Again the variable i shows Flash which item to use from the SWFarray. The third line of code loads the movie into the target movie clip; the pretty rectangle with the rounded corners and the red border named SWFLoader. The next three lines of code create variables for the answers. The variables correspond to the variables in the dynamic text boxes shown in Figure 16-7. And again a variable is used to pluck the proper item from the AnswerArray. The variable k is used to denote the index position for this array. Remember, you have one country and three possible answers.

The first array element is 0, hence the math to get the right `AnswerArray` element for `AnswerB` and `AnswerC`. Finally you add a `stop` action so the viewer has a chance to respond to the question.

Listing 16-4   Creating Questions and Answers with ActionScript

```
question = "What is the capital of " + CountryArray[i] +" ?";
currentURL = SWFArray[i];
loadMovie (currentURL, "_root.SWFLoader");
AnswerA = AnswerArray[k];
AnswerB = AnswerArray[k+1];
AnswerC = AnswerArray[k+2];
stop ();
```

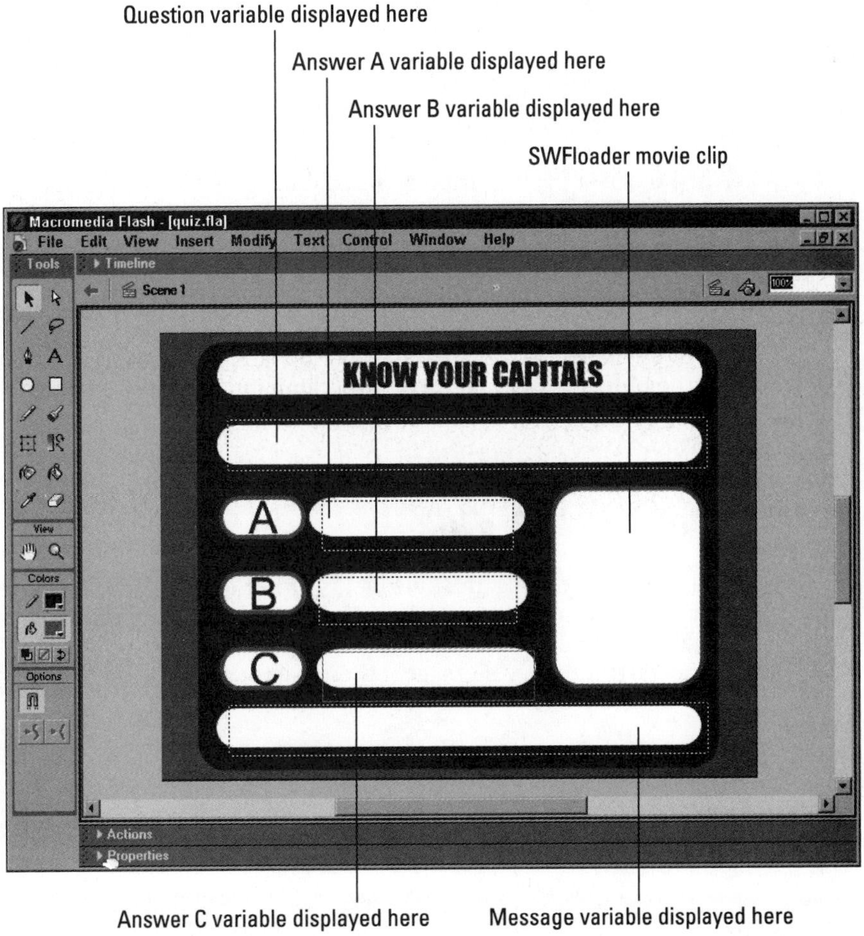

Question variable displayed here

Answer A variable displayed here

Answer B variable displayed here

SWFloader movie clip

Figure 16-7:
If you're gonna see variables, you gotta put 'em somewhere.

Answer C variable displayed here   Message variable displayed here

If you don't know how to get texty (dynamically that is), mosey on over to Chapter 10.

Programming the buttons

This movie has three buttons, one for each answer. The viewer clicks the button that he or she thinks corresponds to the right answer. The button does three things when clicked: it records the viewer's answer, unloads the preceding question's movie, and advances the movie to the next frame where the score is tallied. Listing 16-5 shows the code for the first button.

Listing 16-5 Give Me Your Answer, Please

```
on (release) {
 answer = "A";
 unloadMovieNum (1);
 gotoAndPlay (3);
}
```

When the user clicks button A, a variable named `answer` is set equal to A; this records the viewer's answer as A. In the case of button B, the `answer` variable is set equal to B, which will record the answer as B and so on. The other lines of code unload the currently playing movie (the map of the country in the previous question) and advance the movie to the next frame.

For more information on loading and unloading movies, refer to Chapter 5. For the ultimate information on programming buttons — at least as far as this opus is concerned — leaf through Chapter 11.

Scoring the quiz

After the viewer clicks the button, his or her answer is cast in stone and the movie advances to frame 3 where the answer given is evaluated using conditional statements. If the answer is right, the viewer is rewarded with a point and a congratulatory message, otherwise the viewer gets the sad news that the wrong button has been clicked.

If you've got the Flash movie open as you're reading this, open the Actions panel and click the third frame on the Actions layer. For those of you lounging in your recliner by the pool, refer to Listing 16-6 to see the code that scores the quiz.

Listing 16-6   It All Adds Up. Or Does It?

```
if (answer==AnswerArray[k+3]) {
 message = "Congratulations, that's the right answer.";
 score = ++score;
} else {
 message = "Sorry, that's not the right answer.";
}
k = k+4;
i = ++i;
if (i==12) {
 gotoAndPlay (4);
} else {
 gotoAndPlay (2);
}
```

The first statement checks to see if the viewer has selected the proper answer. Remember that your quiz has three answers and you want Flash to check for the correct one. The first element in an array is number 0, hence 3 added to the variable k will check the element in the AnswerArray that contains the correct answer(A, B, or C). If the answer is correct, the quiz player is rewarded and 1 is added to his or her score. If not, the else action comes into play and the destined-to-be-forlorn player receives the bad news. In this frame code is also added to increase the value of the two variables; i being increased by 1 and k being increased by 4. Remember that k is being used to cycle the elements in the AnswerArray and each question has three possible answers plus an element denote whether choice A, B, or C is the proper answer. The last conditional statement ends the game when the variable i reaches 12; all questions have been used and answered and the movie advances to frame 4. If i is less than 12, the else action takes over, the movie goes to frame 2 where the player is presented with another quiz question.

I show you the conditions involved in creating conditional statements in Chapter 12.

Ending the game

When you create a quiz game and the player has answered all the questions, you can simply advance the movie to a frame and display the player's score or you can end the game with a bit of panache and create a personalized message that varies depending on the number of answers the player gets right. And if you've been the astute ActionScript author, no doubt you already figured out you use a variable to vary the message. In the case of this quiz, you use a conditional statement, the Logical AND operator and the variable message to create different messages.

Spicing up a game

Creating a game in Flash gives you all sorts of opportunity to exercise your creativity. For example, when a player gets an answer right, you can have a movie clip play with the sounds of a cheering or applauding audience; a wrong answer can be accompanied by a movie clip with the sounds of catcalls or boos. To do this, simply create a movie clip with sound only and leave the first frame blank. After the viewer answers the question use the `else` and `if` actions to determine which movie clip will play.

If you've been reading this section at your computer and have the quiz.fla file open, click the arrow to the left of the word Actions to open the Actions panel and click the fourth frame in the Actions layer to see a fine example of the `if`, `else if`, and `else` trilogy at work. If you're reading this section while taking a bubble bath, refer to Listing 16-7 for the ActionScript and for goodness sakes, try not to submerge the book.

Listing 16-7 End the Game with a Conditional Statement

```
if (score==12) {
 message = "Game over. You got every answer
            right.Congratulations. You know your capitals.";
} else if (score<12 && score >=10) {
 message = "Game over. You're a pretty smart cookie. You got
            " + score+ " answers right.";
} else if (score<10 && score>=7) {
 message = "Game over.  You got " + score+ " answers right.
            You can do better than that.";
} else if (score<7 && score>=4) {
 message = "Game over.  You got " + score+ " answers
            right.You need a refresher course in World
            Geography.";
} else {
 message = "Game over.  You got " + score+ " answers right.
            Bury your nose in a good Atlas.";
}
stop ();
```

This code determines what message the player will see in the dynamic text box in frame 4. The first statement checks to see if the player has a perfect score (12 correct answers). If they answered all questions correctly, they are congratulated for the perfect score. If not, the first `else if` action checks to see if the score is greater than or equal to 10 and less than 12 to display a different message. The Logical AND operator is used to evaluate this statement and the following statements. Both conditions in the statement must be true for the entire statement to be true. For example, in the first else if statement, the variable score must be less than 12 and greater than or equal to 10 for the statement to be true. If this statement evaluates as false, the next else if action comes into play. If none of the conditional statements evaluate as true, the else action takes over and the message tells the player to bone up on world geography. And of course the game needs to stop, hence the stop action.

If you need a refresher course in logical operators, I show you how to use the operators logically in Chapter 12.

Part V
The Part of Tens

The 5th Wave   By Rich Tennant

"Well, shoot — I know the animation's moving a mite too fast, but <u>dang</u> if I can find a 'mosey' function anywhere in the toolbox!"

In this part . . .

Here you get a couple chapters that have ten snippets (hence the "Part of Tens" title) of valuable tips and Internet resources that you can use to further your career as an ActionScripter.

Chapter 17

Ten Tips for Trouble-Free ActionScript

● ●

In This Chapter

▶ ActionScript tips

▶ Using comments

▶ Tracing your script

▶ Calling an action

● ●

ActionScript can be so rewarding when you get it right and oh so frustrating when you get it wrong. If you've ever slaved away for hours doing something you knew was right, and yet when you were done with it, it wasn't right, you know what I'm talking about. But then again it wasn't exactly wrong, either; it was sound in concept, but somewhere along the line, some little something you did threw a spanner in the works. In this chapter, I show you how to construct your ActionScript so that it's easy to figure out which right was actually wrong.

Label Everything

One of the easiest ways to troubleshoot a faulty ActionScript is with the Movie Explorer. You use the Movie Explorer's visual outline to find a frame or object you suspect may be causing the hiccup in your ActionScript. By default, a frame is designated by its path and frame number. That makes it kind of difficult to figure out exactly which frame contains the faulty ActionScript. If, however, you give each frame a distinct label, it's much easier to figure out what the frame does. Then when you're troubleshooting faulty ActionScript and scrolling through the Movie Explorer, your built-in sensor (or censor depending upon the type of bug you're after) says, "Aha, I'll bet this is where I've gone wrong." And if you've done a good job of creating a meaningful label for the frame, you're probably right.

When you assign actions to a movie clip object, you are working with a labeled instance of a symbol. Name it right, and it will be easy to troubleshoot with the Movie Explorer.

Use Comments

Another way to make your life as a purveyor of ActionScript less stressful is to use comments. Comments are little notes to yourself and other Flash authors working on the project. A comment can appear in one of two places: in a frame or within the ActionScript itself. When you create a comment, create one that will make sense in three or four months when you have to revise the Flash movie. Also be considerate of other Flash authors working on the same project. They should also be able to decipher the comment easily.

For more information on comments, see Chapter 3.

You can also create comments on keyframes. To create a comment on a keyframe:

1. **Select the keyframe you want the comment to appear on.**

2. **Click the arrow to the left of the word Properties.**

   The Property inspector opens.

3. **In the <Frame Label> field, type two forward slashes (//) followed by the comment.**

   Flash displays the comment on the keyframe preceded by two forward slashes that are colored green. The reason for the two forward slashes is so that Flash reads this as a comment instead of a frame label and also so you and other Flash authors on the project will know a comment from a label If the comment is obscured by other keyframes in close proximity, position your cursor over the keyframe the two green slashes, and a tooltip appears with the word *Comment* followed by your comment. Such efficiency.

Use the trace Action

When you create a complex ActionScript, it's nice to know what's happening in the background; for example, the current value of a variable. Many times you think you've got everything done exactly the way it should be, but for some reason, your variables don't vary. In fact, in many cases, your variables are doing nothing. You don't know that this is happening; your variables are silent little messengers that give Flash a memory. When you use the trace action, the value of the variable you are tracing appears in the Output window when you use the Test Movie command to preview the your movie. If the variable is used as a counter in a loop, you'll see each value of the variable as the script executes.

If you use the `trace` action to trace more than one variable at a time, you'll have an overload of data without knowing which number matches which variable. You can add a message in front of the variable to identify the variable's name. For example, to trace the variable `i`, you can enter the following in the `trace` action's Message field: `"This is the value of variable " + i`. Be sure to check the Expression box. If you're tracing several variables and they scroll down the Output window just a tad slower than the speed of light, set breakpoints for each `trace` action you use.

You can also use the `trace` action to display a message; for example, what you expect the movie to be doing at a particular point. If the movie isn't doing what's expected, send it to its room. No, seriously, if it's not doing what you expected, the `trace` action is attached to the action where you expected the expected behavior to occur, giving you a starting point for your troubleshooting process.

For more information on the `trace` action and setting breakpoints, check out Chapter 13.

Create a Separate Layer for All Frame Actions

Did you ever try to find something and couldn't? You know, like a pair of your favorite socks or stockings? Well, if you put your socks or stockings in their own separate drawer, then you'd know where they are at all times save for an obligatory trip to the washing machine where at least one pair of your favorite socks ends up a solo act — how socks orphan themselves is still a mystery to me. The same thing is true of actions. If you put them all in the same place, then you know where to find them when debugging your Flash movies. When you assign an action to an object, it's always right where it should be, attached to the movie clip or button you assigned the action to. However, a frame action is attached to a keyframe, and if you've got lots of keyframes intermingled among lots of frames that are allocated on lots of layers, the keyframe with the action that has your movie screwed up eight ways to Sunday is going to be hard to find. The antidote is to create a separate layer for all frame actions and position this layer at the top of the hierarchy.

For more information on creating a layer for actions, see Chapter 2.

Create Meaningful Names

Flash names things. And it gives them names you wouldn't wish on your worst enemy. For example, if Flash were in the baby christening business, babies would be named Baby1, Baby2, Baby3, and so on, which of course would make it difficult for the census takers of the world and bill collectors — not to mention the IRS — to identify people. You have so many things that Flash names automatically, and others — such as variables and arrays — that you are responsible for naming; it behooves you to give everything that can be named a name that makes sense, something you can use to identify the object several months from now when you have to revise the movie.

KISS: Keep It Short, Simple

Whenever you label a keyframe, variable, or instance of a movie clip, keep the name short and simple. You never know when you may have to enter the object's name again and when you do, you don't want to wipe yourself out by typing a long name. 'Nuff said.

Use the call Action

When you use the same lines of code several times during the course of the movie, it becomes quite a bother to type it over and over and over again. To avoid this redundancy and to save your wrists from an early onset of carpal tunnel syndrome, call on the `call` action. With the `call` action, you can call (hence the name) a labeled frame, and Flash will execute the actions on that frame no matter what frame in the movie calls the set of actions. To use the `call` action, give a frame a unique name and then create the appropriate ActionScript. For example, if you were creating an ActionScript to keep score of a game, you could call the frame `score`. Then whenever you have a keyframe that you want to use to revise the game's score, create the following line of code: `call ("score");` on the keyframe where you want to revise the score; Flash calls the ActionScript from the `score` keyframe without running up your long distance bill.

When you get really good with ActionScript and start using local variables (that var guy in the Actions panel), they won't exist after the initial script is finished. If you use the call action to call a script with local variables, your call will be in vain.

Save Early and Save Often

Like any other graphics programs, Flash uses a lot of your system's resources. The program generally runs like clockwork, but you never know when your operating system might hiccup and freeze everything up. To make matters worse, certain parts of the country are in energy crisis; you never know when your power may fail and wipe out all your fantastic ActionScript. To avoid a minor — or major depending upon how much work you've done — crisis, save your work early and save it often.

 When you work on a lengthy project and save frequently, you can run the risk of corrupting a file. Save a master version of the document under a different name, and once every day or so, use the Save As command to save a copy of the working file as the master document. If Murphy's Law strikes with a vengeance and your file becomes gibberish, at least you have the last master document as backup and won't have to start from square one.

Think Modular

Objects and effects that you create with ActionScript — especially the cooler and more complex things — involve quite a few lines of ActionScript and generally take a while to create. When you get something that's especially good, there's no sense in recreating it in another movie; convert the effect into a movie clip and then use the Open As Library command to use the effect (which is now a movie clip) in another movie. Here's how:

1. **Select all the frames used to create the object or effect.**

   The frames are highlighted.

2. **Choose Edit⇨Copy Frames.**

   The frames are copied to the clipboard.

3. **Choose Insert⇨New Symbol.**

   The Symbol Properties dialog box appears.

4. **Choose the Movie Clip behavior, name the symbol, and then click OK.**

   Flash enters symbol-editing mode.

5. **Select the first frame and then choose Edit⇨Paste Frames.**

   Flash pastes the frames, objects, and layers into the movie clip using the same layer names.

6. **Click the Back button to exit symbol-editing mode.**

   The movie clip is stored in the document Library for future use.

   If you want, you can delete the frames you just copied and put the movie clip in their place. You can now use the movie clip in other movies by opening the file using the Open as Library command and dragging the symbol on Stage or into the current document's Library. The symbol is now ready for use in the new document.

Use the Extension Manager

"Why work harder when you can work smarter" has always been my motto. Creating ActionScript is fun, challenging, and rewarding. But if the script you need has already been written, why reinvent the wheel? Macromedia has made it possible for you to import Extensions (ActionScript and other items that have already been created) and include them as a menu item. Whenever you need the bit of ActionScript, simply use the proper menu command, and you've got it. Depending upon the extension you add, you'll either find it as part of the Window menu or embedded within another menu such as the Publish settings. To add extensions to your copy of Flash, log on to the Internet and point your Web browser to www.macromedia.com/exchange/flash. The information associated with the file tells you where to look for the extension after you have it installed.

Export and Import ActionScript

If you've been counting sections, you're up to eleven now, and this part of the book is called Part of Tens meaning there's supposed to be ten sections in each chapter. No, I haven't forgotten how to count (although my abacus has been squeaking a bit lately); I just thought this bit was important enough to break protocol and create an eleventh section.

When you create ActionScript, you're creating text that you can export as a file. You can either export it to edit it within a word processor such as the Windows Notepad, or you can export it for use in other Flash movies. To export an ActionScript you're especially proud of or want to use again:

1. **In the Actions panel, click the Options button (the icon that looks like three squares, three dashes, and an inverted triangle in the upper right-hand corner of the Actions panel).**

   The Options menu opens.

2. Choose Export as File.

The Save As dialog box appears.

3. Choose a name and location for the file and then click Save.

Flash saves the file to the selected directory with an .as (ActionScript) extension.

After you've exported an ActionScript file, you can import it when needed. To import an ActionScript File:

1. Select the keyframe or object you want to apply the ActionScript to and click the arrow to the left of the word Actions.

The Actions panel opens.

2. Click the Options button (the icon that looks like three squares, three dashes, and an inverted triangle in the upper right-hand corner of the Actions panel).

The Options menu opens.

3. Choose Import from File.

A dialog box appears, prompting you for the name and location of the ActionScript file (it has an .as extension).

4. Locate the file and open it.

The ActionScript appears in the right pane of the Actions panel, exactly as you saved it.

If you edit an ActionScript in a word processor, be sure to save it with an .as extension. If your word processor defaults to another extension such as .doc or .txt, use your computer's operating system to change the extension back to .as before using it in Flash.

Chapter 18

Ten Internet Resources for ActionScript

In This Chapter

▶ Ten other places to find out about Flash

*T*he following sites provide even more information about Flash. Who knew you could become such an expert?

If you're in the mood for inspiration, check out the CD. I include a bonus chapter on ten showcase Web sites guaranteed to get those creative juices flowing.

Macromedia Support

This section of Macromedia's site (www.macromedia.com/support/flash) features extensive Flash resources. Here you'll find examples of every aspect of Flash as well as a section devoted to ActionScript. The sections are informative with excellent examples of how to do things with Flash. You'll also find links to other Flash resources, downloads, and much more.

ActionScript.org

If you build it, they will come, but if you build it and the ActionScript isn't right, they won't come again. At this site (www.actionscript.org), you can find anything from the mundane to the mahvelos dahlink. This site features tutorials and other useful information. Network with ActionScript gurus to find out what it's all about.

Crazy Raven Productions

This former Macromedia site (www.crazyraven.com) features a choice of interfaces and several interesting tutorials. Check out their tutorial of the day, and you may be on the road to mastering a new Flash skill. Check out their site of the day for inspiration. Crazy raven; like a black crow flying . . . Thank you, Joni.

Flash Kit

If you want access to tutorials about Flash animation and tutorials about Flash ActionScript, as well as other Flash topics, this site (www.flashkit.com) has it all. You can also find royalty-free music loops here, buttons, and other Flash graphics. There is an extensive section devoted to tutorials with source files that you can download and dissect at your convenience. Check out the links section for inspiring Flash Web sites.

The Flash Academy

If academy makes you think of school and school makes you think of studying, it's academic to note that this site (www.enetserve.com/tutorials) is designed to show you stuff. But the stuff this site shows you is very cool and informative. You'll find tutorials here as well as examples of stuff you can do with Flash. Right now there are tutorials only for Flash 4 and 5 (MX is the new kid on the block as this is being written), but before long — which may be now if you're reading this book several months after the release of Flash MX — you'll find tutorials on the latest and greatest things you can do with Macromedia's new baby.

Flash Magazine

So you say you want to know the latest, greatest, most stupendous information about Flash the planet has to offer? Well you can't go too far wrong when you point your Web browser to the Flash Magazine site (www.flashmagazine.com). This online magazine — created with Flash of course — features tutorials, news, and information about third-party applications (software you use to create stuff for your Flash movies that was not created by Macromedia) to use with Flash. About the only thing you can't do with this online magazine is curl it up and swat the errant mosquito that found the only hole in your patio screen while you were enjoying a cool mint julep.

Flash Planet

Eric Wittman, Flash Senior Product Manager, recommended this site (`www.flashplanet.com`) to me. Here you'll find extensive tutorials as well as news about Flash and third-party accessories devoted to Flash. In the Resources section, you'll find clip art and sounds that you can download. Most of the clip art and sounds are royalty free and can be used on your own sites as long as you give credit to the person or company that created the work. Check out the site of the day, yet another source for interesting examples of what you can do with Flash.

Virtual FX

Virtual FX (`www.virtual-fx.net`) is another site that's chock-full of useful resources, ranging from tutorials to source files. The site has a Help Forums section that is broken down into different categories with something for every level of Flash user. You'll also find the occasional contest here where you can win software or other goodies.

We're Here Forums

We're Here Forums (`www.were-here.com/index.shtml`) is yet another site filled to the brim with tutorials, source files, sounds, games, and much more. You'll find more user forums here and links to awe-inspiring Flash sites and software manufacturers.

WebMonkey

The WebMonkey (`hotwired.lycos.com/webmonkey/multimedia/shockwave_flash`) qualifies as one of a Web designer's best friends. In addition to being an excellent Flash resource, this Web site features information about complex topics such as JavaScript and video for the Web. If you desire, select one of the links at `hotwired.lycos.com/email/signup/webmonkey.html` to receive a twice-weekly e-mail newsletter. It's a no-brainer. Do it.

Appendix

About the CD

*O*n the CD, which is only a few short pages away, you'll find lots of good-ies to work with. First and foremost, you'll find a Flash .fla file for every exercise in the book. Where applicable, I've also included the finished file, something you can compare your handiwork against. The files are located in folders by chapter. Where there is more than one file for an exercise, they are neatly stuffed away within their own little folder within the chapter's folder. It's sort of like one of those box puzzles where you open one box that reveals a smaller box, which you open to reveal yet a smaller box, and so on and so forth.

You'll also find some goodies to play with — demo software that you can use in conjunction with your Flash movies. This appendix tells you all about system requirements, installation instructions, and a section that gives a brief description of each goody. Enjoy.

System Requirements

Make sure that your computer meets the minimum system requirements shown in the following list. If your computer doesn't match up to most of these requirements, you may have problems using the software and files on the CD.

- ✔ A PC with a Pentium or faster processor; or a Mac OS computer with a 68040 or faster processor

- ✔ Microsoft Windows 98 or later; or Mac OS system software 9.1 or later

- ✔ At least 32MB of total RAM installed on your computer; for best performance, we recommend at least 64MB

✔ At least 150MB of available hard drive space if you want to install all the software from this CD; you'll need less space if you don't install every program

✔ A CD-ROM drive

✔ A sound card for PCs; Mac OS computers have built-in sound support

✔ A monitor capable of displaying at least 256 colors or grayscale

✔ A modem with a speed of at least 14,400 bps

If you need more information on the basics, check out these books published by Hungry Minds, Inc.: *PCs For Dummies,* by Dan Gookin; *Macs For Dummies,* by David Pogue; *iMacs For Dummies* by David Pogue; *Windows 95 For Dummies, Windows 98 For Dummies, Windows 2000 Professional For Dummies, Microsoft Windows ME Millennium Edition For Dummies,* all by Andy Rathbone.

Using the CD with Microsoft Windows

To install items from the CD to your hard drive, follow these steps:

1. **Insert the CD into your computer's CD-ROM drive.**

2. **Click the Start button and choose Run from the menu.**

3. **In the dialog box that appears, type** d:\start.htm.

   Replace *d* with the proper drive letter for your CD-ROM if it uses a different letter. (If you don't know the letter, double-click My Computer on your desktop and see what letter is listed for your CD-ROM drive.)

4. **Read through the license agreement, nod your head, and click the Agree button if you want to use the CD.**

   After you click Agree, you're taken to the Main menu, where you can browse through the contents of the CD.

5. **To navigate within the interface, click a topic of interest to go to an explanation of the files on the CD and how to use or install them.**

6. **To install software from the CD, simply click the software name.**

   You'll see two options: to run or open the file from the current location or to save the file to your hard drive. Choose to run or open the file from its current location, and the installation procedure continues. When you finish using the interface, close your browser as usual.

Note: We have included an "easy install" in these HTML pages. If your browser supports installations from within it, go ahead and click the links of the program names you see. You'll see two options: Run the File from the

Current Location and Save the File to Your Hard Drive. Choose to Run the File from the Current Location and the installation procedure will continue. A Security Warning dialog box appears. Click Yes to continue the installation.

To run some of the programs on the CD, you may need to keep the disc inside your CD-ROM drive. This is a good thing. Otherwise, a very large chunk of the program would be installed to your hard drive, consuming valuable hard drive space and possibly keeping you from installing other software.

Using the CD with Mac OS

To install items from the CD to your hard drive, follow these steps:

1. **Insert the CD into your computer's CD-ROM drive.**

   In a moment, an icon representing the CD you just inserted appears on your Mac desktop. Chances are, the icon looks like a CD-ROM.

2. **Double-click the CD icon to show the CD's contents.**

3. **Double-click** `start.htm` **to open your browser and display the license agreement.**

   If your browser doesn't open automatically, open it as you normally would by choosing File⇨Open File (in Internet Explorer) or File⇨Open⇨Location in Netscape (in Netscape Navigator) and select *Flash ActionScript For Dummies*. The license agreement appears.

4. **Read through the license agreement, nod your head, and click the Accept button if you want to use the CD.**

   After you click Accept, you're taken to the Main menu. This is where you can browse through the contents of the CD.

5. **To navigate within the interface, click any topic of interest and you're taken to an explanation of the files on the CD and how to use or install them.**

6. **To install software from the CD, simply click the software name.**

What You'll Find on the CD

The following sections are arranged by category and provide a summary of the software and other goodies you'll find on the CD. If you need help with installing the items provided on the CD, refer to the installation instructions in the preceding section.

Shareware programs are fully functional, trial versions of copyrighted programs. If you like particular programs, register with their authors for a nominal fee and receive licenses, enhanced versions, and technical support. *Freeware programs* are free, copyrighted games, applications, and utilities. Unlike shareware, these programs do not require a fee or provide technical support. *Trial, demo,* or *evaluation* versions of software are usually limited either by time or functionality (such as not letting you save a project after you create it). Some trial versions are very sensitive to system date changes. If you alter your computer's date, the programs will "time out" and will no longer be functional.

Author-created material

For Windows and Mac.

All the exercises and examples provided in this book are located in the Author directory on the CD and work with Macintosh, and Windows 98/NT and later computers. These files contain the sample code from the book. Many of the exercises contain multiple assets and are located in their own folder within the chapter folder. The On the CD icon will alert you to where you can locate the necessary files to complete each exercise. The structure of the examples directory is

```
Author/Chapter1
```

Macromedia Dreamweaver

For Windows and Mac.

Do you need to weave your dream Web site for all the world to see? If so, you owe it to yourself to try out Macromedia's Dreamweaver (`www.macromedia.com/software/dreamweaver`). The software is a full-featured WSYIWG HTML editor. Create tables, text, add images, and then add interactive objects like Flash buttons or Flash text. After you're done creating your dream web site, use Dreamweaver's site management tool to upload it to your Web site host.

Macromedia Fireworks

For Windows and Mac.

Macromedia Fireworks makes it possible for you to create and optimize graphics for your Web pages or your Flash documents. If you're creating a document for a Web page, you can add cool stuff like rollover buttons and pop-up menus. The software also features some sophisticated image-editing tools. Go to www.macromedia.com/software/fireworks.

Macromedia Freehand

For Windows and Mac.

If you need to create vector objects for your Flash documents, Macromedia Freehand is a handy tool to use. You can create document and then export them as *SWF files. Documents created in Freehand import into Flash with most of the features from the original Freehand file intact. If you're into creating your own vector objects, you owe it to yourself to give Freehand a try. Please visit www.macromedia.com/software/freehand.

Swift 3D

For Windows and Mac.

Swift 3D is the solution is you're looking to add three-dimensional vector objects to your Flash movies. Swift 3D is a Windows/Macintosh application that you use to create and convert 3D images and animations to 3D vector graphics. Swift 3D exports the completed file in the Flash SWF format. Please visit Electric Rain's Web site at www.electricrain.org for the latest updates on this product.

WildForm SWfX

For Windows.

SWfX is an easy-to-use text animation tool. You can choose from over 200 different effects to create swirling text, swooping text, and fading text, to name a few. The animation you create is exported in Flash's native SWF format. Use animated text to spice up your Flash movies. Please visit WildForm's Web site at www.wildform.com.

Bonus content

Yikes!! I ran out of paper, or is that pages? At any rate, I wrote so much stuff about ActionScript, it won't all fit in this book. Worry not, though — my words have not ended up in my computer's Recycle Bin. Rather, they appear on the CD-ROM as bonus content, and that's not bogus information. For bonus content, you get three appendixes with definitions and information about the most popular ActionScript actions. You also get one full chapter with information about some very inspirational Web sites, and there are two tutorials for you to complete: "Creating Printable Movie Frames" and "Creating a Visitor Response Form." And in case you don't have it on your computer, there's a version of the Acrobat Reader, which is the software you'll need to view the bonus content. Enjoy.

Troubleshooting

If you have difficulty installing or using any of the materials on the companion CD, try the following solutions:

✔ Turn off any anti-virus software that you may have running. Installers sometimes mimic virus activity and can make your computer incorrectly believe that it is being infected by a virus. (Be sure to turn the anti-virus software back on later.)

✔ Close all running programs. The more programs you're running, the less memory is available to other programs. Installers also typically update files and programs; if you keep other programs running installation may not work properly.

✔ Reference the ReadMe.txt: Please refer to the ReadMe file located at the root of the CD-ROM for the latest product information at the time of publication.

If you still have trouble with the CD, please call the Hungry Minds Customer Care phone number: (800) 762-2974. Outside the United States, call 1 (317) 572-3994. You can also contact Hungry Minds Customer Service by e-mail at techsupdum@hungryminds.com. Hungry Minds will provide technical support only for installation and other general quality control items; for technical support on the applications themselves, consult the program's vendor or author.

Index

• *E* •

• **F** •

• *N* •

• *X* •

• *Y* •

Hungry Minds, Inc.
End-User License Agreement

5. **Limited Warranty.**

    (a) HMI warrants that the Software and Software Media are free from defects in materials and workmanship under normal use for a period of sixty (60) days from the date of purchase of this Book. If HMI receives notification within the warranty period of defects in materials or workmanship, HMI will replace the defective Software Media.

    (b) HMI AND THE AUTHOR OF THE BOOK DISCLAIM ALL OTHER WARRANTIES, EXPRESS OR IMPLIED, INCLUDING WITHOUT LIMITATION IMPLIED WARRANTIES OF MERCHANTABILITY AND FITNESS FOR A PARTICULAR PURPOSE, WITH RESPECT TO THE SOFTWARE, THE PROGRAMS, THE SOURCE CODE CONTAINED THEREIN, AND/OR THE TECHNIQUES DESCRIBED IN THIS BOOK. HMI DOES NOT WARRANT THAT THE FUNCTIONS CONTAINED IN THE SOFTWARE WILL MEET YOUR REQUIREMENTS OR THAT THE OPERATION OF THE SOFTWARE WILL BE ERROR FREE.

    (c) This limited warranty gives you specific legal rights, and you may have other rights that vary from jurisdiction to jurisdiction.

6. **Remedies.**

    (a) HMI's entire liability and your exclusive remedy for defects in materials and workmanship shall be limited to replacement of the Software Media, which may be returned to HMI with a copy of your receipt at the following address: Software Media Fulfillment Department, Attn.: *Macromedia Flash MX ActionScript For Dummies*, Hungry Minds, Inc., 10475 Crosspoint Blvd., Indianapolis, IN 46256, or call 1-800-762-2974. Please allow four to six weeks for delivery. This Limited Warranty is void if failure of the Software Media has resulted from accident, abuse, or misapplication. Any replacement Software Media will be warranted for the remainder of the original warranty period or thirty (30) days, whichever is longer.

    (b) In no event shall HMI or the author be liable for any damages whatsoever (including without limitation damages for loss of business profits, business interruption, loss of business information, or any other pecuniary loss) arising from the use of or inability to use the Book or the Software, even if HMI has been advised of the possibility of such damages.

    (c) Because some jurisdictions do not allow the exclusion or limitation of liability for consequential or incidental damages, the above limitation or exclusion may not apply to you.

7. **U.S. Government Restricted Rights.** Use, duplication, or disclosure of the Software for or on behalf of the United States of America, its agencies and/or instrumentalities (the "U.S. Government") is subject to restrictions as stated in paragraph (c)(1)(ii) of the Rights in Technical Data and Computer Software clause of DFARS 252.227-7013, or subparagraphs (c)(1) and (2) of the Commercial Computer Software - Restricted Rights clause at FAR 52.227-19, and in similar clauses in the NASA FAR supplement, as applicable.

8. **General.** This Agreement constitutes the entire understanding of the parties and revokes and supersedes all prior agreements, oral or written, between them and may not be modified or amended except in a writing signed by both parties hereto that specifically refers to this Agreement. This Agreement shall take precedence over any other documents that may be in conflict herewith. If any one or more provisions contained in this Agreement are held by any court or tribunal to be invalid, illegal, or otherwise unenforceable, each and every other provision shall remain in full force and effect.

Installation Instructions

The *Macromedia Flash MX ActionScript For Dummies* CD offers valuable information, tutorials, and source code that you won't want to miss. See the "About the CD" appendix for detailed instructions on installing the items from the CD to your hard drive.